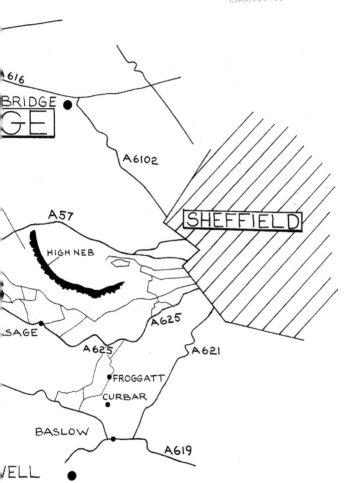

Peak Rock Climbs

Stanage

Edited and compiled by David Simmonite

From a manuscript by Chris Craggs based on previous editions

Crag diagrams by Malc Baxter
Maps by Nigel Baker

Published by the British Mountaineering Council

1924 *Recent Developments on Gritstone* edited by Fergus Graham. The Stanage section was written by Rice Kemper Evans

1951 *Sheffield Area* (Climbs on Gritstone, First Series, Volume 1) Edited by Eric Byne

1957 *Further Developments in the Peak District* (Climbs on Gritstone, First Series, Volume 4) Edited by Eric Byne and Wilf White

1964 *The Sheffield-Stanage Area* (Rock Climbs in the Peak, Second Series, Volume 1) Edited by Eric Byne

1976 *Stanage Area* by Brian Griffiths and Alan Wright (Rock Climbs in the Peak, Third Series, Volume 1) Edited by Dave Gregory

1983 *Stanage Millstone* (Peak District Climbs, Fourth Series, Volume 1) Edited by Geoff Milburn

1989 *Stanage* (Peak Rock Climbs, Fifth Series, Volume 1) Edited by Graham Hoey

2002 *Stanage* Edited by David Simmonite

A catalogue record for this book is available from the British Library

796.522

ISBN 0-903908-42-5

Front Cover: Mick Carr climbing the classic *Left Unconquerable* E1.
Photo: David Simmonite.
Rear Cover: Stephen Coughlan on *Flying Buttress* V Diff.
Photo: David Simmonite.
Rear Endpaper: Percy Bishton climbing *Not To Be Taken Away* E2.
Photo: David Simmonite.

BMC Participation Statement
The BMC recognises that climbing, hillwalking and mountaineering are activities with a danger of personal injury or death. Participants in these activities should be aware of, and accept, these risks and be responsible for their own actions and involvement.

Prepared for printing by the Editor and Ian Smith
Produced by Joseph Ward Colour Print
Distributed by Cordee, 3a De Montfort Street, Leicester LE1 7HD
Copyright British Mountaineering Council
Copyright of photographs remains with photographers

Contents

INTRODUCTION

> **The climbs in this guidebook have been described from right-to-left. Traditionally this crag has always been described from left-to-right but it was felt it would be more logical to start with the Popular End. The diagram numbering is also right-to-left.**

This is the first time in the many guidebooks which have covered the rock climbs on Stanage that the Edge has had a guide to itself. This is an obvious consequence of the increasing number of climbs on this five kilometre-long gritstone rampart and may portend the eventual working out of its store of, as yet, undiscovered secrets. From J W Puttrell, in his tweed knee breeches and nailed boots and nothing but a rope in the way of gear making the first exploration in the 1890s to the gear-festooned youngster of today is now over a century. It has been a century of amazing changes in every aspect of life but, despite the erosion of its most popular routes and the tracks to its foot, Stanage is still there, Britain's most popular crag in terms of visitor numbers, ready to give the unique pleasure of gritstone to the climbers of the next century, providing that we respect it and its traditions.

You would think that this massive curtain wall, extending the length of a climbing career, would be utterly impregnable. We can all stand under a climb and believe that we will never be able to climb it — and that our experience of Stanage will live forever. In its vast lifetime, from its early granite grain beds in an ancient sea, to its final washing away, many millions of years hence, it will remember in a blink the time of climbers — let it not be a time when it lost its natural splendour.

Stanage Edge is a crag of major international importance. It is probably the world's busiest crag with a quality of rock and routes that is difficult to match. Climbing will occur on almost every day of the year and has done so for over a century. Such is the appeal of Stanage.

The coarse family of gritstones that gave birth to this unique edge are sedimentary rocks laid down in estuaries and shallow seas and derived ultimately from weathered and washed-down granite deposits. Rivelin Grit at Stanage is very hard-wearing, particularly the quartz pebbles, and has only a small amount of feldspar.

The escarpment is set upon high peat moorland, a rare landscape unique to the Atlantic seaboard of Europe. What we have is very special. There is very little moorland outside the UK, and international attention is given to its protection and study. We know that the harsh conditions associated with moorlands sustain only low densities of a few species of wildlife which struggle hard to survive.

Although Stanage is so accessible from major urban centres, it has been sheltered from the worst atmospheric pollution — unlike the higher Kinder Plateau, which is more exposed to prevailing winds. Stanage and its surrounding moorland still has living Sphagnum moss, making it especially significant locally, regionally and globally. The Stanage of today is an important area of landscape and, despite its accessibility, it is little changed since the forest clearances some 7,000 years ago.

Don't arrive too early at the crag, birds and other wildlife are most active first and last thing during the day, so give them a chance to feed. Parking has now been formalised and the principle aim of this is to limit erosion and minimise the number of approaches to the crag. The land we cross to get to our routes is particularly valuable. Boggy areas or Sitches are among the prized assets of The Peak, they are home to many small invertebrates — for breeding Reed Bunting and Whinchat, amongst other birds. By only having one route across the Hooks Carr Sitch, it is hoped these birds will flourish. But imagine one dog, or one party of climbers sauntering through the middle of this area every day… then that's another year with no nesting. Please stick to the paths and keep your dog under control, particularly when approaching the crag. Use the car parks, they are not an attempt to exploit climbers, they are there to protect the environment — the same one in which we want to enjoy climbing.

While belaying at the top of the crag, take a look behind you and imagine; the new feeder road, all those tents, the camping barns and the litter bins. Ever since the dogs chased off the last Merlin, Raven and Golden Plovers, the fires stripped out the remaining vegetation and… you know sometimes you don't notice what you've got till it's gone. Take another look behind you, isn't it magnificent?

People come from all over the world to look at the purple heather, cotton grass and living bog — aren't they strange? Give them something to look forward to.

So please…
No bolts
No chipping
No resin
No camping
No fires or idle cigarettes
Do keep dogs under control or on a lead
Do park sensibly
Do keep to the footpaths where possible
… picking up litter is only the start of looking after Stanage.

SITUATION AND CHARACTER

Stanage is the longest edge of the eastern escarpment, extending for some five kilometres from Stanage End in the north to the Cowper Stone at the southern end. The edge lies some 10km west of Sheffield and three kilometres north of the village of Hathersage at an elevation of approximately 450m and is marked on O.S. 1:50,000 Sheet 110, OS 1:25,000 Outdoor Leisure Number 1 (Dark Peak) Harvey 1:40,000 Peak District maps.

Facing south-west, Stanage catches the sun from late morning onwards. Less fortunately, it catches the other elements too, receiving its full share of wind and rain. The Edge is, however, quick-drying with only a few routes affected by seepage. For gritstone devotees, Stanage is at its best on those rare, not too cold, clear days in winter when the friction is brilliant and the views stunning. Perhaps the most reliable period for enjoyable climbing lies from Easter through to late June. In July and August on overcast, windless days the midges can drive you to distraction. Insect repellent, liberally applied reduces friction to almost zero. On sunny days in summer it can be almost too hot to climb and the high, refreshingly cool, edges of Kinder are a better bet.

Stanage offers routes to suit all styles of climbing, from the overhangs of *The Dangler* or *Quietus* to the slab technicalities of *Daydreamer* and from the thuggish jamming of the aptly-named *Vice* to the brilliant finger-jamming and laybacking of *The Asp*. Classic routes of all grades are available on every area of the edge.

For the first time visitor, if only for the sheer number of quality routes at every grade, the right-hand 'Popular End' must be recommended, though Wall End runs it close. Later, visits might be made to High Neb or the buttresses above the Plantation, where routes the equal of any on the edge may be found. Stanage

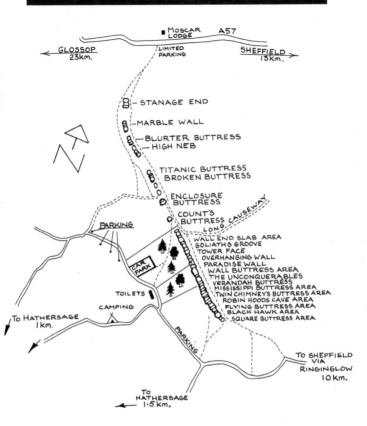

End is often quite deserted, even when, on sunny Sunday afternoons, other areas have become almost unbearably crowded. Escape from the hordes is often possible simply by moving a few hundred metres along the edge, say to Count's Buttress from Wall End.

THE ROCK

The gritstone of Stanage, while not so smooth as that of Froggatt Edge, nor yet so rough as that of Ramshaw Rocks, is almost everywhere exceedingly sound. Some three hundred million years ago the erosion products of a range of granite mountains in what

7

is now Scandinavia were swept southward in a great river which dropped the water-worn fragments in a great delta over what is now the North of England. The South was not so lucky. The thick deposits of silt and sand and pebbles have consolidated into a series of beds of gritstones, shales and, even, where forests developed on the marshy beds, coals. We are not so fortunate as to have the depth of the homogeneous beds which give the Montserrat conglomerates, for instance, but we are blessed in having several horizons of our almost unique rock.

The gritstone edges running down the east bank of the River Derwent are the north-east limb of the huge anticline (upward fold) which gives gritstone to the north-east and south-west of the central limestone plateau. Glaciation and the Derwent itself have contributed to the production of the gritstone edges, Stanage dominant among them, and added to their sculpting and the scattering of boulder fields below them. The deposition processes have given the edge noticeable horizontal features and the typical current bedding. Pressures on the rock during its consolidation and folding have given the vertical joint lines. These two features, horizontal and vertical, weathered over the centuries of their exposure to the weather, give the sublime jamming cracks over which local exponents eulogise and which puzzle the newcomer. The other typical feature of gritstone, the overhanging neb, also results from the weathering of horizontal weaknesses. Nature has done its job perfectly in every respect other than giving us twice as much, twice as high.

By the early 1950s the use of nailed boots was dying out but classic easier routes were already heavily scarred. The plimsolls which superseded nails and the smooth-soled rock boots which followed them have a less disastrous effect but the scarring continues. Even gritstone has its glassy holds and Stanage more than many edges. Drying and cleaning one's boot soles will be safer for the climber and lessen the sandpaper effect of the grains upon the holds.

ECOLOGY

Although the climber's activities will be confined to the narrow region on, above and below the rock face the edge is a boundary between two heather moorlands. Grouse are still raised below the High Neb end and the Ring Ouzel, which is very scarce farther south, is still present. Curlew and Snipe can still be seen and (at dusk) the quiet observer may be rewarded by sight of birds of prey at the hunt. Climbers are asked not to stray from the accepted paths on their way to the crag and to leave as much of the moorland as possible undisturbed.

EROSION

As at many Peak District crags the ground at the foot of the rock is suffering badly and its level being rapidly lowered. The approach to Stanage is easy and trainers, or wellingtons in wet weather, should be sufficient rather than heavy boots. Keep to the obvious and indicated paths and avoid removing rocks from the foot of the crag.

DROUGHT AND FIRE RISK

The controversy of recent years occasioned by the exclusion of climbers from crags during periods of high fire risk whilst walkers are still allowed, by law, to use rights of way over the moors in danger still continues. Clearly, prolonged periods with little or no rain increase the possibility of surface vegetation and the underlying peat catching fire. Whatever their cause, WHERE FIRES OCCUR THEIR EFFECTS ARE DISASTROUS. The wildlife, both vegetation and animal, and just as important, the livelihood of the local population can be destroyed. The potential erosion consequent upon the removal of the protective vegetation cover could destroy an area for ever and consequently the BMC ADVISES ALL CLIMBERS TO BE VERY CAREFUL IN USING ANY COMBUSTIBLES such as MATCHES, CIGARETTES and STOVES, PARTICULARLY IN PERIODS OF DROUGHT. At such times SUCH MATERIALS SHOULD BE LEFT IN THE CAR OR AT HOME.

If you are on a crag during such high-risk periods, please keep an eye open for any signs of smoke or indications of fire and report the incident to the fire brigade, on 999, immediately. Be sure to give as accurate description of the location as possible and offer to act as a guide by meeting the brigade vehicle at some easily describable rendezvous.

LITTER

Very slowly publicity, education and even example are improving the behaviour of the public in open country with respect to litter. Each new generation needs encouraging or chiding and we can only appeal for no-one to leave any litter of their own and to take home any that they find. Carrying a tough plastic bag with you on any visit to this, or any other edge gives you the chance to improve the condition of our easily damaged resource. People in charge of groups will do well to study the BMC's booklet *The Peak Group Book* which offers much useful advice. The Stanage caves still attract bivouackers, climbers and others along with a residue of cans and bottles, but for the most part people's behaviour is improving. May it continue to do so. You can help it.

TOILET TRAINING

The increased number of well-fed people visiting the edge could lead to an unpleasant environmental situation and even health risk. GO BEFORE YOU GO is good advice i.e. use the toilet at home, or in the nearest village, or at your hut or camp site rather than the shelter of the boulders below the edge. Toilet paper, and paper tissues are particularly unpleasant residues to leave behind.

As the American poet said: "If you have to wipe your ass, use grass." There is a toilet next to the road near the Plantation car park at the top of the footpath leading from the North Lees camp site.

THE BMC

This definitive guidebook is produced for The British Mountaineering Council by the BMC Guidebook Committee on a voluntary basis and any surpluses generated from the sales of guidebooks are used to support future publications or for other purposes beneficial to climbers. In addition 5% of the cover price of every guide sold is contributed to the Access and Conservation Trust. This fund is used to campaign for access to and the conservation of crags and mountains throughout the United Kingdom and is a vital contribution to preservation and furtherance of the freedom of all climbers, mountaineers and hill-walkers to pursue their sport.

The BMC was formed in 1944 and has been involved in guidebook production in the Peak District since 1964. The organisation has (in 2002) over 57,000 members and is recognised by Government and the various Sports Councils of the UK as the National Governing Body of the Sport.

The British Mountaineering Council promotes the interests of climbers, hill-walkers and mountaineers and the freedom to enjoy their activities.

Through a democratic representative structure the BMC will:

Negotiate access improvements and promote cliff and mountain conservation

Promote and advise on good practice, facilities, training and equipment

Support events and specialist programmes, including youth and excellence

Provide services and information for members.

The BMC Guidebook Committee is responsible for the compilation, publication and distribution of rock-climbing guides to the Peak District. The committee is always looking for fresh volunteers to help in the production of new guidebooks. In addition, tracking down good climbing photographs for use in Peak District guides is always a difficult task. Anyone interested in supporting any aspect of the the work of the Guidebook Committee is urged to contact the BMC by email or any other means.

Correspondence

Any correspondence should be addressed to the
BMC Headquarters, 177-179 Burton Road, Manchester M20 2BB
Tel: 0870 010 4878 Fax: 0161 445 4500
email: office@thebmc.co.uk   web: www.thebmc.co.uk

ACKNOWLEDGEMENTS

Taking on the role of editing a guidebook to, arguably, the most famous and popular crag in Britain is no easy task and first of all thanks must be made to all of the editors and volunteers involved in previous editions of guidebooks produced to Stanage. Without this valuable work, all based on the successful system adopted by the BMC and most other guidebook producers in the country of guidebooks written by volunteers whose only reward is to be part of the ongoing tradition, the compilation and editing of this guidebook would be a far greater task.

With so many people involved with route checking, script work and checking and everything else that goes on behind the scenes it is difficult to pick out any particular individuals. However, mention must be made of Chris Craggs who took on the enormous task of turning the Stanage routes around by describing the Edge more logically from right-to-left rather than the traditional left-to-right and producing the original script from which this guidebook is based. We should also doff our caps to artist extraordinaire Malc Baxter who, in many peoples opinion, has produced the finest set of drawings yet seen in a British guidebook.

The BMC guidebook system is undergoing a transition at present and the past members of the BMC Guidebook Committee should also take credit for their faith in the volunteer ethic and for the sterling work put in on this book. These include Dave Farrant, Dave Gregory, Brian Griffiths, Graham Hoey, Geoff Milburn, Geoff Radcliffe, Keith Sharples, Andrew Wood and Chris Wright. Adge Last was the last Chair of the Guidebook Committee and oversaw the delicate matter of the transition to new methods of producing guidebooks.

Many people gave up their spare time to help Chris Craggs on the original manuscript and these include Dave Gregory, Geoff Milburn, Dave Spencer, Graham Parkes, Jim Rubery, Colin Binks and John Street (who uncovered the location of many unclimbed gaps with his topo guidebook) and to any others I have missed out, I apologise.

Since being thrust into the role of editor to this guide I have had help from many people and these include: Neil Foster, Terry Gifford,

Brian Griffiths, Paul Harrison, Pat Horscroft, Dave Musgrove, Mo Overfield, Graham Sutton, Richard Wheeldon, Tony and Sarah Whitehouse and Martin Whitaker who all gave valuable comments on the manuscript. In his meticulous way Mike Snell checked and double-checked the first ascent details for errors and, talking of first ascents, Vivienne Smith wrote a fine history to the edge. Niall Grimes, Percy Bishton, Jon Barton and Mike Lea all wrote parts of the introductions to each section of the crag, the bouldering, environmental notes and the graded list. Henry Folkard made comments on sections of the script and, more importantly, represented climbers at numerous meetings of the Stanage Forum. Nigel Baker drew the maps for which I thank him.

This guidebook contains many fine photographs and these have made it a much richer product. Cheers for all of those who contributed; Viv Durrant, Niall Grimes, Rich Heap, Ian Parnell, Jez Portman, Carl Ryan, Ian Smith, Ron Townsend, Dave Wilkinson, Ray Wood and Chris Williams for the use of his father, Paul's, photograph. Many thanks to you all and sorry to those who I've forgotten; producing guidebooks does funny things to the memory.

And, finally, I've saved my biggest thanks until the end for Ian Smith, who despite having a seemingly full workload, put in a huge amount of time in helping typeset and edit this guide. Without his expertise this thankless task would have been desperate.
David Simmonite

OWNERSHIP, ACCESS AND APPROACHES

The days of keepered restrictions to Stanage have gone but the northern section of the edge, beyond the iron fence and the so-called Roman road, is still in the private ownership of Mr J. Archdale. He currently (2002) allows that section of the Edge to be used for climbing. Climbers are asked to keep near to the rocks and not to approach across the open moor between Stanage and Bamford Edges. There may be occasions when shooting is taking place on that section of moor and climbers are asked to comply, politely, with any requests from the shooting party to keep away from particular sections of the Edge. The remainder of the crag is managed by the Peak District National Park Authority and the public has freedom of access, including for rock-climbing. Climbers, particularly those who use the various possible sites for bivouacking, are asked to take their litter home.

We are fortunate that we have almost unrestricted access to gritstone's premier crag. Since the last full Stanage guidebook the national number of rock-climbers has increased, owing to the effect of climbing walls and outdoor education centres. Stanage, of course, has seen increased usage but the fears expressed as to the worsening pressures on the edge have not come to pass.

ACCESS DIFFICULTIES

No difficulties should arise on Stanage, but should they, please report them to the BMC or the Peak District National Park Authority.

British Mountaineering Council
177 - 179 Burton Road,
West Didsbury,
Manchester
M20 2BB
Tel. 0870 010 4878

Peak District National Park Authority
Aldern House,
Baslow Road,
Bakewell,
Derbyshire
DE4 IAE
Tel. 01629 816200

STATEMENT BY THE PEAK DISTRICT NATIONAL PARK AUTHORITY

The Peak District National Park Authority owns the North Lees Estate, which includes the most popular southeastern half of Stanage Edge. Through its management, the Authority seeks to work in partnership with others to demonstrate:
• how to conserve and enhance the area's special qualities
• to provide opportunities for their enjoyment and understanding and to improve the quality of life for the people who live, work and visit.

The Authority welcomes climbers from all over the world and recognises the international importance of Stanage for both climbing and bouldering. Stanage/North Lees is also important for a number of other reasons. Local people care passionately about the area and hundreds of thousands of visitors come each year to enjoy a wide range of activities, surrounded by its natural beauty. It is also internationally important for wildlife. There is a whole range of habitats from flower-rich pastures and hay meadows to woodlands, crags and boulder slopes. Stanage Edge itself is home to birds such as Ring Ouzel. The moorland and raised bog of White Path Moss, above the edge, is of particular importance for its breeding population of rare wetland birds, including Curlew, Snipe and Golden Plover. It is a Site of Special Scientific Interest and a Special Protection Area. There is also a working farm, managed by Derby College and a number of important archaeological features. Management of the Estate is

15

therefore often a careful balancing act to ensure that all of these things can co-exist without endangering the long term sustainable future of the special qualities that we all love about Stanage today.

STANAGE FORUM

The Authority believes that, in order to manage the Estate effectively, everyone with an interest in the area or who is affected by its management should have the opportunity to become involved. The stated aim of the Forum is:

to involve all those with an interest in Stanage/the North Lees Estate in the development of an effective management plan, to ensure that it remains a special place, where people can live, work and visit for enjoyment.

At the time of writing you can also have your say on the web discussion board. Visit the website at www.peakdistrict.org and look for the Stanage Forum link. You could also use the more traditional forms of communication — by writing or phoning.

For further information, please contact the North Lees Estate Manager at: Peak District National Park Authority, Aldern House, Baslow Road, Bakewell, Derbyshire, DE45 1AE.

APPROACHES

The approach depends on what part of the edge you wish to visit, from where you are coming and your means of transport. The walk to the crag is never more than 20 minutes from the nearest car park.

BY PUBLIC TRANSPORT

There is a railway station at Hathersage, which lies on the Sheffield to Manchester line. For timetable and fare enquiries telephone 08457 48 49 50. Having successfully caught your train, alight at Hathersage and from the station follow Station Road to its junction with Main Road opposite the George Hotel. Turn right, cross Main Road at the pedestrian crossing and continue to the Hathersage Inn. Turn left into Baulk Lane and with the edge in sight on the distant skyline, follow the lane and footpath past Brookfield Manor to reach the road that runs below the edge.

Hathersage and Stanage Edge are served by a number of bus services, which have been listed below. It goes without saying that these are subject to alteration. For more information telephone Derbyshire Busline on Buxton 0870 608 2608 or the Hope Valley and High Peak Community Rail Partnership on 01663 746377.

174 Matlock – Baslow – Hathersage – Castleton. Matlock can be reached by train from Derby.

175 Bakewell – Eyam – Hathersage – Bamford – Derwent – Snake Inn – Castleton.

272 Sheffield – Hathersage – Bradwell – Castleton.

274 Sheffield – Ladybower – Bamford – Castleton.

276 Chesterfield – Baslow – Hathersage – Castleton.

395 Manchester – Glossop – Ladybower – Castleton. (Sundays and Bank Holidays only)

796 Chesterfield – Bakewell – Hathersage – Derwent.

The Fox House Inn, SK 267803, on the A625, can be reached by 272 service. From there, one can walk up the Burbage Valley and across the Ringinglow road to the Cowper Stone end of Stanage and the first climbs on the edge.

For climbers based in Sheffield who can read a map and a bus timetable various other public transport or shanks's pony possibilities exist.

BY CAR

Whenever possible share a car with someone else. From Sheffield, the easiest approach is via Bents Green along Ringinglow Road past the Norfolk Arms and bearing right just beyond Upper Burbage Bridge (O.S. Ref. SK 260830) until the edge comes into view on the north (right-hand) side of the road.

From the filling station in Hathersage, go up through the village in the direction of Sheffield (A6187 - A625 on older maps). Just beyond a narrowing of the road near the chemist's shop, turn left into School Lane. Continue on, passing the Scotsman's Pack pub, to The Dale and so up the steep hill to join the road that runs in the shallow valley below the edge.

From Manchester, follow the A57 (Snake Pass road) towards Sheffield, until Ladybower Reservoir is reached. Turn right onto the A6013 towards Bamford. Just beyond the Yorkshire Bridge pub (on the right), turn left (eastwards) up a narrow lane, past Bamford Edge and onward until in 3km Stanage comes into view. Once on the road that runs below the edge, park in one of three car parks depending on your ultimate destination (see map).

Hooks Car, O.S. Ref. SK 275829, serves the southern or 'Popular End'.

Hollin Bank, known by climbers as the Plantation Car Park, O.S. Ref. SK 239837 is a large pay and display car park that serves the area from Wall End to the Unconquerables.

Denis Knoll, O.S. Ref. SK 227843, is situated at the junction of the so-called Roman Road and the road that runs below the edge.

17

From there the climbs on High Neb and Count's Buttress are accessible in 20 minutes.

For those wishing to climb at the Cowper Stone and True North areas, cars may be parked in the car park at Upper Burbage Bridge. From there the edge can be reached in 10 minutes by following the obvious path that runs westwards from the hairpin bend in the road 50 metres west of the car park entrance. Alternatively, limited roadside parking is available between Upper Burbage Bridge and Overstones Farm (O.S. Ref. SK 254826) on hard standing at Cabin Track, just before the road commences its steep descent to Hooks Carr and Hathersage.

If you intend to climb at Stanage End, Marble Wall or Crow Chin, then the nearest approach is from the A57 (Snake Pass road), opposite Moscar Lodge (O.S. Ref. SK 231879) where there is very limited car parking on the south side of the road. From there the edge may be reached in 20 minutes along an old track.

Due to the high incidence of theft from cars, climbers are advised not to leave anything of value in their vehicles.

DOGS

Many of the birds living on these moors nest on the ground and it is imperative that dogs are not allowed to run over the moors off the lead. Loose dogs are the greatest irritant to landowners and if you cannot keep your dog under control, it would be better to leave it at home. The same comment applies, with greater emphasis, with regard to sheep. They can be severely harrassed, particularly if they are in lamb, or have lambs by what a dog-owner may regard as a playful dog. Landowners have the right to **shoot** dogs that are harrassing sheep.

FACILITIES AND AMENITIES
ACCOMMODATION

Surprisingly, there are very few camp sites within the Peak Park. The most popular climbers camp site is North Lees, situated a 15-minute walk from the crag, (01433 650838). The camp site is run by the Peak Park and is fully equipped with toilets, showers etc. In the summer months, particularly at weekends, you will need to book in advance, as many a climber has arrived late on a Friday night only to spend an uncomfortable night in the car because the site is full. Discount rates are available for people who have proof (i.e. a ticket) they travelled by public transport.

Alternatively, the Eric Byne Memorial camp site (01246 582277) offers basic camping facilities. This is situated on the Baslow to Chesterfield road, 150m west of the Robin Hood Public House, under Birchen Edge. Stocking Farm (01433 630516) at Calver also provides good basic facilities. Laneside camp site (01433 620215) in Hope offers very well-equipped facilities, **although no single sex groups are allowed**.

Also popular with climbers are camping barns which can be booked through the Camping Barns Reservation Service on 01200 420102. There are also several climbing club huts in the area. Information on these can be obtained from the BMC. There is bunkhouse accommodation at Thorpe Farm, Coggers Lane, Hathersage, telephone 01433 650659.

For those wanting the ultimate luxury of clean sheets and a cooked breakfast there are several B&Bs in the area. Contact Bakewell Tourist Information on 01629 813227.

CAFES

For those dependent on starting, or ending, the day with calorie 'cranks' and caffeine injections the following are within easy reach of the crag and offer popular rendezvous.

Longland's above the gear shop, Outside, in Hathersage. (01433 651978)
Mondays 11.00 - 17.00
Tuesday - Friday 10.00 - 17.00
Weekends 9.00 - 18.00

Grindleford Station Café   (01433 631920)
Monday - Friday 8.30 - 18.00 (16.30 in winter)
Weekends 8.30 - 18.30 (18.00 in winter)

GEAR SUPPLIERS

Having arrived at the crag and finding your climbing rack woefully inadequate for the demands of the coming day, a full range of equipment can be purchased at the following suppliers. (Don't forget midge repellent, essential in the summer months.)

Hitch and Hike, Bamford (01433 651013)

Outside, Hathersage (01433 651936)

OTHER SERVICES

There are several general stores situated in Hathersage village which may be of interest to the visiting climber. The Spar, at the petrol station on Main Road (next to the gear shop Outside) is open seven days a week, 7.00-22.00. The One Stop on Station Road is also open seven days a week, 8.00-22.00. A bakery (opposite One Stop on Station Road) sells a wide variety of freshly made hot and cold sandwiches. The Hathersage Pharmacy (on Main Road) supplies everything from toothpaste to 24 hour film developing. There are two banks in the village, The Royal Bank of Scotland and The Nat West, both are on Main Road and both have cash dispensers.

Of course, after a day of heart stopping (hopefully, not permanent) epics pushing one's grade, thoughts turn to liquid refreshments.

PUBS

There are several pubs in the village, the ones of most interest to climbers are The Millstone Inn (Sheffield Road), The Scotsman's Pack, (School Lane) and The Little John, (Station Road). All but The Millstone Inn are within a 20 minute walk from the crag. They all offer a wide variety of bar meals and are open all day during the summer months.

CLIMBING WALLS

Surprisingly, it does rain in the Peak District. If, after spending months planning your trip, you are unlucky enough to experience this rare phenomenon the following climbing walls will provide hours of entertainment. Although none are located within the Peak Park itself, all are within a 30-minute drive.

The Edge, Sheffield (0114 2758899)
The Foundry, Sheffield (0114 2796331)
Glossop Leisure Centre, Glossop (01457 863223)

ETHICS AND STYLE

The two most basic rules here are be honest and don't damage the rock. Beyond that, it's entirely up to you, although in terms of style, some ascents are considered better than others. The best is still the on sight flash, although few, if any, first ascents are currently done in this fashion. In fact, several first ascents on grit are the subject of top roping campaigns which have gone on for months, as have any subsequent ascents. However, this is currently acceptable, as long as the final result is a clean lead of the route, ideally placing protection en route. Several examples of new routes led with pre-placed runners exist and while they are acknowledged, this practice is seen as far from perfect. The grades given are a reflection of the difficulty to be found on an on sight ascent, even if this is currently theoretical. Many routes have also become established with side runners for protection. Where this is so, it will be mentioned in the text and the grade will reflect this fact. And, finally, on a happier note, aid points and rest points have now disappeared from the areas covered in this book, and it is unlikely that a new route containing either would be seen as acceptable.

Any wire brushing of holds is extremely damaging to the fragile outer skin of the rock. If a hold must be brushed, a nylon-bristled brush is more than adequate. Another destructive practice worming its way into use is the use of Fontainebleau type resin, which gives the user benefit, but ultimately destroys the frictional quality of a hold. **Please do not use it**. The rock may seem abundant, but any of these practices can all too quickly turn a classic route or problem into a sorry eyesore.

Never remove vegetation from new or existing routes, nor from boulder problems. Clumps of heather and bilberry on small ledges and on top of boulders are particularly sensitive since these provide ideal (not to mention much watched) nest sites for Ring Ouzels.

QUALITY

Route quality is indicated by the star system. On a lot of grit crags almost every route is worth doing, being solid and clean in most cases, but a route with a star is particularly good. A two star route should be of very high quality, and among the better climbs in the area, while a three star route should be measurable with the best climbs in the country and not found wanting.

A dagger symbol beside a route is now commonly used to donate a route which the guidebook team has been unable to check in order to confirm the grade or quality.

THE CAPITAL CRIME

There are hundreds of good chip shops all over the North of England and that is as near as the word chip should get to any gritstone crag. There is no reason to chip holds or initials or graffiti on this or any other crag. Once the rock is spoiled it cannot be restored to its completely natural state. What may seem to one generation to be a blank piece of rock needing only one little chipped hold could be the three-star E10 of years to come. Leave the rock for the future. It should be pointed out that many of the local activists are rough, uncouth, belligerent northerners who might remonstrate strongly with any transgressors. One disadvantage of the otherwise wholly acceptable development of modern protection gear is that it can get stuck. Please do not damage the

rock in your efforts to get out any trapped gear. Accept your share of ill-luck with good grace. With the possibility of the gear's getting stuck and the wedging effect of modern gear in mind, one should be careful with equipment placements. A fall onto a camming device or a wedge-shaped nut could prise off a flake, leaving an unsightly scar (on you as well as the rock).

CHALK

The use of chalk on gritstone is now almost universal. On those occasions when you are choosing to climb well below your capabilities, do you really need chalk? At the top of climbs, close the chalkbag so that the wind or the friction of the descent does not cover the area in chalk dust if the bag upends. The gritstone area has an acid soil and the altered pH consequent upon a liberal dressing of chalk does not contribute to its well-being.

FIXED PROTECTION

Fixed protection in the form of bolts, pegs, threads or hammered wires is, thankfully, virtually absent from Peak grit. Never, ever, think about placing any, be it on a new route or any subsequent ascent. However, there is the occasional 'hand-placed peg' which refers to pegs slid into horizontal placements and not hammered in any way. On some notable incidents, ascensionists have resorted to giving the iron a few helpful taps with a hammer. So, please, if you must use hand-placed pegs, listen to the angel on your shoulder and not the devil, and resist the temptation to drive it home.

BOULDERING MATS

These delightful pieces of kit have made bouldering an altogether more pleasant activity and it need no longer mean plastic knees by the age of 40. However, their use has spread to more traditional routes and can turn what was previously an all out charge through

the sweaty jaws of death into a boulder problem with glory. Their use, just like chalk and sticky soles before them, is here to stay. Just remember that having them below you, as with any practice such as headpointing, abseil inspection, preplaced protection etc, changes the grade of the route downwards, often by some considerable degree. This, of course, is an entirely personal choice, but if an E5 can be fallen off safely, then it is most likely no longer E5. Hopefully, what will not happen, is that these routes which can be done with the safety of mats, will be taken as right for the grade, while other monsters which cannot be tamed in this way, will be upgraded. Try to remain honest with yourself, to see each achievement for what it is. Please remember that, traditionally, grades have been explained as representing the difficulty and seriousness for an on sight and mat-less ascent.

FIRST ASCENTS

All efforts have been made to get first ascent information correct, but undoubtedly, genuine mistakes will have been made. If anyone can add to the information provided here, their help would be gratefully accepted.

YEAR OF FIRST ASCENTS

If a range of years is given as the date of the first ascent e.g. 1962-69, then details of the ascent in question are incomplete, but it is thought that the route was put up within the time span indicated. If dates occur separated with a slash e.g. 1965/75, the former date indicates the route may have been ascended using aid or rest points. The latter date indicates an improved style of ascent, such as a free ascent, without a rest or use of side runners.

GRADES

It should of course be remembered that grades are primarily a form of entertainment and only a fool would take them seriously in the first place. The full realisation of this fact will improve the quality of any climber's life. As a brief humorous interlude, there now follows an explanation of how grades work. The system of grading for climbs in this volume is the traditional British style, with two parts, a combination of the adjectival and technical grades and assumes the leader has a normal rack, including camming devices, nuts quick draws etc, sticky rubber and no more or less than two of each limb. It may seem esoteric and confusing to those not used to the system, as well as being full of inconsistencies but, once mastered, it succeeds in providing a good indication of what is to be expected from a particular climb. Here is a brief explanation of how these grades work, which probably makes no sense whatsoever. Good luck.

ADJECTIVAL GRADES

The adjectival grade is the first part of the grade and attempts to give a sense of the overall difficulty of a climb. This will be influenced by many aspects including seriousness, the sustained nature of the climb, technical difficulty, exposure, strenuosity, rock quality and any other less tangible aspects which lend difficulty to a pitch. It is an open ended system and currently runs from Easy, which is barely climbing, to E10, which has been barely climbed. Along the way, and in ascending order, are Moderate (Mod), Difficult (D), Hard Diff (HD), Very Difficult (VD), Hard Very Difficult (HVD), Severe (S), Hard Severe (HS), Very Severe (VS), Hard Very Severe (HVS) and Extremely Severe, the last category being split into E1, E2, E3 etc. As with all grades, these catagorisations are subjective; there are no cut off points. VS runs smoothly into HVS, HVS runs into E1. Also, some climbers are better at safe, technical routes, some better at bold easy ones. Some climb well on delicate slabs, some on overhanging fist cracks. All this leads to that all too often splutter: "That's never a Moderate." where a route of one grade is claimed to be harder than one from the next grade up. Well, this just happens. All you can do is, if you find a route easy for its grade, give yourself a pat on the back. If it seems hard, blame the guidebook.

TECHNICAL GRADES

The second part of the grade, the technical grade, is there to give an indication of the hardest move to be found on the route, irrespective of how many of them there might be, how strenuous it is, or how frightened you are when you do it. They come onto the scale somewhere around 4a and currently run thus; 4a, 4b, 4c,

5a, 5b, 5c, 6a, 6b, 6c, 7a, 7b. It is an open ended scale, although while climbs continue to get harder and harder, this is usually reflected in the E grade, with climbs tending to become more serious and more strenuous rather than more technical. Real 7a is still a rarity on routes. Boulder problems have also traditionally used this system and while more fitting grades are used in specialist guides, if boulder problems are mentioned in this book, they still are rated by the traditional system.

COMBINED GRADES

Going back to the combined grade, you should see how the combination of these two grades goes to suggest the difficulty of a climb and what type of difficulty this might be. As a help, climbs of a particular adjectival grade, will often have an associated average technical grade. Roughly these are S 4a; HS 4b; VS 4c; HVS 5a; E1 5b; E2 5c. Above this the technical grade starts to slow down in relation to the adjectival grade, and by the time you get to E6 6b is more of an average grade. However, by the time you get to E6, you should have started to understand grades for yourself, so don't worry about that point. So, for your final lesson, if, for a particular adjectival grade, the technical grade is high, (e.g. VS 5a, E1 5c) then you can expect the route to be technical in character, with maybe a single, hard, well-protected move. If the technical grade is low for the adjectival grade, (e.g. HVS 4c, E3 5b) then expect either a very sustained and strenuous struggle, or a route with relatively easy climbing, only in a serious situation. Which one of these two it might be can hopefully be determined by looking at the climb. The final point is that these rules are broken more often than they are obeyed, so use this explanation only as a guide and stay open-minded.

OTHER PUBLICATIONS

Further information on climbing in the Peak can be obtained from the BMC publication, *On Peak Rock* and other guidebooks to the area. For those who've tired of carrying ropes and racks, can't be bothered with the intricacy of complex route finding or have simply done all the routes on the crag, a wealth of bouldering awaits in the immediate vicinity. Full details are available in the *Peak Bouldering* guide, published by Rockfax.

NEW CLIMBS

Details of new climbs including full descriptions, first ascensionists, date of ascent and any anecdotes etc should be sent to the BMC using either the post or email (office@thebmc.co.uk or guides@thebmc.co.uk). There is also a New Routes book at Outside in Hathersage.

GROUP USE

Insensitive use by organized groups has sometimes caused serious problems of erosion and of conflict with other climbers. Good practice advice for organized groups of climbers is given in the BMC's Peak Group Book (which is being re-issued at the time of writing).

MOUNTAIN RESCUE

In the event of an accident requiring the assistance of Mountain Rescue:

Dial **999** and ask for **'POLICE — MOUNTAIN RESCUE'**

Note: All mountain rescue incidents in the Peak District area fall under the responsibility of Derbyshire Constabulary. If in any doubt request **Derbyshire Police Operations Room.**

Historical

by Vivienne Smith

At the turn of the last century, when a small group of men were braving the weather and gamekeepers to explore the whole Peak District, Stanage Edge was just one of the crags where they searched for gullies and chimneys. It was later that it became the premier crag of gritstone partly because of its proximity to Sheffield but mainly because of the superb quality of its rock which was to be most appreciated when smearing tiny indents on cold sharp mornings. Thus it has become Stanage, needing no further elaboration and a crag on which almost every climber with a love for 'virgin rock' has created a climb reflecting the age and style of its time.

Thus, before the First World War, Stanage received intermittent attention from the main pioneers of the time. J. W. Puttrell scrambled up such gullies as *Hollybush Gully*, *Count's Chimney*, *Mississippi Chimney* and *Twin Chimney*. E. A. Baker records visiting 'the noblest part of Stanage Edge, a long half mile of black massy cliff, overhanging a wood sprinkled hillside' in springtime. It is clear that the Kyndwr Club, formed in 1899, and its Sheffield arm including Henry Bishop and Puttrell, climbed several chimneys and gullies but hardly any of this activity has been recorded. Within such a small group, word of mouth was clearly sufficient. It is known that *Black Hawk Chimney* was climbed in 1904.

Bishop's enthusiasm encouraged a group of fine climbers in a wave of discovery from 1912 to 1914. They ventured out of the gullies and climbed many routes which have subsequently changed their name. Notable existing climbs include *Inaccessible Slab* and *Tango Crack* on High Neb and *Wall End Crack*, *Bishop's Stride* (*Black Hawk Traverse*) and *Castle Crack* (*Black Hawk Slit*). It is at this time that Helfenstein made his first and only adventure on gritstone struggling for hours and eventually being pulled out to create an eponymous route. F. C. Aldous recorded their efforts in the first guidebook of the area which appeared in the *Rucksack Club Journal* Volume 2 Number 4 in 1914.

This team were broken up by the brutality of the First World War. In their place came H. M. (Harry) Kelly and, somewhat reluctantly, his wife Emily, along with the outstanding Norwegian, Iver Berg. They dramatically raised climbing standards. This was epitomised by Berg's solo of *High Neb Buttress*. He had spent the night under the buttress with Alf Schaaning and intended only to have a look but proceeded to the top. He also created *High Neb Girdle* while Kelly climbed *Inaccessible Crack*.

The post war period saw many young men venturing into the Peak as well as exploring other areas of the country. Climbing on Stanage was easier due to friendly gamekeepers kept sweet with small barrels of beer supplied by the American vice-consul based in Sheffield, Rice Kemper Evans. He was the 'presiding spirit of those days' and although he may not have written his name on Stanage as he had hoped, he has left us with the phrases to 'layback' and 'cute little layback'. A. S. Piggott and Morley Wood named *Doctor's Chimney* and *Manhattan Chimney* in his honour. They began a new era of climbing with the use of the shoulder belay and rubbers. In 1921 this group's achievements reached their climax when they completed the *Girdle Traverse of High Neb*. In October, with perfect conditions, Kelly soloed it from right to left in 15 minutes. The idea of waiting for sharp mornings and good friction is not the invention of recent years.

After this Piggott and Rucksack Club members were lured to the Lakes while others moved steadily along the Edge picking out many buttress climbs such as *Flying Buttress*, *Leaning Buttress* and *Right-Hand Buttress Direct*. Cyril Ward and Lewis Coxon maintained the high standards of the Edge with routes such as *Inverted V* and *Twin Chimneys*. The publication of *Recent Developments on Gritstone* by Kemper Evans in 1923 recorded 48 routes and marked Stanage as a notable and increasingly important part of climbing in the Peak District.

Exploration of unclimbed rock continued and several routes were found that were to become classics. Morley Wood's tremendous lead of *Kelly's Overhang* was the hardest route on the Edge by at least a grade although some have questioned its authenticity because a photograph rather than a written record marks the ascent and because of its uncharacteristic boldness. In 1928 enthusiasts from the Manchester University Mountaineering Club joined the Rucksack group and created routes such as *Christmas Crack* by George Bower, *Black Slab* by A. B. Hargreaves and *April Crack* by Herbert Harley. Further exploration in this area resulted in the completion of the *Trinities*.

Madge Cobb and Peggy Coates on *Jitter Face*. Photo: Ron Townsend

As the Depression began to bite from 1930 there were more young men with time, but little in the way of finance, who ventured into the Peak. Thus university clubs were joined by other groups who were prepared to explore, repeat routes and put up some bold additions. Notable amongst these was the Sheffield trio, Harry Dover, Gilbert Ellis and, their leader, Frank Elliot. They not only repeated all the major routes in nailed boots but also added many new ones, few of which they recorded. They climbed *Wall End Slab Direct*, probably the hardest route in the country at the time. Clifford Moyer and Eric Byne also began exploring the edge adding about 20 climbs including *Count's Buttress* and *Count's Crack*. Knowledge of these routes was passed on when groups met by chance or arranged to meet and were shown recent developments and areas with no climbs. Thus Maurice Linnell and Alf Bridge enlightened Moyer and Byne. At this time they also discovered and named *The Unconquerables*. Bridge was renowned for his spectacular ability to fall safely, a technique he had perfected by leaving his house via the upstairs window. He used this skill to fall 30 feet or so from routes such as *Black Slab*, *Christmas Crack* and *Black Hawk Wall*. One snowy day Bridge pioneered *Robin Hood's Innominate* and later *Cave Gully Wall*, an impressive climb at the time. Colin Kirkus also impressed with his ascent of the steep *Grey Wall* and *Kirkus's Corner* overcoming the bulge to the right of *Flying Buttress* and finishing up an unprotected scoop. This was a route avoided by almost everyone for the next 20 years although Arthur Dolphin soloed it in nails after the Second World War.

Stanage became much busier with the formation of the Sheffield Climbing Club and the Sheffield University Mountaineering Club in 1933 and the increased use led to a determination to create a guidebook. From the university came Fred Jones and Tom Stobart, the Everest cameraman, and the Doncaster brothers, Michael and Tony. They ventured as far as *The Unconquerables* and climbed the first part of *Goliath's Groove* but escaped rightwards towards protection to create *Doncaster's Route*. A large group of working class men and women explored the edge including Rubert Brooks, Frank Burgess, Byron Connelly, Reg Damms, Fred Glaister, Jack McLeod, Clifford Moyer and Bert Smith. Consisting of weightlifters, boxers, wrestlers etc, this group was rarely troubled by gamekeepers. They were free to explore the Wall End area and add a host of new routes notably, *Tower Face*. Byron Connelly soloed down the right-hand *Unconquerable* but no one climbed up although several came close to success.

Tony Brookes on *Twin Chimneys Buttress*. Photo: Ron Townsend

Albert Shutt on *Black Slab*. Photo: Ron Townsend

Black Car Burning **E7 6c** (page 50)
Climber: Robin Barker Photo: Jez Portman

Mantelpiece Buttress Direct HVS 5b (page 57)
Climber: Laurent Derioz Photo: Rich Heap

Other clubs also occasionally ventured to this edge such as members of the Polaris Club led by Bernard Simmonds who put up the fine routes of *Mississippi Variant* and *Agony Crack*. Activity came to a virtual stop after 1939 as the Second World War meant the break up of these clubs and friendships. However, the guidebook begun in 1933 was ready and was sent off to a Birmingham printer where it was lost in a bombing raid. Even after the war you could wander along the edge and see no one else. For many Stanage was not the main focus of attention since it was still keepered, especially the northern part above the Robin Hood Area. There were many other areas within easier reach by public transport, petrol was still rationed. Yet guidebook development, under the careful eye of Byne, resumed, not quite from scratch, since Byne and others had some notes from the previous version.

The post-war period saw many changes, the introduction of nylon ropes, Vibram soles and the use of slings and karabiners. A handy stone was the usual method of protection but gradually climbers began to engineer their own individual varieties of nut. In tennis shoes, Peter Harding, climbed *Harding's Superdirect* and, with the help of a stone for a belay stance, *Goliath's Groove*. Soon after this the Derby-based Valkyrie Club began to visit the edge and from 1949 a tremendous wave of exploration began. Chuck Cook climbed *Rugosity Wall* and Wilf White, *Valhalla*. Joe Brown then led both the *Unconquerables* and the new standard was set. Subsequently it was realised that Tom Probert of the Peak CC had already led the left-hand crack. Without protection, both ascents remain outstanding as the authors of the 1951 guidebook warned 'But, would be "tigers" note – they are no easier for their vanquishing'.

The publication of the guidebook marked the end of one era and the beginning of another as with increasingly better equipment, particularly footwear, climbers were able to attempt bolder climbs. Although extremely successful this activity meant that the guidebook was out of date even before publication. The Valkyrie members, many then in the Rock and Ice Club continued their activity with ascents that maintained the new higher standard: *Overhanging Wall*, *Tower Crack*, *Terrazza Crack*, *The Styx*, *BAW's Crawl*, *The Nose*, and *The Unprintable*. Peter Biven and Trevor Peck, being able to travel by car, could reach Stanage fairly easily. They ascended *Surgeon's Saunter* and *Congo Corner* as well as placing one peg and top-roping what was to become *Quietus*. Don Whillans had the confidence to try this route, but took a flier leaving Brown to climb it using a pre-

33

placed runner. Biven too was to make more impressive leads culminating in *Tower Face Direct* and *B P Super*.

Inspired by such climbing, others looked in new ways at the edge. Byne and Charles Ashbury climbed *Jitterbug Buttress*, *Crack and Cave* and *Via Roof Route*. R. A. Brown, Donald Wooler and Frank Fitzgerald attacked the challenge of *Black Hawk Bastion* using pitons. They then moved on to High Tor and did not damage Stanage again. *Flying Buttress Overhang* was also led using aid four years later reflecting a common means of ascent on certain crags, at the time, Millstone being one of the areas where it was acceptable.

All of these new routes appeared in the guidebook published in 1957. The new bold standard was made clear to all and it showed that despite 255 routes there was clearly much unclimbed rock. Ron Townsend, a consistent new router on Stanage, continued to put up routes along with members of the Rock and Ice. Joe Brown led *Esso Extra* and *Jeepers Creepers* while Willians added *Centaur*. Allan Austin and Brian Evans came down from Leeds to climb *Pullover* and Geoffrey Sutton added the *Validiction* routes.

From 1957 to 1960 it was members of the Alpha Club who were in the vanguard of development. Al Parker was the spearhead of this putting up routes such as *The Blurter*, *Lusitania*, *Fina*, *Titanic* and *Nightmare Slab*, whilst Bob Brayshaw led *Hangover* and Desperation and Paul Nunn led *Genesis*.

By 1962 there were over 300 routes on Stanage and the guidebook was out of print. Time for a new series, which acted as a spur to new routes. Pete Crew led *Orang-outang*, Clive Rowlands climbed *The Vice* while Paul Nunn added *Old Salt* and Whillans, *The Knutter* and *Don's Delight*. Len Millsom led the unprotected and bold line of *Millsom's Minion*. *B P Super* and *Tower Face Original* were now found to be impossible due to vital holds breaking off. Further along the edge, many more routes were created, the finest of which was probably *The Tippler*, climbed by Barry Webb. Don Morrison produced his *Redoubt*, *Thrombosis*, *Rigor Mortis* and *Paralysis*, so called because "one tends to stick awhile and ponder."

A year later the new guidebook was ready and ensured that Stanage had a place as one of the finest rock-climbing areas in Britain. It was now within easy reach, by car and motorbike and many came to test their skill. After so much pre-guidebook activity it is not surprising that the pace of development now

Ron Townsend on *Cave Innominate*. Photo: H C Bryson/Townsend Collection

35

slowed. This was acknowledged by the guidebook writers, 'true the pace may be somewhat slower and the difficulties great, but the lines are there for those who have eyes for see'. Many of those who had eyes to see looked elsewhere for their new routes but a small group, including Alan Clarke and Mike Parkin chose to make the new guide obsolete climbing several routes including *Quantum Crack*, *Queersville* and *Yosemite Wall*. Jim Perrin also filled some obvious gaps in 1967 with routes such as *Pedlar's Rib* and *Censor*.

However, the following few years was a period of continued controversy surrounding the use of aid. While some chose to remove it others preferred to 'bludgeon routes into submission'. Consensus now is firmly against such activity particularly, on the Stanage grit, as the guidebook writers testify, but attitudes at the time were not so clear cut. Thus John Gosling created *The Gibbon* and *The Buffoon*, Mike Simpson used a peg on *Calvary* and Ed Drummond on *The Guillotine*. Many routes were ascended clean, the most spectacular being G Dimmock's ascent of *B P Super* and *Tower Face Original*. Paul Gray was able to complete *Flying Buttress Overhang* with only one peg as a runner. Drummond then demonstrated his ability and boldness by the inspired leads of *Wuthering* and *The Archangel*. The use of aid was over.

Further major breakthroughs would need developments in protection and a climber with the ability and boldness to rise to the challenges that remained. This person was to be John Allen, one of the most significant gritstone pioneers. He began by putting up a new route to the right of *Wuthering*, *Premier*, at the age of 12. His successful partnership with Steve Bancroft was to yield a superb number and range of routes over the next few years. *Old Friends*, already cleaned and tried by others, reflected the bold commitment of this pair. It is not surprising that their exploits were compared favourably to Brown and Whillans. They also set about showing that the routes previously aided could be climbed clean, thus, they freed *The Gibbon* to create *Nectar*. Another member of the group, the much underrated Gabriel Regan, similarly freed *The Buffoon* to create *Goosey Goosey Gander*.

The ascent of *White Wand* in 1975 broadened the grade of Extreme still further. This line had long been viewed as impossible due to the lack of protection, despite the recent developments in nut protection. One morning Drummond top roped it and then left it, presuming to climb it later. During the afternoon Allen and Bancroft also top-roped it and Allen felt confident enough to solo it. A few hours later Drummond too soloed it but too late. Drummond's consolation prizes were *The Asp* and *Chameleon*.

The 1976 guidebook aimed to reflect these new standards and developments. Like previous writers they had difficulty collecting accurate information about new routes since there was no efficient mechanism to do this. Since the beginning of activity on Stanage not all routes had been recorded. This situation was made more difficult as the popularity of climbing grew and more people had the time and the means of transport to access a variety of crags. The reporting of new routes in *Crags* magazine was to aid this situation although it might also be argued that it acted as an impetus for people to reach out for new routes. At the same time the grading system was becoming an inadequate reflection of the new standards and the debate about an 'E' grading system had begun.

As might be expected a new guidebook enables activists to see any gaps. John Allen, in a rare pairing with Tom Proctor, was the first to cut the vicious roof crack above *Terrazza Crack* down to size to create *Harvest*. He followed this the next year by *Not to be Taken Away* on the large boulders below *Goliath's Groove*, a well-known problem that had been waiting for a bold ascent. Perhaps the most suprising gap filled was Phil Burke's *Dark Continent*, on a buttress that everyone had thought was worked out, once again demonstrating that some had 'eyes to see'. Similarly Al Parker, a consistent gritstone pioneer, impressed all with his ascent of the tricky *King Kong*. Bancroft similarly impressed with *Boc No Buttress* to the right of *The Asp*.

The difficulty of accurately recording climbs was demonstrated when both Gabe Regan and Gary Gibson thought they had climbed a route on the right of *Martello Buttress*. Gabe named it *After the Fire* and Gary, *Fading Star*. Investigation showed that Gary had climbed it two months earlier than Gabe. Both continued to find new routes with Gary creating over 50, one of the most impressive and serious was *Vena Cave-in*.

Activity continued in preparation for a new guidebook and with the help of continually improving protection. Yet Graham Hoey's *No More Excuses* required a 'hand-placed peg' as a runner, and still does. Jonny Woodward made an early impression with *Paranoid* on The Tippler Buttress. *The Hathersage Trip*, by Bob Berzins, was a brave lead with little protection and a possible long fall because of its position. The

Albert Hattersley on *Leaning Buttrress*. Photo: Ron Townsend

seriousness of this route has subsequently been reduced with Friends and small wires.

The new Stanage guidebook in 1984 had E grades and recorded 648 routes, all aid-free. Giles Barker pointed the way for future exploration, which had begun as the guide was being finished, towards the shorter buttresses and the large boulders. Paul Mitchell was to make a breakthrough on The Cowper Stone with *Snug as a Thug on a Jug*. Jerry Moffatt was the first to show the benefit of the new sticky boots by his spectacular solo, after toproping, of *Ulysses*. This was an arête many had looked at but it had no protection as well as being 6b. Such bold, committed climbing follows in the long tradition of exploration of Stanage Edge. It was to be continued by John Allen on his return from the New World and the new kid on the block, Jonny Dawes. Allen was to begin, almost where he left off, picking off the good lines to create *Pacific Ocean Wall* and *Wall of Sound*. *Bob's Jolly Jape* was named after Berzins who had fallen while attempting an on sight solo of the route. This was followed by the long admired line on Shock Horror Slab, *Shirley's Shining Temple*, unroped. However, one of the last great problems of the edge, the wall to the left of *Old Friends*, was climbed by Ron Fawcett to create *The Crypt Trip*.

Dawes put up several impressive leads, *Weather Report* was at the top end of E5, *Saltation* was another obvious line known by many but with extremely technical unprotected moves its ascent was aided by a hand-placed peg. Dawes's on sight solo of the holdless slab to create *Silk* reflected the characteristic style of the man.

Seemingly blank walls and arêtes were now looked at anew and skilled and bold 'gritstone gods' were able to shock mere mortals with their prowess. Allen started with *Boys will be Boys* and *Grace and Danger*. He also straightened out *BP Super* to create *Indian Summer*. It was Fawcett, after practising jumping off from ever increasing heights who climbed the left arête of *Not to be Taken Away* on the Plantation Boulders. *Careless Torque* at 7a heralded a new grade of technical difficulty for Stanage.

Dave Thomas found *My Herald of Free Enterprise*, an obvious route on an upper tier which had been missed and Neil Travers discovered *Turtle Power* on Cleft Buttress. 1992 marked the ascent of three important lines including one of pure tenacity. It was a tale of the two Barkers, who despite being unrelated had one thing in common, plenty of ability. First off was the younger of the two, Robin, with the much fancied and often attempted, *Unfamiliar*, the near perfect arête on the large boulder below *Pegasus Wall*. Andy Barker struck not long after adding *Scapa Flow* to the edge's repertoire, but Robin came back a month later when he added the unlikely looking roof left of *B.A.W.s Crawl* with *Shine On*. Fawcett, with a feat of endurance and stamina, amazed many when he traversed the entire length of the crag to give the longest route of its kind in the UK.

The search for gaps was helped by the publication in 1993 of a topo guide to Stanage by John Street, supported by the BMC Guidebook Committee. The first to be produced for gritstone, the pages were eminently photocopiable and easy to draw lines on. The subsequent climbs added to the edge were many although it is highly likely that some at least had been climbed before but never recorded. Robin Barker continued his quest to search out the hardest lines on offer when he added *Black Car Burning* to the True North Buttress and Richie Patterson was quick to follow with *Skinless Wonder* in the same area.

There were, however, still a few desperate well-known blank areas to crack, many would try them but success was hard won. Neil Foster took it on himself to scour the edge and his persistence paid off with four high quality routes. Probably his best was *Carpe Diem*, a fine solution to a long-standing problem on Robin Hood's Buttress. Even more impressive was the left arête on Tower Face, *Flight of Ideas*, climbed by Simon Jones, a very talented individual who could see holds where others couldn't. Both of these routes remain unrepeated.

A history of Stanage cannot ignore the important part that this edge has played in the development of bouldering. It contains some of the most difficult and famous problems in the UK. Many of the leading climbing activists have bouldered on various parts of Stanage throughout the century so bouldering is nothing new, but with the growth in its popularity since the nineties, it is something for which Stanage has become internationally renowned. At the time of its creation, in 1995, Jason's Myers's *Brad Pit* was one of the hardest bouldering problems in the world and was achieved using the 'jump' method. Jerry Moffatt's *The Ace* has some of the toughest moves on gritstone and is one of many routes to be worked on by exploring the boulders scattered below and around the edge. Thus this branch of the sport attracts talented climbers from around the world and suggests ways Stanage might develop in the future.

However, as the end of the century drew near Stanage continued to provide further technical challenges both on the Edge and in the bouldering areas. Dawes created a 7b with *Warmlove*, a direct finish to his own *Sad Amongst Friends* on The Cowper Stone. Joe Brown was obviously no less talented than his predecessor and put up the impressive *Cemetery Waits* on the left arête of B.A.W.'s Crawl Buttress which at E7 reflected the new standards of the time.

The next barrier was to be Stanage's first E8, *Marbellous* on Marble Wall climbed by Robin Barker. This highly technical wall was one of the last remaining gaps. The desperate *Little Women* by John Welford filled the penultimate gap on the North Buttress. The final gap was climbed by *Groove is in the Heart* by Neil Bentley. At the end of the old, and going into the new, millennium Mike Lea created, with the highly technical 7a, *Dreadnought* and *Klingon*.

Is that it? Is there no more rock left virgin on Stanage? Since the 1960s it has been considered harder and harder to find new lines. Maybe Stanage, from being a relatively unimportant crag at the beginning of the 20th century, is one of the first to reach full maturity at the end. Having received attention from almost every important climber of their day it has now become the crag which still requires a visit from every climber, however talented or experienced. Who would be brave enough to admit they have never climbed on Stanage?

Stanage has reflected every new development in gear and style, attracted climbers from Britain and overseas and had its share of controversy. It remains a beautiful, harsh, imposing crag. With even more boldness, technique, skill and unforseen developments in technology it may yet yield further delights for those 'who have the eyes to see'.

This extensive and ever-popular cliff starts in a rather inauspicious fashion with the east-facing wall of Chippy Buttress, which emerges from the wasteland of White Path Moss. It is home to four oddly titled routes on very rounded and often rather dirty rock. Whether the names stem from the rock being greasy or the routes being tasty offerings is open to question. In front of Chippy Buttress stands the tilted block that forms The Cowper Stone and running to the south-east, there is a series of low walls that culminate in True North Buttress below the prominent trig point.

CHIPPY BUTTRESS

As on all of the rest of the cliff, the routes are described from RIGHT to LEFT. The most prominent feature is a rounded arête split by a short discontinuous crack, the line of Chips.

Peas 10m E4 5c (1985)

Start at the nose of the buttress and climb up rightwards, tackling the bulges via a difficult mantelshelf. Step right and follow the right-hand side of the upper wall to finish left of the arête.

1. Peas	E4
2. Chips	E3
3. Salt and Vinegar	S
4. Pudding	E1

Chips   7m   E3 5c   (1985)
Climb the cracked arête to the left of Peas to cross the main
bulge and continue up the left-hand side of the upper wall.
Rounded in the extreme.

Salt and Vinegar   6m   S   (1993)
Step from a boulder to climb the obvious right-slanting crack,
finishing by a bulging fissure above.

Pudding   7m   E1 5c   (1985)
The wall to the left of the obvious crack is climbed via rounded
breaks and sloping holds.

Standing in front of Chippy Buttress is:

THE COWPER STONE

The Cowper Stone, standing like a huge rolling cowpat guarding
the northern end of Stanage Edge is, in some ways, not part of the
crag at all. The rock is rougher, the grains much larger and coarser
and its rounded black bulges attract an entirely different
personality and mood from those who are headed to the nearby
Popular End. Yet to many devotees, this ugly lump, this bastard
offspring, is the very essence of gritstone climbing, for without
the requisite amounts of balance, technique, power and
determination, the climbs will be impossible. However, for those

1. Breakdance	E3
2. Snug as a Thug on a Jug	E4
3. Sad Amongst Friends	E6
4. Whatever Happened to Bob?	E3

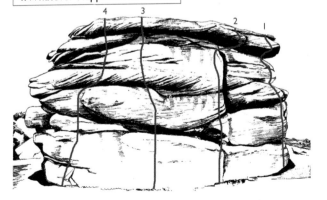

43

in possession of these qualities, the Cowper Stone will provide some of the most perversely satisfying moments on grit.

As said, the rock is extremely rough, and the climbing tends to be based around contortions over gruesome bulges and gaining and passing wide breaks which all seem to slope in every dimension. A good variety of camming devices will prove useful for most routes, as will very thick skin and the ability to handle rejection. If you have never climbed on gritstone, the evil sloping nature of the routes on this block makes it probably the worst place that you could choose to start your apprenticeship. However, this section of the cliff is the only part of Stanage to receive early morning sunshine (apart from the Old Friends wall) and so it is a suitable winter venue on cold, clear days.

Head Spin   6m   E1 6a   (1986)
The right-hand side of the right-hand wall of the buttress leads steeply past four rounded breaks to finish on a sloping ledge.

Leroy Slips a Disc   6m   E2 6c   (1986)
The pocketed wall between Head Spin and the arête of Breakdance is well-named. Contort, slap and struggle to exit on a shelf.

Breakdance   7m   E3 6a   ★   (1985)
The bulging right-hand arête of the leaning front face of the buttress is climbed by a series of weird contortions that prove strangely satisfying. The finish is rounded but not markedly more than the rest of the route.

Traverse of the Gritstone Gods   14m   E4 6b   ★★
                                                               (1986)
A superb and highly arduous right-to-left traverse of the buttress starting up Breakdance and finishing as for Whatever Happened to Bob? following the highest horizontal break throughout using a series of sloping holds and flared jams.

Happy Amongst Friends   7m   E6 6c   ★   †   (1996)
A tough eliminate up the bulging wall to the left of Breakdance, finishing as for Snug as a Thug on a Jug.

Snug as a Thug on a Jug   8m   E4 6b   ★★★   (1983)
Start up a flared crack in the right-hand side of the face. Follow this to flutings on its left followed by a move right to a short flared corner and an horrendous faith-and-friction mantelshelf finish. Described by the first ascensionist as 'a must for masochistic thugs' it remains just that. A direct finish,

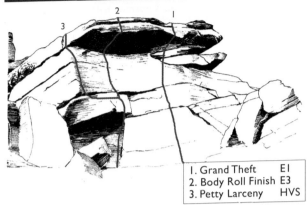

1. Grand Theft	E1
2. Body Roll Finish	E3
3. Petty Larceny	HVS

Warmlove E6 7a ★ † (1995), utilises a pebble attained by a long reach. A very strict approach to using the pebble must be adhered to mantain this grade.

Sad Amongst Friends 8m E6 6c ★★ (1984)
Climb the impossible-looking central section of the face to finish past a protruding iron carbonate 'blister' on the lip of the final overhang. The lower section is bold but the finish is well-protected and quite unique. Hard and very technical at the grade, the solo first ascent was audacious.

Whatever Happened to Bob? 7m E3 5c (1983)
Start at the left-hand side of the overhanging face and follow flakes initially rightwards then back left to finish. One of the easier routes on the buttress but still no pushover. The above climb corresponds in part at least to **Little Weed** E3 5c (1989), which starts at a hanging flake three metres left of Sad Amongst Friends and goes directly up the wall.

Bodypopping 7m VS 5a (1997)
From a small cutaway just left of the left-hand arête of the front face of the buttress, climb the left side of the arête and the wall above to a rounded finish.

Three hundred and thirty metres to the left, past several low outcrops that offer good bouldering, is a flat wall capped by a long roof.

Grand Theft 6m E1 5c ★ (1982)
Climb the middle of the flat wall using a series of thin cracks

45

trending slightly rightwards to a position below the roof. Make a long reach left over the roof and finish with an awkward mantelshelf. **Small Time Crook** E2 6b (2000) ascends the wall just left to the break beneath the widest part of the roof. Pull round this to finish (not so) gracefully.

Petty Larceny   5m   HVS 5c   (1982)
Make steep moves over the cutaway just to the right of the overhang on the left-hand arête (crux) and move left to finish up the arête; good moves but, unfortunately, escapable. The **Body Roll Finish** E3 6a (1989) surmounts the cutaway but continues up to, and over, the left-hand side of the roof above.

Eighty metres farther left and past short walls that have been climbed on for years, are a couple of slabs that offer some pleasant problems of no great difficulty. The first slab takes the form of a short rib with a crack on each side.

Scrag End   5m   VD   (1992)
Climb the flaky crack on the right-hand side of the rib to a steeper exit.

Spare Rib   5m   VD   (1992)
The centre of the rib is followed pleasantly, passing a couple of tiny overlaps.

Twelve metres to the left is a similar but broader slab.

Miny   5m   HS 4b   (1992)
The face is climbed keeping one metre left of the right-hand edge of the slab.

Meeny   5m   HS 4a   (1992)
Climb directly up the centre of the slab using an assortment of sloping breaks and finish just right of the projecting beak.

Eeny   5m   HVD   (1992)
Climb the slab keeping one metre right of its left-hand arête.

Thirty metres to the left things begin to get more impressive in the form of a leaning face capped by a trig point. This is:

TRUE NORTH BUTTRESS

The long drawn-out section of the edge strewn between the Cowper Stone and the beginning of the Popular End, several hundred metres away, is mainly made up of rather short and

1. Miny	HS	
2. Meeny	HS	
3. Eeny	HVD	

sporadic buttresses which, while they are still made from good quality rock, never quite reach a satisfactory height to be good routes. Jaded boulderers, however, can eke out many an exploratory session throughout the whole length of this section of crag, with problems ranging from obscure sitdown sequences to hard traverses on the finest of Stanage slopers never being more than a few metres apart. Solitude and a sense of discovery are the rewards here.

However, standing proud above the small outcrops is the powerful True North Buttress, an architecturally stunning piece of rock that crowns this whole area. Severely undercut and overhanging, with evil holds set at almost Cowper Stonesque angles, it is home to the highest concentration of hard climbs on the whole escarpment. It is most easily recognized by a concrete trig point on the summit, the abandoned millstones tossed at the base and the lack of chalk on the poor holds.

On the right-hand side of the buttress is a boulder-filled cleft with the narrow projecting prow of Mating Toads to its right. Starting from the ancient quarried ledges right of the prow is:

Massacre 7m E1 5b (1982)
Climb the wall utilising slopers to a break. Swing leftwards along the break with reckless abandon to finish on the arête. A direct finish above the slopers is possible.

Mating Toads 6m HVS 5c (1982)
Ascend the narrow, blunt rib immediately to the right of the

47

block-filled gully. This is harder than it looks and the crux is one move higher than you might expect, as you reach past the small overhang.

The right-hand side of the main face is bounded by a blunt arête to the left of the boulder-filled cleft. Two routes have been claimed around this feature but it is difficult to work out their exact relationship to each other. This is the present understanding of these climbs.

True North 9m VS 4c   (1961-63)
Climb on to the large boulder jammed in the gully and continue up the right-hand side of the blunt arête to the left. Finish up the final short wall by a long reach.

1. Massacre	E1
2. Mating Toads	HVS
3. True North	VS

In the 1964 guidebook the description for True North was:
'ascend the sharp arête with difficulty to the overhang. This is
taken on its left side using good horizontal cracks to the top',
which sounds very much like the next route. In the 1976 guide
the route was omitted and by 1983 the first description was in
regular use. By this time another route had appeared in the
form of:

Magnetic North   9m   E3 5c   ★   †   (1982)
Start to the left of the gully and climb the arête on its left-hand
side using the diagonal crack, with a hard move to gain a
projecting ledge on the right. Continue up the arête with a hard
swing left at the overhang to an easier finish. HVS was the
route's original grade, a recent ascent gave the E3 grade.

Black Car Burning 9m E7 6c ★★ † (1993)
An exceptionally arduous climb following a line up the vertical
face to the left of the right-hand arête. Start under the shallow
feature of Groove is in the Heart and trend rightwards to a
poor hold under the roof. Make a hard move to a hold on the
lip and finish more easily by long reaches.

The attractive, open scoop to the left is:

Groove is in the Heart 8m E7 7a ★★★ (1998)
The shallow central groove of the buttress was once one of the
last great problems of the edge. Small (pre-placed) RPs protect
a series of technical and fingery moves through the stacked
overlaps to a rounded finish. Awaits a lead without the pre-
placed RPs.

Little Women 10m E7 7a ★★ † (1997)
Another high-quality modern desperate. Gain the sloping shelf
to the left of the previous route and place protection in the
slanting break up to the left. Make gruesome moves moves right
along the lip, aiming for a big jug on the hanging nose in the
middle of the buttress. If successful, a long lock-off will bring
rapid relief.

Stanage Without Oxygen 9m E5 6c ★★ (1983)
The easiest route on this section of wall climbs directly up the
left-hand side of the front face of the buttress aiming for the
right edge of the capping roof to a finish up the chipped holds
of Apparent North. The crucial move requires a fierce pull on a
sloper that is barely discernible from the vertical rock that
surrounds it. The grade is height dependant.

Skinless Wonder 9m E6 6c ★★ (1993)
Yet another hard route, which takes a direct line through
Apparent North with a powerful start and a hideous
mantelshelf finish. Start up a small hanging arête at the left-hand
corner of the face and make a hard move to reach the break of
Apparent North. Move one metre to the right and climb
directly over the hideous shelving top of the buttress.

Apparent North 15m HVS 5b ★★ (1961-63)
Around to the left is a short steep crack springing from a large
recess. Climb the crack to reach a horizontal break and follow
this rightwards on to the front of the buttress. Finish via the
obvious break and the chipped holds on the slab above.

1. Mating Toads	HVS
2. Black Car Burning	E7
3. Little Women	E7
4. Stanage Without Oxygen	E5
5. Apparent North	HVS
6. Skinless Wonder	E6
7. Eminence Grise	E2
8. My Crazy Head	HVS

Led a Dance 18m E1 5b ★   (1984)
Start as for the previous climb but follow the break all the way
to the right-hand edge of the buttress. A remarkable exercise
in horizontal jamming. A plentiful supply of large camming
devices would be useful.

Eminence Grise 7m E2 6a   (1983)
Climb the vertical crack of Apparent North to the roof, which
is usually surmounted with something of a battle.

Frigid Witch 6m HVS 5b   (1983)
The bulging wall to the left of the vertical crack at the left-hand
end of the buttress leads to a gripping finale.

The right arête of the clean wall a few metres to the left of Frigid
Witch provides **My Crazy Head** HVS 6a (1993) with a couple of
excellent moves.

Forty metres to the left is a small but attractive flat buttress split
near its left-hand side by an obvious crack.

EASY JAMMING BUTTRESS

Scary Canary 6m HVS 5b (1993)
The right-hand arête of the buttress has good moves linking the breaks.

Twin Cam 6m E4 6c ★★ (1984)
A series of desperate moves lead up the blank wall to the right of the crack passing three horizontal breaks and a cluster of tiny pebbles. Sadly the flake at the start has been chipped.

The Real 20-foot Crack 6m VS 4c ★ (pre-1989)
The superb crack one metre to the left of the centre of the wall.

Trainer Failure 6m VS 5a (pre-1989)
The pumpy left-hand arête of the face is followed.

Easy Jamming 6m HVD (pre-1989)
The crack one metre to the left is misnamed.

Easy Walling 6m HVS 5c (1970s)
Climb straight up the centre of the wall to the left with a far from easy start.

1. Scary Canary	HVS
2. Twin Cam	E4
3. The Real 20-foot Crack	VS
4. Trainer Failure	VS
5. Easy Jamming	HVD

To the left the line of the edge is marked by boulders and the occasional small buttress. Many good problems can be found there on exceptionally sound rock. Eighty five metres to the left is a more continuous section of rock with three short problems. **Gripple One** 5a starts one metre right of the green streak and uses pockets and sloping holds to reach easier moves. The green streak is climbed by **Gripple Two** 5a via a useful pocket. Finally **Gripple Three** 5a takes a line one and a half metres left of the green streak passing a slanting pocket

Three hundred and seventy metres to the left and overlooking the Hope Valley is the start of the magnificent main escarpment of Stanage Edge and this first section is known, for reasons which will become obvious, as the Popular End.

The Popular End is the shopping mall of Stanage where, if you don't mind a bit of a crowd, you can get the best and most of whatever you could ever want. It begins with End Buttress and from there extends south-west as a continuous outcrop of the best gritstone to be found anywhere. The concentration of very, very high quality outcrop climbing is unsurpassed and for one, two and three star climbs in the lower to middle grades, it's hard to imagine anywhere better. The rock is peerless and just about every route is worth doing. This concentration of fantastic quality extends without the merest pause and passing some of the proudest buttresses on grit, as far as B.A.W.'s Crawl Buttress. Only there does its energy start to fizzle out.

Throughout its length, a refreshing variety of styles will match most moods. Jam cracks, overhangs, corners and delicate slabs are all in abundance to please the beginner and expert alike. Only the lover of the awkward thrutch will walk away disappointed, although with careful searching, even he will end up with a smile on his face. The cost of this popularity is busyness, especially on summer weekends, although with Stanage being what it is, one need not walk very far to find some peace and quiet if it all gets a bit much. It also means that the terrain is badly worn, although considering the traffic, the climbs are standing up well.

END BUTTRESS

Takes the form of a square-fronted buttress undercut along its front face and split by a wide crack close to its left-hand edge. It is bounded on the right by a steep corner and to the right of this is a short wall with a couple of problems that have almost certainly been climbed before. **The End of All Things** S (1997) climbs to a triangular roof and moves round it to easier rock. To the right

The Be All and End All VD (1997) gains a small triangular niche just right of the corner and exits rightwards to continue pleasantly to the top.

Fire Curtain 8m VD   (1992)
The angular corner on the right-hand side of the buttress.

Happy Hips 8m HVS 6a   (1993)
The right-hand side of the rib to the left is followed throughout. The difficulties ease as height is gained.

Finale 8m HVS 5b   (1961-63)
The undercut right-hand arête of the buttress is gained from the right with a thin pull and a tricky step round the arête. Continue carefully up shelving rock. **Finale Direct** HVS 6a (1983-89) gains the easier upper section of Finale by technically difficult moves starting from a jam under the right-hand edge of the roof.

Suzanne 8m HVS 6a ★   (1965)
A classic problem up the centre of the face of End Buttress. Reaching the large break above the overhang often involves mounting frustration and eventually a lurch, although the strong may do the moves fluently. Continue to the top up shelving rock.

Ding Dong 8m VS 5b   (1961-63)
The arête to the right of the crack that splits the left-hand edge of the buttress is easier if recourse is made to Gashed Crack.

Gashed Crack 7m VS 5a   (1961-63)
The crack on the left-hand of the buttress overhangs awkwardly at the start, but eases above the bulge.

Gashed Knee 7m VS 5a   (1993)
The projecting left arête of Gashed Crack is climbed on its left-hand side, avoiding the use of the (in)convenient blocks. The wall just left is 4c.

Eight metres to the left and beyond an area of rocks too low to be of interest is a square buttress protruding from the edge.

SQUARE BUTTRESS

Square Buttress Corner 6m D   (1961-63)
Climb the short corner on the right.

Square Buttress Wall   6m   S 4a   ★   (1961-63)
Climb the centre of the right-hand wall of the buttress. It is
steep and pleasant.

Square Buttress Arête   6m   VS 4c   (1961-63)
The right-hand arête is climbed mostly on its right-hand side.

Square Buttress Direct   7m   HVS 5b   (1961-63)
The centre of the front face of the buttress is taken directly.
Start up undercut rock and, with a difficult pull, gain the ledge at
half-height.

Monkey Crack   6m   VD   (1923-51)
The shallow, undercut corner crack immediately left of Square
Buttress is awkward to start and remains steep throughout.

Square Chimney   6m   M   (1923-51)
The chimney two metres left bounds the left edge of Square
Buttress. Climb this and escape out left at the capstone.

Square Chimney Arête   6m   S 4b   (1997)
With sufficient discipline it is possible to climb the arête just to
the left of the chimney on its right-hand side using a finger
crack to the right.

DESCENT ROUTE
Just to the left is a short chimney that is steep and somewhat
awkward towards the bottom.

On the left-hand side of a recess is a small buttress with three
previously unrecorded climbs, though they have almost certainly
been climbed for many years.

Velcro Arête   6m   VD   (1993)
The right-hand arête of the buttress has its moments.

Toggle   8m   S   (1993)
The centre of the narrow face just to the left is climbed passing
a small crack at two metres and a tricky move just below the
top.

Button Wall   6m   VD   (1993)
The crack to the right of the left-hand arête of the buttress.

DESCENT ROUTE
To the left a short open corner leads down to a good ledge,

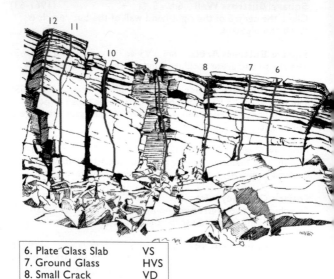

6. Plate Glass Slab	VS	
7. Ground Glass	HVS	
8. Small Crack	VD	
9. Hoaxer's Crack	VS	
10. Nicheless Climb	S	
11. Rugosity Crack	HVS	
12. South Sea Charmer	HVS	

below which, short cracks lead to the foot of the cliff. This is rather easier than the descent route described to the right.

To the left is a V-shaped cleft with a block at its base.

Zip Crack 7m M   (1961-63)
The line is obvious.

To the left is a more prominent buttress with a series of stacked roofs on its left-hand side. This is:

MANTELPIECE BUTTRESS

Mantelpiece Right 7m D   (1923-51)
Climb the depression just left of the right-hand edge of the buttress to a ledge and continue up the wall above.

1. Suzanne	HVS
2. Square Buttress Direct	HVS
3. Button Wall	VD
4. Mantelpiece Buttress Direct	HVS
5. Mental Peace	E2

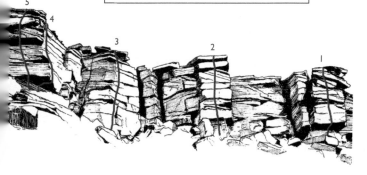

Fragile Mantel   7m   VS 5a   (1993)
Climb the wall passing the right-hand edge of the disappearing
roof with a long reach for the ledge; finish easily.

Mantelpiece Buttress Direct   8m   HVS 5b   ★   (1961-63)
A short crack splits the nose of the overhang. Taken direct this
gives excellent strenuous climbing which eases above the roof.

Mental Peace   8m   E2 5c   (1993)
Start under the left-hand side of the tiered overhangs of
Mantelpiece Buttress and climb through the centre of these to
a tough finish.

The initial strenuous moves on Mantelpiece Buttress Direct can
be avoided from the left by one of the following variants.

Mantelpiece Lower Hand-Traverse
10m   HVS 4c   ★   (1951-56)
The lowest break via a swinging hand-traverse joins the regular
route just above its crux.

Mantelpiece Upper Hand-Traverse
10m   HVS 5a   (1989-97)
The break below the roof gives a crab-like shuffle until it is
possible to step around the arête.

Mantelpiece Buttress 7m D (1923-51)
The oddly-named slanting flake crack which bounds the left-hand side of the steep buttress. It is most easily reached by starting under the roof and traversing left to the base of the flake, though a more direct start has one polished move of 4b to reach the initial ledges.

Mantelpiece Crack 7m M (traditional)
The crack that bounds the right-hand side of the steep slab to the left.

To the left is a pleasant section of slabby rock, popular in the 'olden-days' hence the state of some of the footholds that were ground into patches of shiny rock by the passage of many hobnail-booted climbers.

PLATE GLASS SLAB

Carborundum 7m VS 5a (1993)
The slab just right of the well-scratched start of Plate Glass Slab has a couple of long reaches.

Plate Glass Slab 7m VS 4c ★ (1923-51)
The centre of the slab has a glassy start from a boulder up two well-scratched flakes. The route then eases.

Ground Glass 7m HVS 4c ★ (1923-51)
Ascend the shallow corner in the wall to the right of the prominent crack that bounds the left-hand edge of the slabby section of rock, with a tricky move just below half-height.

Small Crack 6m VD (1923-51)
Just to the left climb the straight and narrow crack that bounds the left-hand edge of the slab. The footholds are glossy and the crack is not the most useful width.

Blunt Arête (Trivial Pursuit) 6m VS 5a (1976)
From just left of Small Crack climb directly to a ledge, continue straight up past a suspect flake to an awkward finish.

Hoaxer's Crack 7m VS 4b (1961-63)
Just to the left, and immediately right of a narrow chimney, climb the thin, steep finger crack to a reach for solid jams.

DESCENT ROUTE

Not surprisingly the easy chimney just to the left is called Easy Chimney. It has now been relegated to a descent route and is rather tricky towards the bottom.

The square tower to the left is split by a wide crack/narrow chimney that runs out at half-height. There are several closely packed routes there as climbers of yesteryear tried to climb every piece of the buttress.

RUGOSITY CRACK BUTTRESS

Right Edge 9m S   (pre-1964)
Climb the stepped arête immediately to the left of Easy Chimney with steep moves at half-height to reach ledges on the right, just below the top. Finish up a short awkward crack close to Easy Chimney. Not a very satisfying route.

Nicheless Climb 9m S 4b   (1951-56)
Start below a wide crack in the centre of the wall to the left of Easy Chimney and ascend the short steep wall to a good ledge. Finish up the wide crack above.

The Christiania Swing 10m S 4b   (1912-14)
Start up the chimney crack that splits the centre of the buttress and climb to a niche then gain a ledge on the right. Move right and finish up Nicheless Climb.

Niche Wall Direct 10m S 4b ★   (1976-1983)
Climb the chimney crack to a good ledge and head up the steep continuation finger crack above. This gives pleasant, well-protected moves. The original route **Niche Wall** (1954) moved right from the good ledge to finish up the wide crack of Nicheless Climb at the same grade.

Rugosity Crack 9m HVS 5b ★★   (1961-63)
The prominent thin crack which splits the narrow tower to the left is a little gem and is indicative of the quality of things to come. Climb to a ledge then finger-jam the crucial central section before pressing on directly up the face above. A variation **South Sea Charmer** HVS 5b ★ (1978) follows the previous route to its crux then swings out to gain the left-hand arête of the buttress.

Around to the left is a stygian chimney and a platform that runs along the base of the cliff.

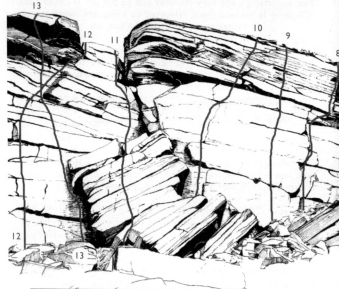

8. Green Wall	VS	11. Grotto Slab	D
9. Reagent	E5	12. Heather Wall	VS
10. Grotto Wall	HVS	13. Chimp's Corner	VS

Black Chimney 9m D (1923-51)
Plumbs the depth of the chimney and not a route for the claustrophobic.

To the left a fallen block lies at the foot of the cliff and the top of the block is a platform with some vegetation surviving near its left-hand edge. This is the start of the:

GULLIBLE'S TRAVELS AREA

The 3-D Wall 8m E2 6a (1979)
Ascend the wall from the right-hand side of the platform and keep between one and two metres from the chimney. Good, but escapable, climbing which features long reaches and proves to be harder for the short.

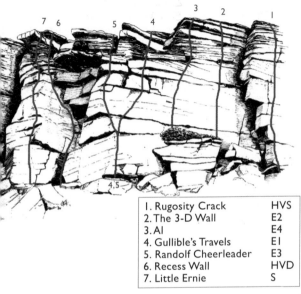

1. Rugosity Crack	HVS
2. The 3-D Wall	E2
3. Al	E4
4. Gullible's Travels	E1
5. Randolf Cheerleader	E3
6. Recess Wall	HVD
7. Little Ernie	S

Al   8m   E4 5c   (1985)
From the gorse-covered left-hand end of the platform, climb
the faint scoop trending right to finish up the wall. Rarely
repeated for several reasons; it being dirty, hard, reachy and
poorly protected are the most obvious.

Gullible's Travels   10m   E1 5b   ★   (1961-63)
Start at the left-hand corner of the wall and trend right with
reachy and delicate moves at mid-height. Good technical
climbing, protectable with small cams.

Randolf Cheerleader   10m   E3 6a   (1983)
Climb the rib at the left-hand edge of the wall to a bulge. A
mean rock-over and a long reach brings the short crack to the
left within reach. Easier ground remains.

To the left is a deep V-shaped recess capped by a large triangular
roof.

Right Wall Route 10m HVD (1923-51)
A steep slab forms the right-hand side of the recess. Climb this
and move right to finish up a crack that cuts round the right
edge of the roof.

L Gareth 24/05/03
S Nancy ——//——

✓**Recess Wall** 10m HVD (1923-51)
Climb the right-hand edge of the steep slab that forms the left-
hand side of the recess, passing the left-hand edge of the
capping overhang.

In Earnest 10m HVS 5a (1993)
The square left-hand arête of the recess has an awkward short
wall for starters followed by a couple of pleasantly delicate
moves before it eases.

Big Chris 10m E1 5b (1993)
The centre of the face of Little Ernie is climbed directly, starting
up a thin flake and finishing up the crack splitting the final
overhang.

Little Ernie 8m S 4b (1961-63)
Start at the left-hand edge of the small buttress which forms
the right-hand side of the obvious blocked chimney and climb
on to a ledge before trending rightwards to reach easier
ground.

Capstone Chimney 10m D ★ (1910s)
The wide, capped chimney to the left forms a good introduction
to chimney techniques.

A smooth wall stretches away to the left featuring a slumped slab
at its left-hand side. This is the:

GROTTO SLAB AREA

Green Wall 10m VS 4b ★ (1958)
On the right-hand side of the smooth wall is a flake-crack.
Climb this until a traverse right gains the final, usually green,
chimney crack which is awkward to enter.

Reagent 12m E5 6a (1984)
An unprotected and rarely repeated route up the smooth wall
just to the left. From just left of the start of the flake of Green
Wall, rock up and stretch left to reach a good hold. An
enormous span from this (or a jump at E6 6b) gains small holds

followed by a further reach for better ones. From the break climb, more easily, up the often dirty wall above.

Grotto Wall   14m   HVS 4c   ★   (1923-51)
A pleasant but neglected climb up the left-hand side of the smooth wall. Start immediately right of the slumped flake of Grotto Slab. Gain the shallow left-facing groove and climb this to its top. Exit awkwardly and finish up the final wall trending rightwards on generally good but elusive holds.

Jersey Boys   14m   E1 5a   (1989)
Start from the 'pit' behind the right-hand side of Grotto Slab. Climb the easy corner to the top of the slab to take the blunt rib on the right. Move right to pass the roof and continue up the wall on large sloping holds.

To the left a large tilted slab rests against the wall and gives a pleasant beginners' route.

Grotto Slab   14m   D   ★   (1912-14)
Start at the toe of the slab and ascend to its apex by any one of a series of variations. A couple of short corners then lead to the cliff top.

DESCENT ROUTE
Grotto Slab is often used as a way down by the suitably competent.

Chimp's Corner   12m   VS 5b   (1961-63)
The overhanging corner that bounds the left side of Grotto Slab is climbed in a rather simian fashion. Above this, move up and left to a large ledge and pull over the final roof using a superb jug on its rim.

To the left of Grotto Slab is a fine crack-riven wall with one excellent climb and a couple of variations.

Heather Wall   12m   VS 4c   ★★   (1923-51)
Climb the excellent steep face to the left of Grotto Corner using a series of meandering cracks, to a deeper vertical crack. Difficult moves above this gain a ledge then a right-trending scoop. From the large ledge at the top of the scoop finish up the corner on the right. **Heather Wall Variation** HVS 5a (1976-82) follows the thin cracks just to the right of the regular route and immediately left of Chimp's Corner. From a deep horizontal break move left to join the parent route.

6. Tier Climb	S
7. Manchester Buttress	HS
8. Beggar's Crack	VS
9. Anatomy	VD
10. Physiology	VD

Crack and Corner   15m   S 4b   ★★   (1923-51)
Set in the arête to the left is a right-angled corner. This is
started with difficulty using a variety of polished holds and has
long been a well-known sandbag. Continue up the excellent
groove to a comfortable platform below an overhanging block.
This is overcome at its left-hand corner by a final ungainly
move. The arête immediately right is **War Zone** E1 6a (1976-
79), the start is hard but eases with height; unfortunately
escapable.

Lancashire Wall   12m   HVS 5a   ★   (1978)
The centre of the wall to the left has a delicate start from a

Eliminator HVS 5b (page 71)
Climber: Chris Craggs Photo: Ian Smith

9 O'clock Watershed   E6 6c   (page 73)
Climber: Neil Foster   Photo: David Simmonite

Paranoid E6 6b (page 73)
Climber: Mike Lea Photo: David Simmonite

Kirkus's Corner   E1 5b   (page 77)
Climber: Chris Wright   Photo: David Simmonite

1. Heather Wall	VS
2. Crack and Corner	S
3. Lancashire Wall	HVS
4. Cakestand	S
5. Two Tier Climb	VS

block and a moderately thrilling finale up the leaning front face of the final detached block. Fortunately the good holds keep on arriving.

Cool Groove 10m S   (1961-63)
Just to the left the obvious open groove leads easily to a capping overhang, the passing of which provides the fun.

Cakestand 9m S 4b   (1961-63)
Immediately left of the open groove is a narrow buttress comprising a series of stacked blocks, follow this, with the

occasional long reach, to a narrow ledge just below the top. The true finish up the rounded buttress is tough, though there is an easier corner immediately to the left.

Two Tier Climb   12m   VS 5a   (1961-63)
In the back corner of the bay is an easy groove and left of this is a two-tiered buttress. The lower section is slabby and leads to a bouldery ledge. The continuation wall is hard to start, not well-protected and with a poor landing but fortunately short-lived. Another sandbag that was graded V Diff for 30 years.

DESCENT ROUTE

To the left a chimney with a large, sloping chockstone provides an easy but devious way down.

The next buttress projects forward with a slabby front face and a steep left wall. This is the ever popular:

MANCHESTER BUTTRESS

Tier Climb   12m   S   (1961-63)
An unsatisfactory climb up the right-hand edge of Manchester Buttress. Climb the lower tier via a troublesome V-shaped groove to reach a good ledge to gain the short steep crack above the right-hand edge of this; finish steeply.

Manchester Buttress   15m   HS 4b   ★★★   (1932-33)
Climb the crack in the arête before moving left in an exposed position underneath the overhang. Go up to a deep horizontal break then make an awkward traverse back to the right and around the nose to get established on a ledge. Finish directly. A more direct alternative is **Manchester United** HVS 5b (1988). Climb up the face right of the starting crack of Manchester Buttress, to the horizontal break. A long reach gains the ledge of the parent route and a common finish.

The steep left wall of Manchester Buttress is home to three routes. Oddly enough the original description of Tip Off (in the 1983 guide) clearly describes it as taking the flake at the left-hand edge of the face, though by the 1989 guide it had mysteriously moved to the hanging groove on the right-hand side of the face.

Moss Side   13m   E4 6a   (1994)
Climb the obvious shallow polished scoop via a tough mantelshelf to reach the break. Continue up the centre of the well-brushed upper wall via an essential pebble.

Tip Off Right   14m   E1 5b   (1983-89)
Climb the blunt rib on the left to a move to the right and head
up the hanging flake directly above the point where Manchester
Buttress swings round the corner. Not really very inspiring.

Tip Off   14m   E2 5c   (1978)
Climb the blunt rib on the left then gain and climb the flake
crack close to Beggar's Crack. Not much better than its right-
hand neighbour.

Beggar's Crack   13m   VS 5a   (1923-51)
The wider crack that bounds the left-hand edge of the face has
an overhang at mid-height. The main difficulty is getting
established in the crack.

Tinker's Crack   13m   VS 4c   ★   (1961-63)
The narrow wall to the left is split in its upper part by an
indefinite crack. Pull over a bulge to gain the crack and follow it
with a couple of tricky moves in the middle section where it
briefly disappears.

To the left is a recess with climbs up both corners and also one
up the narrow central face. This is a popular venue with top-roping
hordes, an explanation for the unpleasantly-glossed nature of these
climbs.

Anatomy   13m   VD   (1923-51)
The right-hand corner is climbed with a move left at the
awkward overhang. Finish up the continuation corner. An
alternative is **Another Ology** VS 4c (2000) which climbs the
corner followed by the wide crack directly above.

Sociology   13m   S   (1923-51)
The centre of the narrow face on the left is best climbed
directly, initially up the front face of a block.

✓ **Physiology**   13m   VD   ★   L Gareth 29/05/03   (1923-51)
                                  S Nancy
The left-hand crack is followed throughout and is the best of
this trio.

To the left is a fine projecting buttress with an overhang at two
metres. This is:

GARGOYLE BUTTRESS

Dry Rot   13m   E2 5b   ★   (1981)
From the right-hand toe of the buttress step left along the

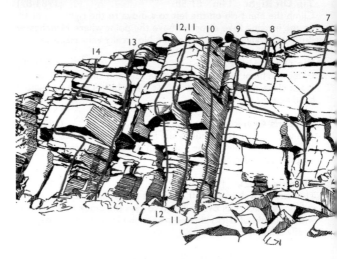

horizontal break, then pull up and right with difficulty before
following the precarious and poorly protected right-hand edge
of the slab to finish over the capping stone.

Gargoyle Buttress 14m VS 4b ★★   (1949)
Start at the right-hand toe of the buttress and follow a
horizontal crack out to the left. Pull up (and definitely not out)
on a slightly suspect perched 'boulder' and finish up the centre
of the wall above.

Gargoyle Variant HS 4b ★   (1955-56)
This begins under the hanging left-hand arête of the buttress
and climbs the wide crack to the overhangs. A traverse out
right joins the regular route just before the suspect 'boulder'
and a common finish.

Moriarty 16m E3 6a   (1989)
The overhanging stepped arête left of Gargoyle Buttress is
climbed starting as for Gargoyle Variant. Continue by difficult
undercut, shin-grinding laybacking.

To the left is a deep chimney followed by a fine flat wall running
leftwards into a steep right-angled corner. This is the ever-popular:

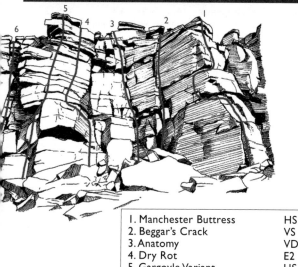

1. Manchester Buttress	HS
2. Beggar's Crack	VS
3. Anatomy	VD
4. Dry Rot	E2
5. Gargoyle Variant	HS
6. Black Hawk Hell Crack	S
7. Providence	E1
8. Black Hawk Traverse Left	VD
9. Castle Crack	HS
10. Eliminator	HVS
11. Black Hawk Bastion	E3
12. Chameleon	E4
13. The Y Crack	VS
14. The Tippler	E1

BLACK HAWK AREA

Ugly Mugs   15m   VS 4c   (1997)
Start at the open polished corner below the main chimney and
bridge up this to ledges in the base of the chimney proper.
Traverse out right at the lowest possible level to reach and
climb the juggy and exposed arête.

Black Hawk Traverse Right   16m   D   ★   (1912-14)
Start to the left of the prominent chimney and follow scratched
footholds rightwards to a crack; climb this to bulges. At the
level of these, step right and climb the main fissure to the
capping overhang which is skirted on the left. Known as
Blizzard Chimney for a time.

Black Hawk Hell Crack   14m   S 4a   ★★   (1932-33)
This excellent route takes the steep, well-protected, crack to
the left of the chimney.

In the centre of the face is a well-polished vertical crack running
into a zone of smoother rock.

Tribute to Kitty   15m   E6 6c   ★   (1985/1999)
Pull over the overhang to the right of Providence and continue
up the wall above on any remaining pebbles and poor sloping
holds. This route was originally E5 6b but was unrepeated for
14 years since the loss of one of the pebbles used to surmount
the roof. It has now been reclimbed, but more pebbles may have
since disappeared.

Providence   15m   E1 5c   (1978)
In the centre of the wall is a shallow niche above which is a
left-slanting crack. Climb into the niche to reach the bottom of
the slanting crack. Lean rightwards and use small holds to climb
up to the ledge above. Step right and ascend the final wall
directly.

Black Hawk Traverse Left   17m   VD   ★★   (1912-14)
Climb Providence to the shallow niche and make the wide
'Bishop's Stride' move round the bulge to the left. Continue up
and leftwards to a good ledge with a potential belay site; the
'Parapet'. There are various finishes, with the obvious crack on
the right being the best, the wider crack directly above being
the most popular and the chimney on the left being the easiest.

Burgess's Variation   17m   S 4a   ★★   (1930s)
This climb avoids the long stride on the previous route by an
ascending leftwards traverse. Follow Black Hawk Traverse Left
to the niche and move left to follow the left-slanting crack until
it is possible to climb the right-hand of a pair of cracks in the
left-hand side of the final wall.

Divine Providence   16m   HVS 5b   ★   (1991)
Start in the V-shaped groove just left of the start of Black Hawk
Traverse Left. Climb this to polished ledges, step right and
climb the thin leftward-slanting crack on Providence until near
its top. Pull straight up to reach ledges and finish directly up the
wall above with a tricky finish.

Black Hawk   15m   HS 4c   ★★   (1932-33)
This route uses bits of earlier climbs but offers a good direct
line in a surprisingly modern way. Just to the right of the corner

bounding the left-hand side of the wall is an overhanging flake (Elliott's Eliminate). Climb this and from the top step continue rightwards to follow a shallow crack which leads to the 'Parapet' ledge. Finish up the right-hand crack above (as for Burgess's Variation).

Elliott's Eliminate   17m   HS 4c   ★   (c.1934)
A true eliminate with good moves and exciting positions. Climb the flake to the right of the corner to its top then traverse leftwards into the main angle. Climb this to a good ledge on the left and traverse leftwards to finish up the exposed shallow corner in the tower above the left-hand wall of the corner. The thin crack just right of the final corner offers a harder finish.

Castle Crack   18m   HS 4b   ★★   (1912-14)
The obvious slippery corner-crack is climbed to reach a ledge. Finish directly or by moving either left to a crack in the tower, or right to a crack in the main face. Known for a long time as Black Hawk Slit.

Eliminator   15m   HVS 5b   ★★   (1965)
A fine climb up the square arête and hanging wall to the left of the angular corner. Climb the technical arête and move right to a short vertical crack. Strenuous climbing leads up the short wall above on good, but spaced, holds to a finish up the final shallow corner of Elliott's Eliminate.

Black Hawk Bastion   16m   E3 6a   ★★   (1952/1975)
The stepped corner to the left turns nasty at the large overhang. Climb to the roof where committing moves lead left to an exposed finish up the hanging left arête of the final groove. An alternative finish can be made over the roof: **Black Adder's Fortress** E5 6a ★ (1986) crosses this by trending first leftwards towards the arête and back rightwards to finish.

Chameleon   16m   E4 6a   ★★★   (1975)
An excellent and intimidating route up the hanging front face of the tower. Climb the narrow lower wall to the overhang that cuts across the buttress. This is crossed with difficulty (harder for the short) to reach a rightward-slanting ramp. It is usual to hand-traverse up this then move rapidly to the right-hand arête and better holds. It is also possible to finish directly.

Master of Disguise   16m   E6 6c   ★★   (1994)
A short but exciting problem up the hanging arête left of Chameleon. Start round to the left of Chameleon at a white marked wall, climb this and make a cramped traverse right under

the roof to the undercut on Chameleon. Stretch round to gain a disappointing break leading left to the arête. Slap up this to easier ground.

Black Hawk Tower   24m   VD   ★   (1932-33)
A devious but pleasant climb with interesting positions and even more interesting rope work. Ascend the deep, dark chimney to the left of the previous route until an obvious traverse along a ledge on the right leads round the arête and out on to the front face. Continue rightwards around the next arête and climb the final shallow corner groove of Elliott's Eliminate.

The Famous Ed Wood   20m   E1 5b   (1976-82)
A more direct version of the previous route. Climb the chimney for a few metres to a ledge and lean across to reach finger holds above a small overhang on the right. Use these to climb the wall to a ledge before finishing up the rounded left-hand arête of the tower.

Castle Chimney   20m   M   ★★   (1904)
This deep and dark chimney on the left of the buttress is a rarely repeated speleological route of some quality. Enter it over blocks and progress 'Sheffield-wards' until it is possible to bridge up to daylight at a large platform. A variety of routes lead to the cliff top. Inveterate practical jokers may be interested in the fact that it is possible to enter the chimney and then scramble round to the right behind Black Hawk Tower to a point close to daylight behind Castle Crack. It is then possible to spook climbers on that route by making weird noises. Known as Black Hawk Chimney for a time.

The Go Player   8m   E4 6b   (1989)
The short, sharp, hanging arête to the left of the chimney is climbed on its right-hand side; side runners protect.

The Z Crack   18m   VS 4c   ★   (1952)
The hanging buttress to the left is split centrally by a hand-crack in the back of an undercut groove. The *in situ* pigeons add spice and other things of a less tasty nature.

The Y Crack   18m   VS 4b   ★   (1919-23)
The deep cleft to the left is often green, though in dry weather it gives a good direct line. Climb the corner steeply to ledges and finish either left or right.

The face to the left is split by ominous overhangs and fierce cracks which provide a series of strenuous and difficult climbs. Most of these have been gritstone test-pieces of their era and ticking the five classic routes offers a challenging day for the middle Extreme climber. This face is:

TIPPLER BUTTRESS

The Muted Trumper 14m E6 6c ★ †   (1999)
The centre of the right-hand wall of Tippler Buttress is climbed to a horizontal break below the final 'blank' section. Climb this 'via vague seams and an over-arm pop for a slopey jug'. Tough.

The 9 o'clock Watershed 15m E6 6c ★★   (1994)
The right arête of Tippler Buttress gives a powerful and scary lead. Starting on the shelf in the base of The Y Crack, climb the side-wall to the main break and step left into The Tippler. Using a perfect undercut in the roof, stretch round to a flat hold at the base of the arête. Finish up the arête.

The Tippler 20m E1 5b ★★★   (1964)
A classic route that provides a tough challenge at the grade. Start on the front face of the buttress and go up the right-hand edge passing an overlap to a resting place below the big overhang. Make a fine, but scary, traverse left to a crack in the lip of the overhang. Grope up and left for a horizontal break then make the crux moves to get established on the final wall.

Tippler Direct 16m E3 6a ★★★   (1976)
A great piece of roof climbing with one especially taxing move. Start in the centre of the wall and climb through the overhangs to a position hanging from the footholds used by the regular route. With great difficulty reach the break under the final roof. Once established, finish up the parent route.

Paranoid 17m E6 6b ★★   (1981)
A hard and rarely repeated eliminate. Follow Tippler Direct to below its final roof then move two metres to the right and make a desperate pull around the overhang on poor holds. Those lacking in stature will probably need to finger-traverse the lip which is even harder; easy ground remains.

The Dangler 16m E2 5c ★★★   (1954)
A classic and strenuous roof crack. On the left-hand side of the wall are two thin cracks. Take the right-hand one into a cramped cave. Make a long reach to gain the horizontal break at the lip and follow the upper crack with difficulty.

8. The Unprintable	E1
9. Censor	E3
10. Jitterbug Buttress	S

The Unprintable 16m E1 5b ★★ (1952)
A struggle for many and its grade is frequently debated. Follow
the deceptively awkward left-hand crack into the cramped cave.
The exit from this to gain the crack above is difficult and
swearing doesn't seem to help.

The Cutting Room Floor 15m E4 6a † (1998)
Climb the arête to the left of The Unprintable to join Censor
at its crux. Finish up a crack in the upper wall.

1. Gargoyle Variant	HS
2. Black Hawk Hell Crack	S
3. Master of Disguise	E6
4. The Z Crack	VS
5. The Tippler	E1
6. Tippler Direct	E3
7. The Dangler	E2

Censor 15m E3 5c ★★   (1967)

A route requiring a steady lead. Start from the boulders to the left of the face and trend up and rightwards into a shallow left-facing corner. Climb this to the roof, swing right and commit yourself to the bulge before making strenuous and then delicate moves to gain a standing position on the nose. A final tricky move allows Townsend's Variation to be gained or, better, continue up the still precarious centre of the face above.

Anxiety Attack 15m E3 5c (1981)
A short and worrying eliminate that is rarely repeated. Start as for Censor but swing left to stand on a protruding block. Climb the overhanging wall above to a break below a small roof, pull over this and finish easily up the unprotected arête on the right.

Around to the left is a wide bay, the right-hand side of which is formed by the pleasant slab of:

GREY WALL

All the routes on this wall are poorly protected and require a steady approach.

Townsend's Variation 13m HVS 4c ★★ (1949)
Take a line up the right-hand edge of the face and at mid-height move round on to the exposed front face before making committing moves up the rib to reach superb finishing jugs. This is possibly the easiest HVS on the cliff (technically speaking that is) but it is no better protected nowadays than it was in 1949.

Jitter Face 13m S ★★ (1961-63)
This aptly named route starts below the centre of the face and climbs this until shelving holds lead diagonally right towards the arête. Go up this for a couple of moves, then traverse back left to join and finish as for the The Kirkus Original. A pleasantly devious but unprotected way up the face.

The Kirkus Original 12m HVS 4c ★ (1934)
The original route on the face starts on a block to the right of the base of the gully that bounds the left-hand side of the face. Go directly up the face to harder moves at six metres which lead to a mantelshelf and then easier ground above; unprotected.

DESCENT ROUTE
To the left of Grey Wall is Avalanche Gully. This proves to be the easiest way down since the right-hand edge of the cliff.

Jitterbug Buttress 12m S 4a ★ (1950)
In the back of the bay just left of the descent gully, climb the flat front face to the capping overhang and avoid this by sneaking off to the right. The obvious direct finish over the nose of the overhang is **Malarête** VS 4c (1990).

To the left of the descent gully is one of the most recognisable profiles on gritstone, the lower slab and steeply banked roof of:

FLYING BUTTRESS

Spasticus Artisticus 10m E4 5c   (1982)
The short right wall of the Flying Buttress is climbed trending slightly leftwards to finish on shelving holds. The start is the technical crux but the rest is dirty and just plain terrifying.

Kirkus's Corner 16m E1 5b ★★   (1934)
Fine climbing which is somewhat lacking in protection on the delicate final moves. Climb the right-hand edge of the initial slab to the right end of the overhangs and pull through these at a short vertical crack. Step left into a shallow scoop from which a delicate rounded exit is made to the welcoming final crack.

Flying Butt 25m E3 5c ★ †   (1999)
Start up Kirkus's Corner and hand-traverse leftwards along the lip of Flying Buttress past Flying Buttress Direct into the corner of the original Flying Buttress route. Finish directly over a rounded bulge. The crux is at the start of the traverse although failing strength will make the later stages seem taxing. Is this the longest roof route on gritstone?

Flying Buttress Direct 16m E1 5b ★★★ (1956/1966)
Exhilarating climbing on large holds which is more bold than technical. Climb the slippery slab directly to below the centre of the roof above. This is climbed, with an initial long reach, using a mixture of heel-hooks and brute force.

Goodbye Toulouse 18m E1 5b ★★   (1978)
An exciting route crossing the left-hand side of the large overhang. Climb the slab to the curving flake in the roof and attack the roof trending rightwards to finish on good flakes and jams just of the final nose.

✓ **Flying Buttress** 25m VD ★★★ ½&L Nancy (1922)
(handwritten: L Gareth 25/05/03 S Clare ½ J Gareth)
A classically varied route, as popular as any on the edge and with the polish to prove it. The 'question-mark' slab can be taken by a number of lines, all of which are unprotected and meet at its top left-hand corner. A steep slippery undercut groove on the left proves difficult to enter and leads to an exposed slab which is climbed rightwards to a large ledge and a fine finish on monster jugs. Belay, then walk off to the right, or for the full tick, climb the short wall at the back of the ledge.

7. Beech Tree Wall	VS
8. Garden Wall	HVD
9. Leaning Buttress Crack	VD
10. Leaning Butrress Direct	HVS
11. Yosemite Wall	E2

Flying Buttress Gully 16m   D   (1923-51)
The gully that bounds the left-hand side of Flying Buttress gives
an unsatisfying ascent and an awkward descent due to the
jammed boulders that impede progress in either direction.

To the left of the gully are two protruding ribs separated by a
narrow chimney.

Wedge Rib 14m   VS 5a   (1961-63)
The bottom three metres of the right-hand fin of rock gives a
'mini-Archangel'. Finish up the easier broad arête above.

Wedge Gully 12m   VS 4c   (1961-63)
The chimney immediately to the left has a capping block.
Crawling under this is easy so bridge up the chimney then
move right around the outside of the block. A desperate
variation finish can be attempted by trying to get on to the
sloping shelf in the corner above, otherwise traverse off
rightwards.

The Wedge 14m   VS 5a   (1959)
Ascend the front of the buttress directly, with a delicate move
to gain its top. Move right across the gully to finish up the blunt
arête of Wedge Rib.

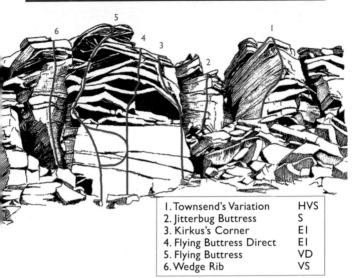

1. Townsend's Variation	HVS
2. Jitterbug Buttress	S
3. Kirkus's Corner	E1
4. Flying Buttress Direct	E1
5. Flying Buttress	VD
6. Wedge Rib	VS

Little Sarah 8m E1 5b   (1983)
Make an awkward move to gain the thin leftward-slanting crack
just to the left of the buttress arête and follow it rapidly
leftwards to chunkier holds.

Mini Micro 6m E2 6b   (1986)
An extended boulder problem up the left-hand side of the
buttress side-wall.

Scrappy Corner 13m D   (traditional)
Around to the left is an angular corner that leads to block-
strewn ledges. The upper continuation of the corner is easier.

DESCENT ROUTE
Scrappy Corner is used as a descent route by the competent
though Avalanche Gully, just beyond Flying Buttress, is
somewhat easier and considerably more pleasant.

To the left a wide wall runs leftwards to terminate where the tall
pillar of Leaning Buttress rests against the face. The wall has a
midway ledge cutting across its right-hand side and a wide chimney
complete with a large chockstone rising from the left-hand end.
This is:

GARDEN WALL AREA

Wild West Wind 14m S (1997)
Start from a flake that leans against the wall two metres left of
the corner and climb straight up the lower wall to arrive on the
midway ledge at a perched block. Move right and climb the
upper wall midway between the flake of Beech Tree Wall and
the easy gully on the right.

Beech Tree Wall 14m VS 4b (1923-51)
Climb the short crack, to the left of the corner to a large
platform. Start just left of the obvious flake and gain it by a long
reach and a quick pull to ledges. Another long reach, just to the
right of a hollybush, gains the top.

Armchair Buccaneer 14m E1 5b (1994)
Climb the short wall left of Beech Tree Wall to the ledge then
climb between it and the upper section of Space Junk using a
pocket and a side-pull and avoiding tendencies to drift to the
right. Finish immediately to the left of the holly barrier.

Space Junk 14m HVS 5b (1979)
The short steep arête at the left edge of the wall is climbed to
the platform. Move four metres to the right and finish up the
wall right of the chimney of Chockstone Direct, initially up a
short crack and continuing direct on rounded holds.

Garden Wall 14m HVD ★ (1922)
Another neglected but worthwhile route. Gain the large
halfway platform by the corner that faces Leaning Buttress or
by the crack in the front face. Climb the narrow chimney above
to the level of the large rounded chockstone. Step left on to
the face and traverse left to finish up the obvious crack-line. A
variation, **Chockstone Direct** S ★ (1930s), tackles the
chockstone direct.

That Sad Man 14m E2 5c (1990)
Climb the very narrow wall between Leaning Buttress Crack
and Garden Wall to reach a break at mid-height. A large pocket
on the right provides much needed protection before a finish
can be made up the centre of the rapidly easing wall above.

At the left-hand side of the wall (which has a halfway ledge) is a
tall, narrow pillar that leans back against the main face forming a
fine, long corner on its right side.

Right On 15m S   (1997)
A route that gives some pleasant moves despite its proximity to
Leaning Buttress Crack. Climb the right-hand of a pair of
corners and make an awkward move to get on to a ledge on
top of a pedestal. The continuation crack gives pleasant moves
and soon leads to easy ground.

Leaning Buttress Crack 15m VD ★★   (1920s)
The well-protected, right-angled, corner crack is climbed
directly. It offers varied moves up a strong line, with good
protection. For **The Bishop's Move** VD ★ starts up Leaning
Buttress Crack and squeezes through the 'window' behind the
buttress to gain access to another world. Finish up the easier
upper section of Leaning Buttress Gully.

Leaning Buttress Indirect 16m VD ★   (1922)
Climb the corner crack to the 'window' then traverse out left
on to the front of the buttress proper and climb its left-hand
edge.

Leaning Buttress Direct 16m HVS 5b ★   (1922)
The long main face of the buttress is taken direct, with a
difficult and serious move to leave the ledge at seven
metres. The difficulties relent above this point. Given (Hard)
Very Difficult in 1951.

Around the corner to the left is a shallow, square chimney blocked
by an overhang at eight metres.

The Old Bag's Head 16m E4 6a   (1991)
The left-hand arête of Leaning Buttress Direct is taken on its
steep left-hand side with the prominent nose providing the
crux.

Hangover 16m VS 4c ★   (1957)
Climb the right-hand crack of the gully past the awkward bulge
to a possible belay. Continue up the easy corner above and exit
right at the final overhang or, illogically but more fun, make a
wild blind swing right round the corner and on to the last few
moves of Leaning Buttress Direct.

Leaning Buttress Gully 15m VS 4c   (1932-33)
The overhang that blocks the gully is passed on the left. Easier
rock leads to the top, passing the final overhang on the left.
Combining the above two routes by bridging is a slightly easier
but more tearful experience.

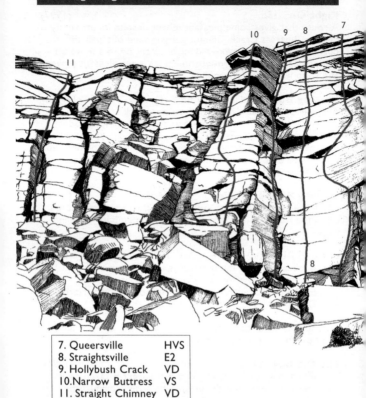

7. Queersville	HVS
8. Straightsville	E2
9. Hollybush Crack	VD
10.Narrow Buttress	VS
11. Straight Chimney	VD

To the left of the square-cut chimney is a wall which has ledges at eight metres and which ends with a rounded rib. This is:

NARROW BUTTRESS AREA

Yosemite Wall 16m E2 5b ★ (1965)
A good route of contrasting styles. Start left of Leaning Buttress Gully and climb into a small recess, leave this by difficult moves leftwards to gain the ledge above (crux). Step up right and teeter up the steep slab using sloping holds to reach ledges and easier climbing up the final arête; poorly protected.
The El Cap Finish E2 5b (1993) follows Yosemite Wall to the

1. Beech Tree Wall	VS
2. Garden Wall	HVD
3. Leaning Buttress Direct	HVS
4. Hangover	VS
5. Leaning Buttress Gully	VS
6. Yosemite Wall	E2

ledges above all difficulties then thrashes over the centre of the roof above.

The Nose 15m E3 6a ★ (1984)
Climb the strenuous bulging arête to the left of the start of Yosemite Wall on good finger-holds until the ledge on Yosemite Wall is reached. Step back left and tackle the more precarious upper section via some tenuous laybacking before things ease.

Queersville 15m HVS 5a ★★ (1965)
Around to the left is an odd projecting flange on the right-hand

side of a rounded bay. Start up this and from its top stretch out left to reach flat ledges and a good resting place above. Climb up to a broken flake below the roof and make a long reach (crux) to the ledge above. Swing rightwards and continue up the pleasant wall above.

Straightsville 15m E2 5b (1987)
Climb directly up the wall one metre right of Hollybush Crack with poor protection unless the thin slanting crack on Queersville is used.

Hollybush Crack 14m VD ★★★ (1926)
The holly has long since gone but this corner-crack remains very clean, very good and very protectable. The lower section is quite tricky but the more imposing upper part is juggy and proves to be especially thrilling for the grade.

Narrow Buttress 14m VS 4c ★★ (1949)
Start up the right arête of the buttress that forms the left wall of Hollybush Crack. Go up and move over on to the left-hand edge briefly before traversing back rightwards again. Climb directly up the right-hand arête to finish in a spectacularly exposed position on the large flutings on the tip of the final overhang. A pleasant eliminate is **Straight and Narrow** HVS 5a (1981) which climbs straight up the centre of the buttress.

DESCENT ROUTE
The broken rocks on the left side of Narrow Buttress are frequently used as a descent by the more capable. There are various ways down the top section and these all unite in an easy blocky chimney in the lower section immediately to the left of the buttress.

To the left is a long low wall that is immensely popular with the bouldering brigade especially towards its left-hand side where it is at its smoothest. This is:

RUSTY WALL

The area is named after the many 'rusty' iron carbonate 'blobs' that decorate it. On the right-hand side there are numerous easier climbs and perversely these have always been less popular than the hard fingery problems farther left.

Albert's Amble 11m HVD (1992)
The first crack in the wall is wide at its base and awkward to start but soon eases.

Albert's Pillar 11m HS 4c (1961-63)
The bulbous pillar immediately to the left of the descent route
again has a boulder problem start and easier climbing above.

Straight Chimney 11m VD (1961-63)
Left again the obvious chimney widens in its centre and
narrows to a crack just below the top.

Oblique Buttress 11m VS 5b (1961-63)
The narrow face to the left can be ascended at 5b by strictly
ignoring the arêtes on either side but the whole thing becomes
much easier if one or both arêtes are employed, VS 4c.

Oblique Crack 11m S ★ (1928)
The crack that bounds the right-hand side of the main section
of Rusty Wall leans slightly to the left. The lower section gives
good jamming and leads to a loose chockstone and a finish up
the rounded face directly above.

Via Dexter 11m E2 5c ★ (1951)
Ascend the wall to the left of Oblique Crack directly.
Purists will attack the centre of the wall with conviction and
will doubtless enjoy the experience. Slinking off right when level
with the thin overlap is HVS 5a.

Via Media 11m VS 4c ★ (1949)
The centre of the wall is split by two thin, converging cracks.
The protectable right-hand crack is easier than its neighbour
and is safe enough to make a good introduction to leading at
the grade. Finish up the short chimney above. A variation,
requiring blinkers, is to climb the narrow wall between the
cracks until it becomes too ridiculous and the cracks can be
used in tandem **Via Trivia** HVS 5b (1980s).

Rusty Crack 11m HVS 5b ★ (1970s)
The left-hand crack on the wall has a tough start using polished
'rusty' footholds and a thin crack. Finish up the short chimney
above.

Rusty Wall 11m HVS 6a ★ (1928)
The wall immediately left of the crack has hard starting moves
on slowly vanishing 'rusty excrescences' above an ankle-
snapping boulder. Once the first good hold (a 4c hop for the
very tall) is reached things relent. Finish up the short wall
immediately to the left of the chimney.

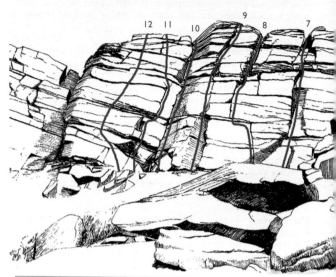

7. Right-Hand Trinity	HS
8. Central Trinity	VS
9. Christmas Crack	HS
10. April Crack	HS
11. The Flange	HVS
12. Hargreaves' Original Route	VS

Rugosity Wall 11m HVS 5c ★ (1949)
The wall two metres to the right of the corner of Green Crack
has a difficult and fingery start leading to marginally easier-angled
climbing with one more tricky pull before things ease. Finish up the
short wall above the ledge.

Green Crack 11m VS 4b ★ (1928)
The square-cut corner on the left-hand side of the wall is well-
named after rain, when it is iridescent and best avoided. When dry
it is usually laybacked until good jams arrive. An interesting
variation is to off-width, then fist-jam, the start before the crack
becomes a more helpful width. Finish up the final narrow chimney.

Topaz 10m E4 6a ★ (1979)
The sharp arête to the left of Green Crack is an odd affair. It is

1. Hollybush Crack	VD
2. Straight Chimney	VD
3. Oblique Crack	S
4. Via Media	VS
5. Rusty Crack	HVS
6. Rugosity Wall	HVS

laybacked on its right-hand side and features one alarmingly long reach above a nasty landing with virtually no protection. Alternatively, follow Topaz to its crux then swing left around the corner and finish up Well Right; **Topaz Copout** E1 5b (1980s).

Beyond the arête of Topaz is a fine wall split by three excellent cracks, the middle one of which has an obvious dog-leg at one third height. The wall also offers fine face climbing and is known as:

TRINITY WALL

Well Right   13m   E2 5c   (1970s)
Start just to the left of the arête of Topaz. Make tricky moves to get established on the face and continue just left of the arête throughout. A route that is delicate and effectively unprotected, though difficulties do ease a little with height.

87

Fergus Graham's Direct Route   13m   HVS 4c   (1920s)
The wall immediately to the right of the prominent straight crack
is followed throughout, avoiding any leftward tendencies. The route
is unprotected though it is possible to lean left and place runners
in the next route, reducing the grade to VS.

Right-Hand Trinity   13m   HS 4a   ★★   (1929)
The first long crack in the wall is climbed directly, initially via a
shallow rightward-facing corner. A step right on to the previous
route can be made to avoid the crux overhang, but is just as hard.
The first of a number of deservedly celebrated routes on this
section of rock.

Meiosis   14m   HVS 5b   ★   (1978)
Ascend the wall between the first two prominent cracks (Right-
Hand Trinity and Central Trinity) via a series of rounded horizontal
breaks. Sustained and reachy, but well-protected.

Twintrin   14m   E1 5c   (1976-77)
Climb the initial thin crack of Central Trinity then press on directly
up the wall above with tricky moves early on.

Central Trinity   15m   VS 4c   ★★★   (1929)
The wall to the left has a vertical crack that ends at seven metres.
Climb this to a leftwards traverse that leads to the base of the
continuation crack. Gain this awkwardly then follow it more easily
into and up a right-facing corner. The base of the upper crack can
be reached directly at HVS 5b ★ (1970s).

Holiday Quartet   14m   HVS 5b   (1997)
Follow the direct on Central Trinity to the base of the crack, step
left and, with a blinkered approach, climb the narrow wall between
Central Trinity and Christmas Crack. Trend gradually rightwards
up the wider upper wall to finish near the arête.

Christmas Crack   15m   HS 4b   ★★★   (1926)
The long straight crack to the left gives one of the finest route of
its grade on the cliff. Approach the thin section of the crack via a
tricky V-shaped groove then follow it with pleasure. The final
leaning corner is awkward. There is an exposed alternative up the
face just to the left. Probably the only route in the country where
a queue is normal on December 25th whatever the weather.

Easter Rib   15m   E1 5b   ★★   (1956)
A delicate undertaking up the blunt arête left of Christmas Crack.
Climb a shallow undercut groove just to the left of the nose

(technical crux) then swing right and go up to a horizontal break. Balance up the rounded rib (psychological crux) to gain access to the final steep, but juggy, rib.

Spring Wall   15m   HVS 5b   (1998)
Start as for Easter Rib but continue straight up the face above with thin moves at eight metres. A runner in April Crack is normal at the grade.

April Crack   15m   HS 4b   ★★★   (1928)
The steep, well-protected crack in the open corner to the right of Black Slab is awkward to start then gives fine sustained climbing that is generally easier than it looks.

To the left is the impressive sweep of Black Slab. Despite the name it is the same colour as all of this section of the cliff. Although it can be climbed virtually anywhere, its three main routes are all independent and well worth seeking out.

BLACK SLAB AREA

The Flange   15m   HVS 5b   ★★   (1956)
Essentially a direct line up the right-hand side of the slab. Steep and strenuous pulls through a cracked overhang are needed to gain the prominent niche at four metres. Above, layback up 'the flange' then press onwards by contrastingly delicate moves between rounded breaks to a finish up a short crack.

Hargreaves' Original Route   16m   VS 4c   ★★★   (1928)
A great route, one of the best VSs on the edge, being both delicate and exposed, though its long-time reputation for being poorly protected no longer stands. Begin at a boulder below an undercut towards the right-hand side of the slab. Pull awkwardly up and out left to gain the base of the slab and then move up and right to a ledge in the centre. Continue upwards always trending slightly rightwards and passing several horizontal breaks to a steep and exhilarating finish.

Macleod's Variation   18m   HS 4b   ★★   (pre-1951)
Not as good as the original but the easiest way up the slab and worth doing. Follow the regular route to a good foot ledge halfway up the slab then traverse leftwards before finishing up the open groove and a short crack near the top left corner.

Echoes   18m   E3 5c   ★   (1995)
A devious line but with some excellent climbing. Start under the base of Black Slab and climb through the overhang using a pocket

before spanning left and hand-traversing to the arête. Swing round the corner and move up to the break on Whillans' Pendulum. Climb leftwards through the roof to reach and climb the leaning arête above, eventually joining the final section of Wall of Sound.

Black Slab has a subsidary face on its left-hand side.

Black Magic 15m HVS 5b ★★   (1976)
Start left of the arête beneath overhangs and monkey rightwards using a prominent shallow pocket and a 'stuck-on' flake until it is possible to gain a ledge on the front face, **Whillans' Pendulum** HVS 5b ★ (1958) or, more easily, and less in keeping with the rest of the climb by a leftwards traverse from Hargeaves' Original Route on the right. Move up awkwardly then step left on to the narrow side face of the slab and ascend this delicately. Large camming devices are useful.

Wall of Sound 17m E6 6b ★★★   (1983)
An arduous and excellent route up the impending scooped wall around to the left of Black Slab. Start up the thin crack then move right via an enormous span to a thin break. From there continue directly, then rightwards, using an obvious pocket to gain the right-hand arête up which the route finishes. Needs a direct finish.

To the left is a recessed bay with a three metre-high pedestal standing in its right-hand side and to the left of this a rib capped by a roof.

Wright's Route 17m VS 4c ★   (1961-63)
Climb the overhanging corner crack on the right-hand side of the pedestal to gain its top and the base of the chimney above, possible stance. A short exposed traverse leads out rightwards across the steep wall and into the bottomless corner, up which the climb finishes.

Pedestal Chimney 15m D ★   (traditional)
The right-hand chimney is entered by climbing the polished crack on the left-hand side of the pedestal at its base. Continue up the chimney and finish under the huge 'corking' boulder.

Hybrid 15m HVS 5b   (1961-63)
Climb directly up the narrow wall between the pedestal and the lower section of Flake Chimney.

Flake Chimney 15m S ★   (1961-63)
The left-hand of the two chimneys in the back of the bay gives classical grunting as far as the boulder that blocks the way.

Squirm ignominiously through the innards of the cliff, or better and more precariously, pass the outside of the boulder (HS 4b). The upper section is steep but much easier.

DESCENT ROUTE
It is possible for the competent to descend the upper section of Flake Chimney (or the easier flake to its right, looking out) then make an exposed move to cross over its lower section and continue down the lower slippery section of Pedestal Chimney. Care is required with this descent.

To the left the edge now thrusts dramatically forward into one of the finest and highest buttresses on Stanage. This is home to several great classics and many routes of only slightly lesser stature.

ROBIN HOOD'S RIGHT-HAND BUTTRESS

The Little Flake Crack   18m   VS 5a   ★   (1930s)
The flat face to the left of Flake Chimney features a hanging flake to the right of the prominent wide fissure of Zigzag Flake Crack. Starting from the chimney make a hard traverse left using polished footholds to attain the base of the flake which is climbed directly.

Ice Boat   20m   E1 5c   ★   (1981)
Start directly below the upper flake of the previous route and climb the wall to the horizontal break at its base. Step up and traverse rightwards almost to the arête before finishing up the wall with a long reach.

Coconut Ice   18m   E2 5b   (1981)
This route manages to force a direct line up the ever-narrowing wall between the The Little Flake and the Zigzag Flake Crack. Moving up past a small nose in the lower section proves to be the crux, low runners increasing the sense of urgency. Above this the route becomes increasingly contrived.

Zigzag Flake Crack 18m   VS 4a   ★★   (1929)
The obvious and impressive flake crack that runs up the face to the right of the arête is precarious and not that well-protected. Shin up it to the good ledge on top of the flake and finish up the easier short wall behind, or traverse out on to the left-hand arête for more exposure. An oddly-named climb as the flake is as straight as an arrow. This route has also been known as The Great Flake and Robin Hood Flake Crack.

7. Straight Crack	VS
8. Thunder Road	E5
9. Robin Hood's Right-Hand Buttress Direct	HS
10. Inverted V	VS

To the left, on the front face of the buttress is a good ledge system above a wide roof. The pioneers of several generations obviously enjoyed climbing on this face with its commodious halfway stance as they criss-crossed it with a series of routes and variations. All are well worth doing and have been rather under-valued in the past.

Brittle Star 18m E3 5c   (1994)
Start at the base of Zigzag Flake Crack but follow the leftward-slanting crack to a ledge below the small triangular overhang in the nose above. Pull over the right side of this and make a hard move to get established on the wall above. Continue over the narrow overhang and finish up the wall.

Zagrete 20m VS 4b ★★   (1962-63)
Start at the base of Zigzag Flake Crack and follow the left-slanting crack to a good platform and a possible belay by the

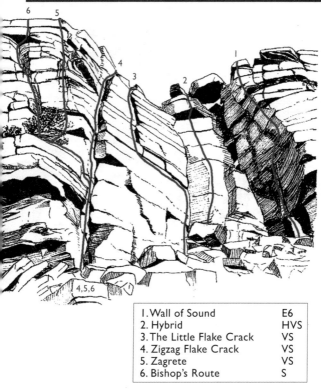

1. Wall of Sound	E6
2. Hybrid	HVS
3. The Little Flake Crack	VS
4. Zigzag Flake Crack	VS
5. Zagrete	VS
6. Bishop's Route	S

hollybush. Step out right and climb the well-positioned thin crack near the arête to a fine finish on flutings at the top.

Bishop's Route (Zigzag Variations)   25m   S 4a   ★★★(1920s)
An excellent wandering expedition that has the distinction of being the longest and easiest way up the buttress. Follow Zagrete to the platform. Continue up the corner-crack to the right of the holly to a higher ledge, then make tricky moves to reach the flakes above. Climb these to a horizontal break just below the cliff top and either traverse left along a ledge system to finish up the upper section of Straight Crack or, harder and perhaps better, finish directly with a long reach.

Two 'problem' routes are possible over the roof below the Bishop's Route.

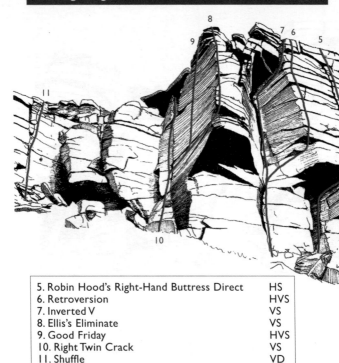

5. Robin Hood's Right-Hand Buttress Direct	HS
6. Retroversion	HVS
7. Inverted V	VS
8. Ellis's Eliminate	VS
9. Good Friday	HVS
10. Right Twin Crack	VS
11. Shuffle	VD

The Actress 9m E2 5c (1965)
Lies under The Bishop. Tackle the overhang directly to slightly
dirty holds and the halfway ledge. Select any way, up or down.

Stage Fright 9m E3 6b (1982)
The hanging left-hand arête is gained with considerable
difficulty, initially by a swinging hand-traverse from the right
then by a fierce pull.

Spring into Action 20m HVS 5b ★ (1996)
Start around to the left and bridge the front of the wide
chimney directly below Straight Crack to gain the right-hand
arête above the overhang. Climb a short wall to a ledge and
possible belay. The centre of the steep wall above and at the
back of the ledge provides the main substance of the route.

I. Black Magic	HVS
2. The Actress	E2
3. Robin Hood's Zigzag	S
4. Straight Crack	VS

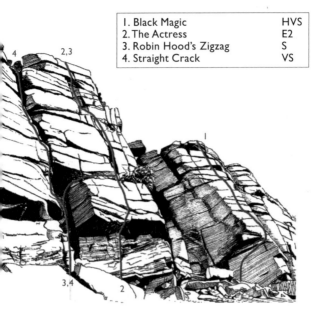

Robin Hood Zigzag 24m S 4a ★★ (1922)
Climb the wide chimney in the centre of the buttress until it
closes. Traverse out rightwards and pass the arête to reach a
good ledge and possible stance. Ascend the crack to the left of
the holly to a ledge and continue up the fine wall to a niche.
Step right and climb the face to the top.

Straight Crack 20m VS 4c ★★ (1923-51)
The central line of the buttress is worthwhile. Climb up into the
wide chimney then either climb to the roof and shuffle left, or
better, climb the flake-crack on the left-hand wall of the chimney.
The two ways unite at the main crack which leads past an
overhang to enter a wide, easy, finishing chimney. A touch hard for
the grade.

Cold Turkey 20m HVS 5a ★ (1973)
Start up the flake in the left rib of Straight Crack. Step left on
to the fine face and climb directly up to and over a small
capping roof. Not a very direct line but a logical way up the
buttress making good use of the neglected upper section of the

95

next climb. The route was effectively 'lost' for 20 years and was reclaimed as Lightning Lane in 1993.

Thunder Road 21m E5 6a (1979)
An unbalanced climb that crosses the centre of the wide roof to the left. It is usually climbed using pre-placed side runners in adjacent routes as a 'baby-bouncer' (E2 6a). Once over the roof, finish up the easier wall behind and as for Cold Turkey.

Robin Hood's Right-Hand Buttress Direct
23m HS 4a ★★★ (1922)
A great route tackling the impressive fist-sized crack splitting the centre of the face to the right of the deep cleft of Inverted V. Climb a wide crack up to the large overhang, then shuffle out right to reach a small ledge below the main crack. From there on the climbing is awkward and not well-protected.

Our Version 21m E3 6a (1985)
A narrow rib to the right of Inverted V provides a difficult approach to the roof below Retroversion. Pleasant moves lead through this via the obvious flake. When the angle eases step right and finish up the slab to the right of the arête.

Retroversion 21m HVS 4c ★★ (1962-63)
Climb Inverted V for five metres, then traverse the right-hand wall along a horizontal break before climbing the bulging wall. When the angle eases finish up the rounded arête in a fine position.

Just to the left is a magnificent crack running up the inside of a perpendicular inverted V-shaped cleft.

Inverted V 21m VS 4c ★★★ (1922)
Follow the crack and groove to the cave, 'The Birdcage'. Either traverse out low to the left and climb the easy arête around the corner, or much better, continue up to the roof and traverse right (thread runners) before finishing up the exposed crack that splits the right edge of the roof. One of the most popular routes on the edge.

Introversion 18m E1 5c (1995)
Start under the huge roof left of Inverted V and climb the slab past a couple of pockets to a diagonal crack under the roof. Move rightwards to the short vertical crack on the side wall of the V then span left to pull over the roof. Continue directly up the steepening side wall to the final roof and exit to the left.

Wall of Sound   E6 6b   (page 90)
Climber: Graham Hoey   Photo: Ian Smith

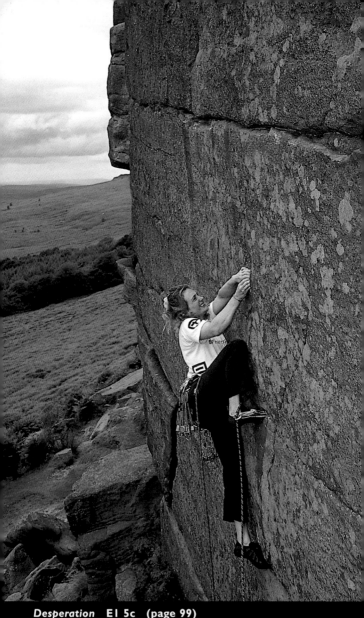

Desperation   E1 5c   (page 99)
Climber: Anne Arran   Photo: Carl Ryan

Cave Eliminate **E3 6a** (page 102)
Climber: Nigel Smart Photo: Dave Wilkinson

Big Dave's Wall   E3 6a   (page 111)
Climber: Percy Bishton   Photo: David Simmonite

Bob's Jolly Jape   15m   E4 6a   (1983)
Climb the small rib below the centre of the traverse of Ellis's Eliminate to its junction with the roof. Using an obvious pocket, and with some difficulty and no protection, gain the break above and right. If successful choose a way on, Good Friday being the obvious choice.

Ellis's Eliminate   20m   VS 4c   ★★   (1950)
A great climb if you are proficient at horizontal hand jamming. Start in the corner on the left-hand side of the buttress as for Twin Cracks and climb up for three metres. Traverse airily rightwards along the obvious horizontal break to a ledge on the arête, up which a finish is made.

Good Friday   15m   HVS 5b   ★★   (1977)
From the middle of the traverse of Ellis's Eliminate make a difficult step up involving a long reach and continue directly up the centre of the wall above.

Right Twin Crack   11m   VS 4c   ★   (1957-60)
The right-hand of a pair of cracks is followed directly. Finish to the right at the huge capstone.

Twin Cracks   11m   VD   ★   (1923-51)
Ascend the right-hand crack for four metres. Continue up the left-hand crack to the capping block and either escape under this or step right and finish as for Right Twin Crack.

Left Twin Crack   10m   S   (1996)
Gain the left-hand crack via the awkward groove and climb it to finish left at the capstone.

Madhouse   12m   E4 6a   (1994)
The hanging black rib is climbed on pockets and flakes to a ledge. Move back left and make a precarious move and one very long reach before sprinting up the final arête.

Grovel, you don't know the meaning of the word
10m   VS   (1993)
To the left, and just right of the descent route, is an inverted V-shaped slot blocked by a chockstone. The climbing is easier but no pleasanter than it looks.

Before Dunne   6m   HVS 5c   (1996)
Climb the undercut nose by leaning in from the left to reach a good but dubious hold and a swing out on to jugs on the front. A short haul remains.

DESCENT ROUTE

To the left is a well-worn descent. Start on top of a flake and cross an exposed gap to finish down the wall past a useful cannon ball-sized hole and a flake. It is exposed and awkward so care is required.

Immediately to the left of the descent route is a short wall split vertically and horizontally by a series of cracks.

Shuffle 10m VD   (1993)
The crack down which the descent route finishes is climbed passing to the left of the cannon ball-sized hole and continuing awkwardly to reach a large ledge.

Soft Shoe 10m VS 5a   (1992)
The narrow wall just to the left of Shuffle is climbed directly, initially up its centre, then pulling through a narrow overlap.

Boot Crack 10m HD ★   (traditional)
This is the obvious wide crack that splits the centre of the wall. It may well be easier in boots.

Cornflakes 10m VS 4c   (1978)
The centre of the flaky wall to the left of Boot Crack finishing up a blunt rib.

Muesli 10m HS 4c   (1992)
The square arête of this short wall is pleasantly technical. Start on the left where a crack aids the initial long reach. Once established, follow the easier arête to a finish on its left-hand side.

Titbit 8m VS 4c ★   (1957-60)
The steep crack on the north-facing side wall leads to an 'interesting' and often gritty exit on to the flat ledge above.

To the left is a short right-angled corner blocked by a jammed boulder and, just left again, a thin crack. Beyond this is a tall, flat wall with a conspicuous thin crack that fails to reach the ground. This is:

DESPERATION BUTTRESS

Stringer 10m HS 4b   (1992)
The thin crack to the left of the angle is tricky while the finish over the blocks is even more awkward.

Kenneth 11m VS 4b (1976-81)

Climb the wall two metres left of the crack by a series of mantelshelf moves. The well-polished starting holds are also used by the next route.

Robin Hood's Staircase 11m VD (1923-51)

This is the obvious weakness running diagonally up the wall just to the left. Climb the wall trending leftwards up a series of sloping ledges to finish up a short corner; poorly protected.

DESCENT ROUTE

Competent climbers regularly reverse Robin Hood's Staircase, proving that the route is well-named. Care is required.

Robin Hood's Staircase Direct 10m VS 4c (traditional)

Start at a short crack just to the left, climb this and continue straight up the pleasant wall to arrive at the foot of the last 'riser' on the regular route. Gain this by a mantelshelf and finish easily.

Rubber Band 20m VS 4b ★ (1972)

Follow Robin Hood's Staircase Direct until two metres from the top of the cliff. Traverse left along the prominent horizontal break on superb jams, crossing the upper wall of Desperation to finish with a touch of Constipation or, more easily, round to the left of the arête.

Desperation 12m E1 5c ★★★ (1959)

The lower section of the smooth wall is climbed via a reachy problem start on the right, (6a for short climbers, 5b for tall ones) to reach the break. Make hard moves up first left then right to gain a thin rightward-trending crack; easier climbing remains.

Pacific Ocean Wall 14m E5 6b ★★ (1983)

A fine route up the smooth left-hand section of the wall. Start as for Constipation then move out right and climb the wall left of Desperation. This features hard climbing on tiny holds and has the potential for a major flier from the final hard moves. Pre-placed side runners in Desperation are used at this grade; it awaits a lead without. Rumoured to have a direct start.

Constipation 14m E4 6a ★ (1973)

The left-hand arête of the wall proves to be a stiff problem. Climb on to a block then make hard moves up the face just right of the arête. The upper part of the arête is much easier unless you are short, where there is one more precarious move just below the

8. Robin Hood's Crack	HVD
9. Paucity	HVS
10. Withered Thing	E2
11. Wuthering	E2

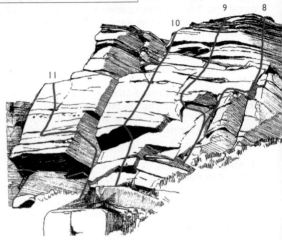

top. The left-hand side of the arête, gained from the left, can be climbed at E2 5c (1976-83) with a side runner in the chimney.

Behind the spacious ledge above Desperation et al is a long low overhang split by two prominent cracks. These both give excellent boulder problems, 5c on the left and 6a on the right, whilst right again the bulges can be climbed using a pocket, a crimp and a long reach at 'classic 6c'. It is worth noting that the low cave to the left was used as an alternative bivouac site to Robin Hood's Cave. Since most of the roof collapsed in the 1970s it has proved less popular.

To the left is a deep, green chimney-groove and left again the fine projecting square tower that forms the right side of:

ROBIN HOOD'S BUTTRESS

Robin Hood's Balcony Cave Direct
20m   VD   ★★   (1919-23)
Climb the large, imposing V-shaped cleft on polished holds to

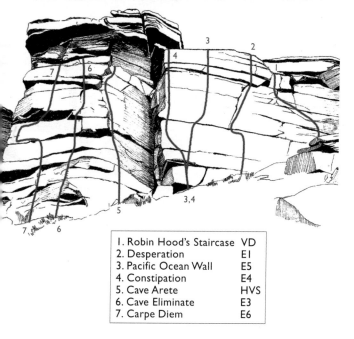

1. Robin Hood's Staircase	VD
2. Desperation	E1
3. Pacific Ocean Wall	E5
4. Constipation	E4
5. Cave Arete	HVS
6. Cave Eliminate	E3
7. Carpe Diem	E6

reach the balcony, its cave systems and a potential belay site. It is possible to escape through the cave or by making an exposed stride over the top of the lower chimney. The true finish goes through the ledgy overhang above and to the left by unlikely-looking moves on big jugs and is S 4a. **Broken Arrow** E1 5b (1999) is the obvious well-protected roof crack directly above the chimney.

Cave Arête 16m HVS 5a ★★   (1961-63)
A fine, photogenic route following the arête to the left of the green cleft. First, gain the ledge below the overhang and make long reaches (5b for the short) to gain better holds and an easing in the angle. The upper section is followed delicately on the right to a stance in the caves. You now have a choice: take the true finish of the previous climb, walk off to the right with an awkward step across the chimney, escape through the back of the caves or move left and finish up Harding's Super Direct Finish.

8. Withered Thing	E2
9. Dithering Frights	E2
10. Wuthering	E2
11. Bee	D

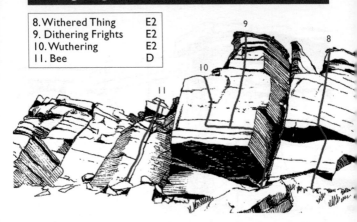

Cave Eliminate 16m E3 6a ★★ (1973)
The only real weakness in the impressive wall to the left of the
arête. A bulging problem start (6a) leads past a prominent
pocket to reach the good ledge at five metres. (This may be
avoided by an easier ascending traverse from the left.) Above is
a step in the overhang, pull past this with difficulty and finish
leftwards up the easier wall above.

Last Bolt 20m E3 5c (1979)
The left arête of the buttress is gained by a progressively
difficult traverse (crux) from the ledge on Cave Eliminate. The
arête itself is reasonably 'steady' but unfortunately is also very
escapable.

Carpe Diem 15m E6 6c ★★ † (1994)
For a long time one of Stanage's last great problems. From the
base of the variation start of Cave Eliminate, climb to a hollow
block at three metres. Continue direct, making a step left on
the Last Bolt traverse, to a good holds beneath the roof.
Stretch rightwards to a pocket on the lip and make a desperate
move to get established on the headwall. Finish directly and
more easily.

The next route starts around the arête to the left where an alluring
thin crack runs up a steep slab/wall into the right-hand of a pair
of prominent rounded caves.

Robin Hood's Cave Innominate 14m VS 5a ★★ (1932)
The thin polished crack at the right-hand end of the gully wall is

I. Constipation	E4
2. Cave Eliminate	E3
3. Robin Hood's Cave Innominate	VS
4. Harding's Super Direct Finish	HVS
5. Cave Gully Wall	HVS
6. Robin Hood's Crack	HVD
7. Paucity	HVS

reached by a precarious toe-traverse from the left or harder (5b) directly up the arête. The crack leads all too soon to the Balcony Cave. Move up and right to a good stance on a higher ledge. Escape easily right or, much better, tackle the next route.

Harding's Super Direct Finish 8m HVS 5a ★★ (1946)
From the stance on the previous route, step left and make a long grope round the roof followed by an exposed pull over on superb holds. Climb the short wall to the top. Well-named as it is both direct and super. Combining this and previous route into a spectacular single pitch proves to be one of the best HVS outings on the edge.

Sands of Time 22m E4 6a ★ (1995)
Climb the slab immediately to the left of Robin Hood's Cave Innominate to the third 'crease' then traverse left for two metres and climb to the base of the 'hour-glass' pillar between the twin caves. Climb the left-hand side of this to a slot and continue up the steep wall above. It is also possible to climb the unprotected initial slab directly at the same grade. Some find this better, take your pick.

Cave Gully Wall   14m   HVS 5a   ★★   (1932)
From the boulders in the gully step right on to the slab and
climb to the right-hand of the twin caves. Continue up the left-
hand edge of this cave and follow the steep shallow groove
above on superb holds to finish at a rocking block. A bold
undertaking for its day when side-belayers were used.

The left-hand cave on the right wall can be reached easily from
the gully and there are two diminutive but exposed and worthwhile
routes.

Just One Cornetto   8m   E2 5c   ★   (1993)
From the large thread in the upper right-hand edge of the left-
hand twin cave pull right on to the wall then climb steeply via
long reaches passing a small roof.

Last Ice Cream   8m   E2 5c   ★   (1982)
Climb the overhang above the left-hand cave and swing on to
the left-hand arête; finish briskly up this. Like its neighbour it is
much better than it looks.

Robin Hood's Cave Gully   15m   HD   (1919-23)
To the left a great block-filled defile leads to a steep and
slippery rock step at mid-height followed by ledges. Above this
is a narrow V-shaped cleft which provides a struggle.

DESCENT ROUTE
Robin Hood's Cave Gully provides a tricky descent route even
for the competent. The tricky upper part can be varied by
squeezing though a small rectangular hole thus removing the
need to climb down the V-shaped groove. It is also possible (and
easier) to walk 15 metres to the north and descend another V-
shaped groove to reach a sloping ledge that runs past a cave
entrance, into the central section of the gully; care required.

Out on the left, part way up Robin Hood's Cave Gully, is the
legendary Robin Hood's Cave, which has been used as a perfect,
weatherproof bivouac site for generations. If you do stop there,
and you should if you consider yourself a true Stanage habitué,
please respect the place, keep it clean and remove any detritus
left by less caring souls.

Tea-leaf Crack   15m   VD   ★   (1959)
In the left wall of the gully is a flake crack with a letter-box slot
in its left-hand wall. Follow the flake to the ledges in front of
the cave, step left and climb the face just left of the cave to the
top.

104

Robin Hood's Crack   18m   HVD   ★★☆ ~~S Nancy~~ (1932-33)
Around to the left is an open groove leading to a long narrow
roof at six metres. Climb the flaky crack in the groove then
pass the overhang on the right. From the ledge climb the face
on the left of the cave as for the previous climb or, bridge the
cave mouth and climb the wall directly above at S 4a. A direct
start is possible up the right arête at VS 4c (1979).

A squeezed-in eliminate, **A Paucity of Independent Climbing**
E1 5c (1997), climbs the groove to the roof and pulls through its
centre to easy ground. Walk off right at the level of the cave.

Paucity   18m   HVS 5b   ★★   (1961-63)
To the left is a shallow depression running up to the left-hand
side of the narrow roof. Climb this to the overhang, step left
and follow the delicate shallow groove to ledges. Finish up the
wall above. An excellent varied pitch. A direct start is possible
via a small roof and a 'groovelet' joining the regular route at the
overhang, **Wearing Thin** E2 6a (1990).

To the left a narrow overlap runs across the steep face and three
routes climb over this feature. Unfortunately and, perhaps rather
unethically, they all resort to pre-clipped protection in adjacent
routes, this providing a 'baby-bouncer' for the crucial moves, hence
the relatively low E grades for the climbs.

Seduced by the Dark Side of Climbing
16m   E3 6b   (1994)
Start just to the left at a small rightward-facing recess. 'Barn-
door' up on to a good foot-ledge then tackle the tough roof
direct before finishing up the much easier slab above.

Withered Thing   17m   E2 6b   ★   (1978)
Start in the centre of the buttress and climb the wall to the
overhang. Pass this via a combination of long stretches and thin
pulls on poor holds to gain the easier upper slab.

Not Much Weak Stack Battered or What
15m   E3 6b   ★   (1975)
Start just right of the right-hand arête of the chimney and make
desperate moves to gain the arête, which is followed, taking the
overhang directly. Protection is normally placed high in the
chimney. An easier start can be made just left of the lower
arête.

To the left is a deep V-shaped chimney and a buttress undercut by
a huge square roof.

Robin Hood's Chockstone Chimney
17m S 4a ★   (1919-23)
The prominent V-shaped chimney that splits the front of the
buttress. It is also possible to finish to the right up an easier
groove. **Connelly's Variation** S 4a ★ (pre-1951) provides a
better finale, moving left above the chockstone to climb the
exposed upper arête.

Premier 18m HVS 5a   (1971)
Climb the chimney to just below the chockstone. A line of
holds on the left-hand wall just above the small overhang leads
to the arête which is followed to join Connelly's Variation after
a couple of moves.

Wuthering 20m E2 5b ★★★   (1973)
A classic solution to the 'unclimbable' buttress. Climb the
chimney until it is possible to bridge out along the lowest line
of holds and make a groin-stretching move to gain the left-hand
arête. Traverse delicately left above the overhang and climb up
and left to finish via a shallow groove just right of the left-hand
arête. Protection is placed high up in the chimney at this grade.

Dithering Frights 18m E2 5b ★   (1995)
Follow Wuthering to the runners in the centre of the slab then
reverse back to a position one and half metres left of the right-
hand arête. Climb straight up the slab on poor pockets and
finish up the well-positioned left-hand edge of the wall above.

The direct start over the enormous roof still looks a couple of
generations away though there is a good hold on the lip and the
broken flakes under the roof suggest that it has been inspected.

Boc No Buttress 14m E5 6a ★★   (1979)
A well-positioned climb that has just enough protection. Climb
The Asp until it is possible to make a thin traverse out to the
right along a line of poor pockets to reach a small ledge on the
arête. When suitably composed, climb the arête which is less
daunting than it appears.

Boc No Buttress Direct 12m E5 6c ★   (1990)
From the base of the thin crack of The Asp use small
fingerholds to make a desperate move/leap for the small ledge
on the arête, if successful, follow this as for the regular climb.

The Asp 10m E3 6a ★★★   (1975)
The obvious slim crack in the steep left-hand wall of the buttress
gives a classic little pitch, which is slow to dry after wet weather

and can be gritty early in the season. Gain the base of the crack from the left or from directly below. Once started the crack gives sustained finger-jamming/laybacking. The finish is easier but bolder.

Robin Hood's Cave Traverse   70m   S   (1922)
A rarely repeated and odd girdle. Start at the top of the edge and descend the easy upper section of Robin Hood's Chockstone Chimney, then go along the easy ramp to Robin Hood's Cave. Cross the gully and Cave Gully Wall to the Balcony Cave, with a dreaded 'bad step' between the two caves on Cave Gully Wall. Balcony Cave is best vacated by ascending the exposed overhang directly above, as for the finish to Robin Hood's Balcony Cave Direct.

DESCENT ROUTE
The stepped gully left of and behind Wuthering provides an easy descent from the cliff top and from the ledge where both Wuthering and The Asp finish.

There are several obvious and well-worn problems in the bay to the left, some of which have been used for a good many years as easy climbs. Belatedly these have been given names and descriptions. You will need to read the five route names in reverse to get the inevitable message. The rock takes the form of a broad buttress split centrally by a shallow V-shaped groove.

Four   12m   VS 4c   ★   (traditional/1992)
Climb just right of the right-hand arête of the central groove and continue up the wall using flakes to reach a ledge. The upper arête is climbed over a couple of small overlaps and can be started on the left or the right.

Bee   12m   D   ★★   (traditional)
The central groove proves to be a pleasant beginner's route. It starts with a classic crack and continues up an easier groove.

Dun   15m   HS   (traditional/1992)
The blunt left-hand arête of the central groove, finishing over a small overhang via a thin crack.

Bean   15m   VS 5a   (1992)
The narrow slabby wall just to the left provides a pleasant eliminate with delicate moves just below the ledges. Finish as for the previous route.

Awl   12m   VD   (traditional)
The left-hand arête of the buttress finishing up the face on the left.

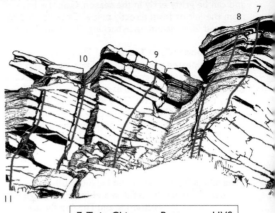

7. Twin Chimneys Buttress	HVS
8. Crack and Cave	VD
9. Paralysis	VS
10. Thrombosis	VS
11. Agony Crack	HVS

To the left a large detached block stands in front of the cliff and beyond this is a buttress split by a prominent Y-shaped chimney, this is:

TWIN CHIMNEYS BUTTRESS

Little Slab 12m S (1992)
To the right of and behind the block that stands in front of the edge is this short and pleasant route starting up a blunt rib and finishing up easy corners.

Little John's Step 25m S 4b ★ (1923-51)
A rambling expedition with some pleasant moves and situations. Start at the large detached block that stands in front of the cliff and pull leftwards over the initial roof (crux), to climb the left-hand side of its sharp outside edge. From the top of the block step awkwardly on to the face, move left and climb just right of Right Twin Chimney to reach its top. Traverse leftwards across the Left Twin Chimney and continue to finish up the final section of Twin Chimneys Buttress. **Dave's Little Route** S 4b (1993) climbs the steep left arête of the starting block to join the original route.

1. Boc No Buttress	E5
2. The Asp	E3
3. Dun	HS
4. Little John's Step	S
5. Right Twin Chimney	VD
6. Left Twin Chimney	M

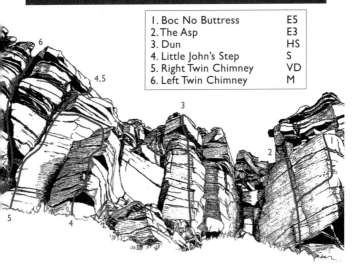

Bobsnob 14m E1 5a   (1983)
An almost independent route taking the smooth unprotected
slab just to the left of the detached block, trending slightly
rightwards throughout.

To the left the buttress is split by the two chimneys that form a V
then unite a short distance from the ground.

Right Twin Chimney 11m VD ★★   (1890-1903)
Go pleasantly up the rib just right of the chimney for five
metres, continue up the chimney as it leans away to the right.
Starting the chimney directly is easier and no less pleasant.

Triplet 17m VS 4b   (1992)
Start up the first five metres of Right Twin Chimney then step
out left to a good foothold before climbing the widening wall
between the rifts.

Left Twin Chimney 15m M ★★   (1890-1903)
This is the left-hand branch of the prominent Y-shaped chimney
system.

Lucy's Joy 15m E1 5b   (1995)
Climb the steep slab on the left to the mid-height bulge, pull
over the right-hand end of this with difficulty and continue up
the narrower buttress above.

Lucy's Delight   15m   VS 4b   (1978)
Follow the previous route to the mid-height bulges but pull
over the left edge of this to join and finish as for Twin
Chimneys Buttress; a poor route.

Twin Chimneys Buttress   17m   HVS 5a   ★★   (1922)
The blunt arête to the left. Start on the left, follow slippery
holds out to the arête and climb to the detached block. A
difficult move gains the upper section which is better protected
and easier. The route was also known as The Crucifix because
of the spread-eagled postures adopted during the ascent of the
mid-height crux. A good effort for 1922.

Around to the left is a steep, north-facing slab with a rounded
cave at its top left-hand edge.

Bill & Ted's Lobotomy   16m   E3 5c   (1992)
The centre of the poorly-protected steep slab is climbed to a
horizontal break; easier, juggier rock leads up the steeper headwall.

Crack and Cave   18m   VD   ★★   (1950)
Climb the prominent wide crack into the cave then traverse
rightwards to finish as for Twin Chimneys Buttress.

Via Roof Route   8m   VS 5a   ★   (1951)
Climb the thin crack on the left-hand side of the slab to gain
the cave. From a stance in the cave gain flakes in the roof and
swing rightwards to the arête where awkward moves lead to an
airy finish up the wall above.

Don't Bark, Bite   18m   E1 5c   (1980)
Start as for Via Roof Route to the cave and its stance, tackle the
thin cracks in the roof and follow these leftwards to a finish up
the hanging left-hand arête. **Rabies** E1 5c (1983) is a direct
start up the centre of the slab just to the right and below the
cave.

DESCENT ROUTE
The stepped crack on the left becomes a gully higher up and
provides an easy descent.

To the left of the descent gully is a wall offering a selection of
short climbs. These improve in quality the farther left you go. The
first two routes start at a higher level than the rest.

Boris the Bold 10m   VS 4c   (1985)
The wall immediately to the left of the descent route provides
a poor eliminate.

Paralysis 12m   VS 4c   (1962-63)
To the left again an awkward, rounded scoop leads to a ledge
above which a steep wall completes the route.

To the left is a prominent crack, the right-hand of a pair. The left-
hand one springs from a recess at a lower level, this is Agony
Crack.

Rigor Mortis 12m   HS 4b   (1962-63)
Climb a short corner crack on the right of Agony Crack then
move out rightwards to a ledge and climb the wider right-hand
crack to the top.

Thrombosis 11m   VS 4c ★   (1962-63)
Follow Rigor Mortis to the ledge on the right followed by the
steep narrow left-hand crack.

Big Dave's Wall 11m   E3 6a ★   (1996)
The slab, roof and wall between the two cracks provide a few
thin moves with a runner in Agony Crack to protect the tough
overhang.

Agony Crack 11m   HVS 5a ★★   (1940)
Climb the awkward thin crack in the blunt arête to an
uncomfortable undercut ledge then attack the well-named
continuation crack that splits the nose above. A traditional
gritstone grinder.

Regret 11m   E4 6a   (1984/1998)
Follow Agony Crack to the roof then step left and climb the
blank-looking wall with a fierce pull on poor pockets and a
harrowing finish well above the runners. Previously graded E2
5c. A direct start (1998) is possible from the block on the left
by making a long reach, followed by an even longer reach.
Unfortunately a detour into Agony Crack is required to place
protection.

N Route 10m   HS 4a ★   (1958)
Start awkwardly from a boulder on the front left-hand corner
of the buttress and follow the shallow groove to the right of
the edge more easily.

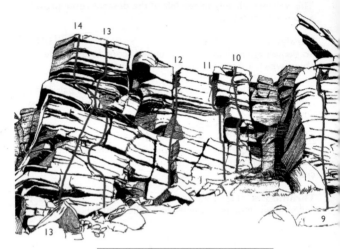

9. N Route	HS
10. Upanover	VS
11. Balcony Corner	D
12. Scoop Crack	HS
13. Centre Stage	HVS
14. Balcony Buttress	S

M Route 11m VS 4c (1952)
Ascend the left-hand wall of the buttress finishing rightwards under a projecting fang; The Green Needle.

Savage Amusement 10m E1 5b (1990)
Probably the edge's most bizarre route traversing the break around the projecting needle above Agony Crack, from right-to-left, or left-to-right. Touching the top is difficult to avoid and reduces the grade.

DESCENT ROUTE
The gully left of The Green Needle is Green Needle Gully.

Twinkle Toes 8m M (1993)
On the left-hand side of the descent gully is a blocky buttress. Climb this trending slightly leftwards and finish up the widening crack to the left of the buttress.

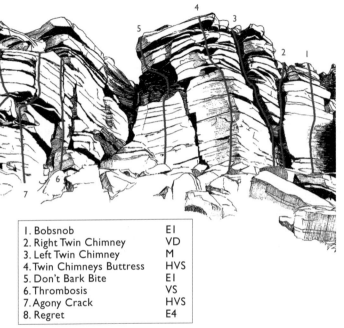

1. Bobsnob	E1
2. Right Twin Chimney	VD
3. Left Twin Chimney	M
4. Twin Chimneys Buttress	HVS
5. Don't Bark Bite	E1
6. Thrombosis	VS
7. Agony Crack	HVS
8. Regret	E4

Upanover Crack 8m S   (1961-63)
Climb the straight crack just to the left. The overhang at one-
third height provides all the fun.

Upanover 8m VS 5b   (1961-63)
A strenuous and awkward overhang on the narrow pillar just
left of Upanover Crack. Finish up the centre of the pillar.

Balcony Corner 9m D   (1961-63)
Just to the left, climb the short lower wall via a rightward-
slanting crack to reach a balcony and finish up the left-facing
corner-crack above.

Rib and Face 12m VS 4c   (1991)
Climb the narrow face (or broad rib), just to the left, to a ledge
and continue up the broader face above.

To the left are two cracks one metre apart.

Scoop Crack   14m HS 4b ★   (1961-63)
Climb a left-facing right-hand corner crack to a ledge and the
undercut continuation crack above, which is awkward to start. A
long standing, and undergraded, V Diff.

Big Yin   14m   VS 4c   (1993)
Climb the initial crack of The Flue then continue up the rib directly
above, between the two wide cracks, finishing up the obvious
scoop.

The Flue   14m   VD   (1961-63)
Climb the straight left-hand crack to a ledge and continue up an
awkward chimney passing to the left of the large hanging
'proboscis'.

(handwritten: L Nancy 25/05/03, S Clare, TR Gareth)

The next prominent feature of the edge is a fine tall buttress with a
heather-clad ledge, The Balcony, at half-height. Understandably this is:

BALCONY BUTTRESS

Balcony Balustrade   16m   HVS 5a   (1996)
Start at the flat ledge below the right-hand side of Balcony
Buttress and climb straight up the wall to ledges and over an
awkward bulge to the heather-coated platform. The final
overhanging arête is climbed on its left-hand side via a useful
pocket.

Balcony Buttress   20m   S 4a   ★★★   (1922)
An old classic, polished in places and with a spectacular finale.
Start at the flat ledge, as for the previous route, and climb the
buttress trending up and left then back right to reach a wide
crack. Climb this to the heathery ledge then traverse to the
left-hand edge of the buttress and finish via a swift layback up
the flake on the exposed arête. The original start (1922) was a
traverse taking the easiest line around the arête from the foot
of Balcony Climb, same grade but not as good.

(handwritten: L Gareth 25/05/03, S Nancy 25/05/03, L Clare 25/05/03)

Centre Stage   18m   HVS 5a   ★★   (1993)
Start at flat ledges below the centre of the face and trend
leftwards then rightwards over the awkward initial bulges
before heading straight up the face passing to the left of the
wide crack of the regular route. From the heather ledge pull
powerfully through the roof to finish at the prominent notch.
The final roof was previously claimed as **Balcony Bulge** HVS
5a (1992).

Exit Stage Left 20m E1 5b ★   (1993)
Start under the left-hand arête of the buttress and climb over
the initial roof to ledges. Tackle the next set of bulges directly,
then finish up the wall around to the left of the flake of Balcony
Buttress.

On the north-facing left-hand side of the buttress is a wide cleft
forming three shallow caves, set one above another; there are
several climbs there.

Balcony Cracks 14m S 4a ★   (1961-63)
Climb strenuously to the upper cave then follow the left-hand
arête and pull awkwardly over the bulge to finish directly via a
series of well-positioned shallow flake cracks.

Balcony Climb 12m HVD   (pre-1923)
Follow the previous climb to the highest cave then traverse out
to the left to reach and finish up the final section of a leftward-
slanting crack. The crack can be reached directly **Balcony
Climb Direct** S 4a ★ (1922).

Polyfilla 14m VS 4c   (1996)
Climb the delicate slab left of the start of Balcony Climb then
move right and climb the wall left of the finish of Balcony
Cracks. As the name suggests it is rather squeezed in.

To the left of the side-wall of Balcony Buttress the cliff swings
round to face west, increasing in size and grandeur the farther
left you proceed. This is the:

MISSISSIPPI BUTTRESS AREA

Fairy Chimney 11m D   (1961-63)
This is the chimney that bounds the left-hand side of Balcony
Buttress, blocked at mid-height by a protruding rib which is
most easily passed on the right.

Pixie 12m VS 5a   (1992)
A pleasant eliminate up the narrow rib just to the left, finishing
up a leftwards-slanting flake crack.

Fairy Castle Crack 11m D   (1961-63)
Ascend the obvious crack to the right of the chimney passing
around the right-hand edge of a protruding square block.

Fallen Pillar Chimney 11m VD   (1961-63)
The deep chimney to the left gets its name from the pillar of

toppled blocks that form its right-hand wall. It provides an archetypal grovel.

The cliff swings round to face west again. The first route follows the arête that forms the right-hand edge of the wall.

Tributary 12m HVS 5b (1996)
The arête immediately to the left of the chimney and right of the prominent flake of Amazon Crack is climbed passing the initial roof on the right (runner on the left in Amazon Crack). Continue to ledges and climb a short crack to take the final bulge directly.

Amazon Crack 12m S 4a ★★ (1923-51)
The undercut flaky crack to the left is best reached from directly below though it is also accessible by swinging in from the right. It is hardest at the start but soon eases.

Melancholy Witness 17m E3 6a (1981)
This forlorn eliminate up the right-hand side of the smooth wall to the left has never proved popular. Start at a short arête just left of Amazon Crack and climb the wall using the arête until it is possible to reach left into the slot of Morrison's Redoubt. Gain small flakes on the right and use these to reach better holds. Step right and continue to a finish in common with Morrison's Redoubt.

Morrison's Redoubt 18m E1 5b ★★ (1962-63)
An excellent climb with a worrying start up the centre of the smooth wall. Climb on to a block and, with little in the way of protection, teeter up the wall (crux) to reach a good horizontal slot and 'bomber' gear. Continue up a very short vertical crack then follow a wider crack trending rightwards to a steep finish. Low in the grade.

Puzzlelock 22m E4 6a ★ (1981)
A bold climb following the blunt arête to the left of the wall. Climb a blocky rib and continue with difficulty to a poor horizontal break. Another thin move brings easier ground within reach. Finish up the crack of The Mississippi Variant.

To the left a wide left-facing corner-crack leads to a notch in the band of overhangs that cuts across the face at four metres.

Stanleyville 22m E4 5c ★★ (1973)
A harrowing lead up the centre of the smooth wall above the overhangs. Climb a groove and bulge to reach a good ledge.

From the middle of the ledge make committing moves to gain a vague horizontal break where a poor Friend 3½ gives little in the way of reassurance for the crucial mantelshelf that follows. Continue trending slightly left to finish over the overhang above The Mississippi Variant.

Orinoco Flow   22m   E2 5c   ★   (1996)
Climb straight through the centre of the large triangular roof between The Mississippi Buttress Direct and The Mississippi Variant Direct to do the crux of the latter route. From the ledge above this step left and climb the wall to the bulges that are split by a flake and trend rightwards through these on rounded holds to reach the top.

The Mississippi Buttress Direct
22m   VS 4c   ★★★   (1929-51)
The leftward-trending flake-line that splits the centre of the buttress is one of Stanage's all time great VS routes, steep and juggy, with good protection. Start in an obvious overhung corner and climb this to a bulge. Pass this awkwardly (crux), then follow the superb crack above.

The Mississippi Variant   24m   HVS 5a   ★★   (1930s)
An old route following a strong natural line. Start as for The Mississippi Buttress Direct and above its crux bulge step out right to reach the obvious flake. Climb this to an overhang and make a difficult move out right to gain a small ledge and an easy finish.

The Mississippi Variant Direct   22m   E1 5b   ★★   (1968)
A good route that is a direct version of the previous climb. Follow Stanleyville to the good ledge and from the left-hand end of this step awkwardly up and left to reach a sloping ledge. Finish as for The Mississippi Variant.

The Mersey Variant   22m   E2 5c   ★   (1980)
A worthwhile eliminate line taking the rib, bulges and wall between The Link and The Mississippi Buttress Direct. Climb the initial stacked roofs between the two cracks to reach a horizontal break. Climb up and left, with difficulty, before continuing up the smooth slab and juggy breaks to the top.

The Link   22m   HVS 5b   ★★★   (1974)
An excellent direct on the original Congo Corner giving a very sustained way up the face. Climb the tough leftward-facing corner crack to a cramped rest below bulges. Continue directly over the overhang on slightly suspect flakes to a swing left

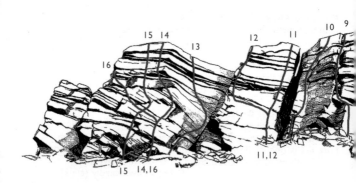

9. Hell Crack	VS
10. Step-Ladder Crack	VS
11. Ashes	E3
12. Saliva	E1
13. The Old Scoop	VS
14. Bloodshot	E3
15. The Scoop/Ozymandias	HVS
16. Martello Buttress	HS

which allows a tricky mantelshelf move on to a good ledge.
Make the crux moves of Congo Corner to reach the beckoning
'horn' and continue more easily to the top.

Congo Corner 24m HVS 5b ★★★ (1954)
Start up the thin crack of The Link and climb this to a rest
below the overhangs. Traverse leftwards below the bulges until
a move up enables a second traverse line to be reached. Follow
this, 'The Tanganyika Traverse', back rightwards to the arête and
make a high step or a mantelshelf to gain a good ledge. From
the ledge a precarious move leads to a good 'horn' and a
sensational finish.

Nairobi 18m E4 6a (1987)
A worthwhile and exciting eliminate through the bulging flake-
crack (as for Dark Continent) and leaning roof one metre left
of The Link, eventually joining it at the 'tricky mantelshelf'.

1. Morrison's Redoubt	E1
2. The Mississippi Variant Direct	E1
3. The Mississippi Buttress Direct	VS
4. The Link	HVS
5. Congo Corner	HVS
6. Dark Continent	E1
7. Mississippi Chimney	VD
8. The Louisiana Rib	VS

Moving left to do the upper section of Dark Continent is the most logical way to the cliff top.

Dark Continent 18m E1 5c ★★   (1978)
To the left, the lowest overhang on the buttress is split by a diagonal flake-crack. Climb this to join Congo Corner and follow it left to the end of its traverse. The wall directly above this point is climbed with the aid of a very long reach. If successful, move slightly left, then finish directly over the bulges in a glorious position.

African Herbs 18m E3 5c   (1985)
Follow Mississippi Chimney to half-height then move rightwards to attack the bold wall and easier rib above.

Mississippi Chimney 18m VD ★★   (1890-1903)
The prominent hanging cleft on the left-hand side of the

buttress is entered by a short difficult crack and followed more easily.

To the left of the chimney is a narrow tower-like buttress, bounded on its left-hand side by a prominent gully, this is:

THE LOUISIANA RIB

The Levée 17m HVS 5b (1993)
Climb the steep little wall one metre left of Mississippi Chimney to a sloping ledge. Continue up the arête above, at first on its left-hand side (as for Louisiana Rib) and finally on its right-hand side.

Finger Licking Good 18m HVS 5a ★ (1998)
An eliminate with some excellent climbing. Start between blocks and climb the centre of the buttress directly on a continuously surprising set of holds.

The Louisiana Rib 18m VS 4c ★★ (1950)
The original route finds a sneaky way up the narrow buttress. Climb the crack to the left of the centre of the rib until a delicate traverse rightwards leads to the arête. Climb this awkwardly for three metres to a move leftwards on to the front face to finish.

Acheron 17m E1 5b ★★ (1967)
An exciting route which climbs the left-hand side of The Louisiana Rib throughout making a long reach and a hard pull from the start of the rightward traverse of that route. Continue up the pleasantly positioned left-hand arête.

Ferryboat Highway 32m HVS 5b ★ (1956)
An arduous traverse of the left-hand and central sections of Mississippi Buttress. Start as for The Louisiana Rib and follow the rightwards traverse of this route into Mississippi Chimney. Continue along the rightward traverse of Congo Corner to the small ledge and a move up to a difficult toe-traverse into Mississippi Buttress Direct. A line of holds runs out rightwards ending with a long step down into the upper section of The Mississippi Variant; finish up this.

Gathering Gloom 10m E1 5c (1992)
The centre of the leaning wall around to the left of Acheron is climbed on mostly (but not exclusively) good holds.

DESCENT ROUTE
The gully that cuts in behind The Mississippi Buttress and The Louisiana Rib provides an easy scrambling descent.

To the left of the descent route is a bulging buttress with a steep central crack-line:

HEAVEN CRACK BUTTRESS

Jean's Line　10m　HS 4a　　　　　　　　　　(1977)
The upper section of the left-hand side-wall of the descent gully wall has a shallow corner, leading to a crack in the upper wall.

Lethe　10m　HVS 5a　　　　　　　　　　　　(1967)
Start at twin flakes slightly higher up the gully than the flake of Heaven Crack. Climb the wall, trending slightly left at the top.

The Aeneid　35m　VS 4c, 5a　★　　　　　　(1979)
This is another of those odd girdle traverses that is probably best soloed to reduce the annoyance to the climbing public. Climb Lethe to half-height then traverse left along the obvious horizontal break to reach and cross the dark cleft of Devil's Chimney. Continue along the same break crossing the Saliva buttress to a possible stance in Martello Cracks. Cross Martello Buttress and finish up the left-hand side-wall via the final section of Zel.

Heaven Crack　10m　VD　★★★　　　　　　(1923-51)
The inviting flake crack at the lower end of the descent gully is climbed by a laybacking 'jugfest' to a final delicate move. It is a great pity that the route isn't three times longer.

Still in Limbo　13m　E1 5b　　　　　　　　(1993)
Climb through the centre of the flat roof between 'Heaven and Hell' and continue on mostly good breaks. Some care is required with a large, but vital, loose block at half-height.

Hell Crack　13m　VS 4c　★★★　　　　　　(1932-33)
The black bulging crack to the left is taken directly. Some of the roughest, toughest rock on the cliff.

Dark Water　14m　E3 6b　　　　　　　　　　(1983)
Start as for Hell Crack then move out left to climb the blunt rib right of Step-ladder Crack by a ludicrous lunge/reach. The upper section is much easier. A side-runner by the crux moves provides an exciting swing if, as is usual, you miss the hold.

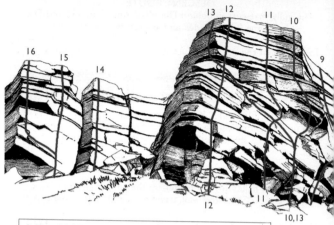

9. The Old Scoop	VS
10. Bloodshot	E3
11. The Scoop/Ozymandias	HVS
12. Another Game of Bowls Sir Walter?	E1
13. Martello Buttress	HS
14. Little Tower	HS
15. The Roundabout	HVS
16. Swings	E1

Step-ladder Crack　15m　VS 5a　★★　　　　(1950-51)
From a short distance up Devil's Chimney, make a difficult
stride right to the thin crack. Climb this and move right to a
deeper flake-crack which is followed by a move right again to
finish up the rib, or a little farther right up the final section of
Hell Crack. A direct start and finish, starting up a shallow
groove with a crack that doesn't quite reach the ground and
finishing directly up the short wall above, is possible at HVS 5c
★★ (1964-76).

Devil's Chimney　13m　HD　★★　　　　(1923-51)
The deep dark 'lum' on the left is climbed in traditional fashion
to an exit on the right-hand wall when the chimney closes. An
alternative is to **Stay in the Light** 13m HS (1999) by bridging
up the mouth of the chimney.

To the left is a steep, smooth slab with a prominent horizontal
overlap at two-thirds height and an undercut on its left-hand side;
this is:

122

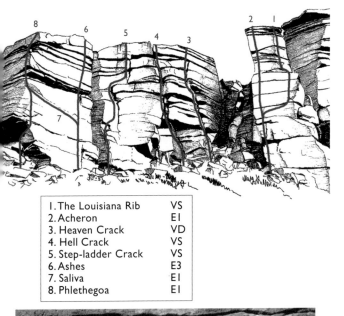

1. The Louisiana Rib	VS
2. Acheron	E1
3. Heaven Crack	VD
4. Hell Crack	VS
5. Step-ladder Crack	VS
6. Ashes	E3
7. Saliva	E1
8. Phlethegoa	E1

SALIVA BUTTRESS

Ashes 12m E3 5c ★ (1981)
Climb a thin crack in the right-hand side of the slab then make
a series of difficult and unprotectable moves up the wall above
to reach the security of a large horizontal break. Continue up
the steep wall above.

Saliva 15m E1 5b ★★ (1955)
Start as for Ashes up the thin crack until it is possible to make
a committing traverse diagonally leftwards to the arête; finish
up this.

Fading Star 13m E2 6a ★★ (1979)
Climb the hanging left-hand arete of the wall with difficulty to
enter a shallow groove. Continue up this and the arête above
to a roof. Move right, surmount the roof and attack the short

smooth wall via a crucial pull on a large pebble. Getting established on this wall constitutes the crux. A direct start at E2 6b ★ (1979-89) can be made by climbing the wall left of the crack of Saliva.

Phlegethoa 12m E1 5c ★   (1967)
Start at the cutaway left of the hanging arête of Fading Star. Swing right onto the arête and, after a tricky move, follow this to the top of the crag. The direct start at E1 6a (1979) climbs Fading Star to the arête of Phlegethoa.

Wax Museum 12m HVS 5c   (1983)
Left of Phlegethoa is a slab severely undercut at its base. From below the cutaway swing up and leftwards to cross the roof by a perplexing move. Continue much more easily up the slab to the left of the arête.

Mistella 12m VD ★   (1923-51)
Ascend Martello Cracks for three metres then traverse rightwards to finish up the centre of the face.

Martello Cracks 10m M ★   (1923-51)
The twin cracks in the slabby angle between Martello Buttress and Saliva Buttress give a pleasant low-grade climb.

To the left is the broad tapering **MARTELLO BUTTRESS** named after its resemblance to the old Martello Fortresses that were built along the south coast of England in 1804 against the threat of a French invasion. There has been some confusion over the years as there appear to have been two separate routes called The Scoop put up on this buttress. The original starts of Martello Buttress and The Scoop/Ozymandias have been switched to give better and more balanced routes.

MARTELLO BUTTRESS

The Old Scoop 15m VS 4b ★   (traditional)
Start just left of the open gully of Martello Cracks at a recess. Climb into and up a short, leaning corner to reach a platform. Follow the left-hand of the Martello Cracks for a short distance until a ledge leads leftwards into the large scoop. Finish directly up the back of the scoop.

Ain't Nobody Here but us Chickens 14m E3 6b (1991)
An eliminate that straightens out The Old Scoop by difficult moves to gain the sloping shelf at the base of the slab; finish easily.

Bloodshot 15m E3 5c ★ (1979)
Start in the same place as Martello Buttress but trend up and
right into a shallow, leaning corner and climb the overhang on
the left using spaced and rounded holds via a harrowing
sequence of reaches. Finish up the easier arête on the left. An
eliminate, **Hebden's Heights** HVS 5a (1996) starts in the
same place and gains the projecting ledge to tackle the steep
wall and bulge directly above. Finish up the left-hand side of the
upper arête on rounded holds; not too well-protected.

Martello Buttress 17m HS 4b ★★ (1922)
The original route of the buttress. Start at the bottom right-
hand corner of the buttress at a projecting tooth of rock. Step
off this and pull steeply up and left to a ledge. Continue,
trending left and up, to a good ledge and an impressive finish up
the left-hand side of the final arête.

The Scoop/Ozymandias 15m HVS 5a ★★★ (1959)
Start in the middle of the buttress and make steep and
awkward moves through an overhang onto a ledge. Move up
into a shallow scoop where a long move left reaches rounded
breaks which lead to the top giving superb, open climbing.

Another Game of Bowls Sir Walter?
15m E1 5b ★ (1992)
Start at the short flake just right of the arête and climb this to
its end, then make troublesome moves to better holds.
Continue steeply, keeping right of the upper arête throughout.

To the left the arête is undercut by a large flat roof three metres
off the ground. The next two routes pass round either edge of
this.

Choux Fleur 15m E1 5c (1992)
Climb past the right-hand edge of the overhang to reach a
difficult pull back left which gains a sloping hold then a black
block. Continue to the final ledge of Martello Buttress before
climbing the wall on the left to the top.

Choux 15m E2 6a (1992)
Climb the left-hand side of the overhang with difficulty to gain
the horizontal break. Continue up the wall using a gritty white
flake, keeping to the right of Byne's Route; finish easily.

Byne's Route 15m VS 4c ★★ (1932-33)
Start round to the left of the buttress and climb into a recess.

Traverse right to a short crack and climb this to a finish up the arête of Martello Buttress.

Zel 13m HVS 4c (1979)
Follow Byne's Route to the start of the traverse and climb the wall trending leftwards to finish up the left-hand arête of the face.

Vanishing Point 10m VS 4c (1981)
Climb the chimney around to the left, moving right above the roof to climb a steep blunt rib.

Narrowing Chimney 7m S (1961-63)
Climb the aforementioned chimney that cuts in behind Martello Buttress.

Trinket 7m S (1993)
This is the short arête left of Narrowing Chimney which is climbed pleasantly on its left-hand side.

Beads 7m S (1961-63)
The narrow wall in the back of the recess is climbed via the central, thin crack-line.

49 Bikinis 9m HVS 5a (1993)
Just to the left of an easy corner, climb the centre of the front face of Little Tower.

Little Tower 8m HS 4b ★ (1951)
Climb the short square arête on the left-hand side of the little tower.

Turf Crack 10m VD ★ (1951)
The corner crack that bounds the right-hand side of the taller tower of Intermediate Buttress.

The last buttress before the rocks become smaller is the narrow tower of:

INTERMEDIATE BUTTRESS

The Roundabout 12m HVS 5b (1956)
Start at the right-hand side of the buttress and make difficult moves up and leftwards across the wall to reach pockets and good horizontal cracks below a shallow groove. The groove is climbed to a steep and somewhat urgent finish pulling directly over the final overhang.

Swings 11m E1 5c ★   (1983)
A more direct version of the previous climb offering a fine
technical way up the buttress. From the centre of the front face
of the buttress move up and right using a couple of rugosities
and an elusive two-finger pocket to reach jugs and runners.
Continue up the steep groove to finish as for The Roundabout.

Second Wind 11m HVS 5c   (1986)
Start in the centre of the right-hand wall of the buttress.
Traverse leftwards and pull up to gain the prominent short
crack with difficulty. Continue up the right-hand side of the
arête, passing an awkward bulge to reach the top.

The Nose 10m VS 4b ★   (1954)
Start under the centre of the left face of the buttress. Traverse
rightwards and finish up the exposed arête.

Jaygo's Pipe 10m HVS 5a ★   (1994)
Start as for the previous route but pull straight over the bulges
and climb the centre of the face to a rounded exit; low in the
grade.

Intermediate Buttress 10m VD ★★   (1923-51)
From the left-hand side of the buttress climb up the left-hand
edge then move slightly right to finish.

5 See Plus 10m VS 5a   (1998)
Start just left of the left-hand arête of the buttress and climb
directly to a typical gritstone finish.

The next climbs are located 30 metres to the left past an area of
low rock.

DESCENT ROUTE
To the left is a low point in the cliff that provides an easy
descent down a couple of rocky steps.

The next section of rock is a buttress with a series of overhangs
on its left-hand face and with the shelving ledge that gives its
name prominent on the right face of the buttress. This is:

VERANDAH BUTTRESS

On the right, the first piece of rock is a short, rounded buttress
seamed with horizontal cracks.

1. Little Tower	HS
2. The Roundabout	HVS
3. Swings	E1
4. The Confectioner	VS
5. Verandah Pillar	HS
6. Greengrocer Wall	E1
7. Butcher Crack	HVS
8. Verandah Buttress	HVD
9. The Guillotine	E3
10. Pedlar's Slab	HVS
11. Pedlar's Arête	E1
12. Punklet	E1

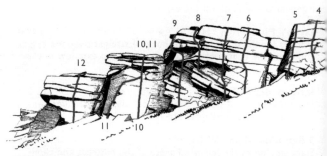

The Confectioner 8m VS 5a (1959)
Climb the short wall on the right via a shallow niche, a couple of long reaches and a rounded exit.

Verandah Pillar 10m HS 4b ★ (1951)
Just to the left of The Confectioner, climb the left-facing flaky weakness in the flat front of the buttress to an awkward finish.

Cocktails 9m VS 4c ★ (1993)
The rounded rib in the centre of the wall proves to be juggy and excellent. Start from the cutaway and trend leftwards over the initial bulges before continuing directly.

Verandah Wall 10m VS 4c (1961-63)
The steep wall to the right of the corner is climbed on a series of rounded holds.

Verandah Cracks 8m D (1961-63)
Ascend the twin cracks in the angle to the left.

Balcony Buttress S 4a (page 114)
Climber: Kate Hughes Photo: David Simmonite

Amazon Crack S 4a (page 116)
Climber: David Trelawny Ross Photo: Ian Smith

Saliva El 5b (page 123)
Climber: Unknown Photo: David Simmonite

Greengrocer Wall   10m   E1 5c   ★   (1951-56)
The wall to the left of the corner has a difficult start using a
thin diagonal crack. Continue directly up the wall passing a
useful boss and finish directly on widely-spaced holds.

One Stop Shopping   10m   E1 6a   (1997)
An eliminate, though with some good moves. Climb the wall
immediately right of the polished start to Verandah Buttress
with difficulty, continue in a direct line with a couple of long
reaches.

Butcher Crack   12m   HVS 5b   ★   (1954)
Start as for Verandah Buttress to reach the sloping shelf. From
there climb directly to the top by a short crack and a long
stretch.

Verandah Buttress   14m   HVD 5b   ★   (1923-51)
The sloping shelf of the verandah can be gained at its bottom
right-hand corner by devious manoeuvres (crux). From the
scoop, traverse left to finish up the exposed arête of the
buttress. Originally there was a block in the scoop which fell
out. The 1951 guidebook simply stated: 'block missing from
scoop, start now rather hard'.

Fit as a Butcher's Dog   12m   E1 5c   (1997)
Do battle with the hideous meat-eating roof-crack to reach the
centre of the shelf on Verandah Buttress. Climb over the

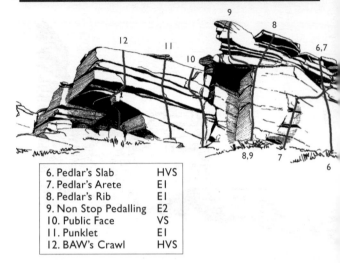

6. Pedlar's Slab	HVS
7. Pedlar's Arete	E1
8. Pedlar's Rib	E1
9. Non Stop Pedalling	E2
10. Public Face	VS
11. Punklet	E1
12. BAW's Crawl	HVS

smaller overhang and, finishing with a long reach, arrive at the left edge of the obvious block.

To the left the main section of the face is cut by many overhangs, forcing the seven closely-packed routes to weave through them in an uncharacteristic fashion for gritstone.

The Old Dragon 14m E2 5b ★ (1968/1973)
Start under the groove on the right-hand side of the overhanging face and climb to a small ledge, from there swarm up the steep groove on 'better-than expected' holds to reach the good ledge on The Guillotine. Escape off right, or better but less logically, finish up the awkward overhanging crack just to the left.

An excellent, if fragile, problem **Mary Whitehouse** E3 6b (1983) swings rightwards across the overhang which forms the right-hand wall of Old Dragon on brittle flakes to reach the left-hand end of the shelf of Verandah Buttress, up which a finish is possible. The landing below is not good and spotters are useful. This climb appears to correspond to **Young Lion** E2 6b (1987) and **Verandah Buttress Direct** E4 6c (1995), though the the latter apparently climbs direct over the roof to the left of Mary Whitehouse and a common finish.

1. Verandah Pillar	HS
2. The Guillotine	E3
3. Off With His Head	E4
4. Plasic Dream	E3
5. Elastic	VS

The Guillotine 16m E3 5c ★★ (1971/1973)
An exciting though devious trip, the first route to tackle the central section of the buttress. Start in the centre of the overhanging face to the left of The Old Dragon and climb to a small ledge. Step left and go up to the lip of the first overhang before swinging right below a prominent scar to reach a good ledge on the right-hand edge of the buttress. Traverse leftwards until just around the arête and surmount the overhang just to the left of the prow.

Guillotine Direct 14m E4 6b ★★★ (1987)
A better, more direct ascent of the buttress. Start as for The Guillotine but at the roof step right and pull over the overhang passing to the right of the rock scar. Above this join the regular route just right of the prow before stepping left for the normal exit.

Off With His Head 14m E4 6a ★★★ (1982)
A fine climb that is almost more direct than Guillotine Direct and has often been climbed in mistake for it. Start as for The Guillotine but where that route moves right trend left past the rock scar and make a hard move over the nose to gain the break under the overhang. Another hard move leads over this using a prominent pocket to reach the better break above; finish easily.

Headless Chicken 13m E5 6b ★★   (1994)
Start two metres left of the previous route. Climb the wall
using a line of juggy flakes before stretching up left to the ledge
below the obvious worrying flake jammed below the roof.
Climb the wall just right of this to the top overhang, step left
and cross the roof with difficulty. Finish more easily leftwards.

Tarzan Boy 10m E3 6a   (1982/1987)
Start below the obvious 'kamikaze' flake and climb straight up
towards this with difficulty. Carefully circumnavigate it and slink
off leftwards below the roof to finish up the left-hand arête of
the buttress as for Plastic Dream.

Plastic Dream 10m E3 6a ★   (1977)
The severely undercut left-hand arête of the buttress is climbed
facing left. Once established follow the rest of the arête
throughout.

To the left is a rather confusing area of corners and pillars which
may well have been climbed in the past and which have certainly
seen considerable development since the last edition of this
guidebook.

Pisa Crack 11m VS 4c   (1951-56)
A tower-like block slumps against the left-hand side of Verandah
Buttress forming a narrowing cleft. Climb the cleft to the
capping overhang and finish up the right-hand edge.

Hidden Crack 10m VD   (1961-63)
The chimney from the start of Pisa Crack leads through a
skylight to a finishing crack in the right-hand side of the bay
above.

Right Side 10m HVS 5c   (1998)
The leaning right-hand edge of the front face of the pillar
features sustained and technical moves.

Pisa Pillar 10m HS 4b   (1992)
The left-hand edge of the front face leads past an awkward
initial overhang to a mantelshelf finish on to the top block.

To the left it is possible to scramble up into a recess behind the
leaning tower of Pisa.

Left Flank 8m D   (traditional)
Scramble into the recess and climb the face on the right to the
top of the tower, continue by crossing over to the main edge.

Viridescent Corner   8m   HVD   (traditional)
Scramble into the recess then climb the well-named angular
corner which proves to be better than it looks.

Topo Mania   8m   VS 5a   (1998)
Climb the narrow rib on the left-hand side of the recess,
transferring to the right-hand side where it steepens. Finish
over the bulge. Unfortunately the difficulties can be avoided by
bridging to the opposite wall of the recess.

Recess Rib   8m   D   (1992)
Climb the pleasant, narrow, stepped rib keeping on its left-hand
side throughout and using the straight crack to the left as and
when required.

Corner Crack   8m   D   (traditional)
The easy corner.

Elastic   10m   VS 4c   (1998)
Climb the centre of the narrow rib without using either edge.

Top Block Rock   10m   VD   (1992)
The rib and/or widening crack just right of Pedlar's Slab; well-
named.

To the left is an attractive, smooth slab with a projecting fang of
rock at its top left corner.

PEDLAR'S SLAB

Pedlar's Wall   10m   HVS 5b   (1998)
Climb Top Block Rock to a small ledge then step left on to the
wall and climb to a tricky finish. This can also be used as a right-
hand finish to the next route.

Pedlar's Slab   11m   HVS 5c   ★★   (1961-63)
The centre of the smooth slab on the left has a technical start.
Continue more easily with care; unprotected.

Keep Pedalling   10m   E2 5c   (1991)
Climb the blunt rib left of Pedlar's Slab directly to the ledge on
Pedlar's Arete. Finish directly on sloping holds

Pedlar's Arête   11m   E1 5b   ★   (1961-63)
Climb the blunt arête using flakes to a ledge. Traverse right and
finish as for Pedlar's Slab.

Pedlar's Rib 11m E1 5c ★★ (1967)
The elegant rib, right of an easy chimney, is awkward to start
and is climbed via a series of small layaway holds to reach a
deep horizontal break. Swing rapidly rightwards to escape. A
variation finish **Non-stop Pedalling** E2 5c (1985) swings left
at the break to scale the hanging prow.

Green Chimney 10m VD (traditional)
The narrow chimney to the left is tricky to enter. Exit through a
hole. The green wall to the left has thin moves and a lone RP
runner. It is hardly a gem, **Paste** HVS 5c (1998).

DESCENT ROUTE
The chimney to the left offers an awkward way down in its
lower reaches.

To the left is a buttress that is severely undercut on its left-hand
edge, featuring an odd collection of up-and-down routes and
sideways shuffling expeditions.

BAW'S CRAWL BUTTRESS

Public Image 15m VS 5a (1989)
Climb the shallow groove just to the left of the right-hand
edge of the buttress to reach the top break. Traverse left to
pass BAW's Crawl, go round the arête and finish up The Punk.
Public Face VS 5a (1970s) finishes directly from the shallow
groove.

Punklet 9m E1 6a ★ (1976)
The right-hand wall of the buttress is taken up its centre with a
difficult move at the start and a sense of urgency to finish.

BAW's Crawl 10m HVS 5a ★★★ (1952)
Start from a boulder below the centre of the big roof. The
object is to install yourself, or at least your feet, in the slot high
on the right. Once ensconced, shuffle along the slot until a
standing position on the face on the right is achieved. Finish
with a long reach.

Shine On 9m E7 6c ★★★ (1992)
The main overhang of the buttress is tackled by an excellent
and arduous outing. The final crack of The Punk is reached from
below by traversing the thin expanding flake in the roof,
followed by difficult moves using two obvious pockets on the
headwall.

Cemetery Waits   9m   E7 6c   ★★   (1995)
The hanging, left-hand arête of the buttress is started from the
left and proves to be taxing in the extreme. You need a certain
amount of vision to see the route and the useful flakes under
the roof are as brittle as they look.

The Punk   10m   VS 4b   ★   (1973)
The obvious crack in the front face of the buttress is gained
from the gully by a startling hand-traverse above jagged
boulders.

Old Smoothie   15m   VS 4c   (1998)
Start in the depths of the cleft behind the buttress and traverse
the highest break passing beneath the capstone and around
onto the front face to a finish up a crack.

Continuing leftwards the edge deteriorates somewhat. Despite
this the next section of rock is always a good place to avoid the
crowds on busy weekends and might be considered a major venue
if it were part of a lesser cliff.

To the left of the deep chimney up which The Punk starts, is a
shorter, square-fronted buttress and to the right of this an angular
corner and an arête almost in the chimney.

Probably Done Before   8m   S   (1998)
The arête is followed on its right-hand side.

Obviously Done Before   8m   S   (1998)
Climb the recess to a bulge followed by an awkward move to
enter the hanging corner.

Little Pete   8m   HVS 5a   (1994)
The main arête of the buttress is climbed on its right-hand side
passing a small overlap and then continuing delicately using a
shallow crack. A problem start over the roof to the left is 5c.

Eyes   9m   VS 4c   (1992)
The right-hand arête of the north-facing wall is climbed on its
left-hand side.

Jon's Route   9m   S 4a   (1992)
The centre of the north face is climbed directly.

The Nays   8m   D   (1999)
Climb the edge of the wall to the left of Jon's Route starting
with a mantelshelf.

DESCENT ROUTE
To the left lower rocks offer several easy ways down.

Thirty metres to the left, past the shorter rocks, is a buttress with a deep recess flanked on the right by a large hanging flange-like rib. The whole buttress is deviously called:

THE CLEFT WING

The next route starts on the face on the far right of the buttress.

Wing Wall 11m D (1923-51)
Climb the shelving right-hand edge of the slabby face that forms the outside of The Wing to reach a ledge with a prominent hollybush. Walk left along the ledge and finish up a wide crack.

Taking a Winger 12m E2 5c (1996)
Start on the front face, left of a block and climb small flakes to reach the ledge on Wing Wall. Continue up the easier upper wall trending rightwards to finish.

Spearing the Bearded Clam 11m E2 5c (1983)
Start under the hanging arête and make a couple of taxing moves on poor holds to get established on the face above and right. Once established, step left to reach easier ground. A spooky and poorly-protected pitch with a highly dubious name.

Trimming the Beard 11m E3 6a (1989)
The hanging arête of The Wing is climbed initially rightwards as for the previous route, but swing back left under the first bulge and layback boldly up the left-hand side of the arête to reach easier rock; finish directly.

Cleft Wing Superdirect 12m VS 4c ★ (1958)
Climb up into the back of the gloomy V-shaped groove then take a deep breath and hand-traverse the overhanging right-hand wall in spectacular fashion. Swing round the arête and finish up easier bulging rock with relief.

Cleft Wing 12m HVS 5b ★ (1953)
Start on the left-hand wall of the deep cleft at well-scratched footholds. Make sketchy moves to reach the flake crack that runs up to the overhang. Face the opposite wall of The Wing and, when suitably 'psyched-up,' fall across the gap making sure to catch the holds on the other side as failure to do so may well result in a cleft skull. Swing around the arête to reach

easier climbing as for the previous climb. One of Stanage's more bizarre routes.

5.9 Finish 12m E1 5b ★   (1977)
Follow the previous climb to the roof then, rather than risk the 'fall' across to the other side, cross the overhang rightwards by means of a thin flake and a couple of strange upside down moves to a 'beached whale' landing.

Wing Buttress 13m HVS 5b ★   (1923-51)
Start on the left-hand wall of the deep cleft at the well-scratched footholds of the previous climb and make delicate moves to better holds then swing leftwards along a horizontal break. Go around the arête and climb the steep side wall to finish up a short crack.

On a Wing and Prayer 12m E1 5c   (1996)
From the left of the hanging arête, delicately gain the small ledge three metres up the arête to continue awkwardly over a nose to finish up the side wall immediately left of the capping roof. Top out at a rocking stone.

Wing Buttress Gully 12m D   (1923-51)
The obvious deep cleft to the left is yet another of those classic grit chimneys.

To the left of the gully is the well-fissured:

DOVER'S WALL

The Grey Cliffs of ... 12m HVS 5b   (1999)
Climb the little facet to the left of Wing Buttress Gully and right of Dover's Wall, Route 4 to a triangular overhang. Go over this and finish up the arête.

Dover's Wall, Route 4 11m VS 4b   (1964-76)
Climb the awkward crack immediately left of the right-hand arête of the wall to reach a ledge. Finish over a bulge.

Dover's Wall, Route 1 12m S 4a ★   (1930-33)
A narrow crack (second from the right) leads to a small projecting tooth of rock at the top of the buttress. An eliminate **Dover's Wall, Route 1.5** VS 5a (1999) climbs the rock between Dover's Wall Routes 1 & 2 and avoiding holds on both.

5. Dover's Wall, Route 4	VS
6. Dover's Wall, Route 1	S
7. Dover's Wall, Route 2	HVS
8. Dover's Wall, Route 3	VS
9. Newhaven	HD
10. Beady Eyed	VS

Dover's Wall, Route 2 12m HVS 5a ★ (1930-51)
Climb the thin crack (third from the right) to reach an exciting
finish up the overhanging flakes in the centre of the face.

Nothing to do with Dover 12m HVS 5a ★ (1978)
Start just to the left and tackle the smooth lower wall and
stacked bulges above. A pleasantly gymnastic pitch.

The next feature to the left is the rightward-rising ramp that is
used by Dover's Wall, Route 3. Starting just right of this is:

Falaise de Douvre 7m VS 4c (1996)
Start just right of the foot of the ramp and cross this to climb
straight up the bulging wall left of the steep flake-crack of
Dover's Wall, Route 3.

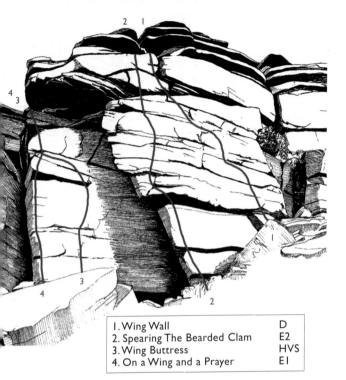

1. Wing Wall	D	
2. Spearing The Bearded Clam	E2	
3. Wing Buttress	HVS	
4. On a Wing and a Prayer	E1	

Dover's Wall, Route 3 12m VS 4b   (1961-63)
Ascend easily rightwards up the ramp at the left-hand end of
the wall. Climb the bulging crack to a difficult finish.

Dieppe 7m VS 4b   (1992)
From three metres right of the corner and at the foot of the
ramp, climb the thin left-slanting crack and finishing directly up
the steeper wall.

Ramsgate 7m S   (1996)
The wall one metre right of the corner is pleasant enough.

Newhaven 7m HD ★   (traditional)
The agreeable corner at the left-hand side of the wall has often
been overlooked.

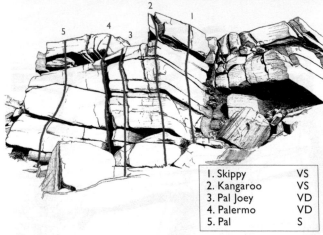

1. Skippy	VS
2. Kangaroo	VS
3. Pal Joey	VD
4. Palermo	VD
5. Pal	S

Long Reaches? 7m HVS 5c   (1996)
The centre of the narrow wall left of the corner is climbed to
an awkward exit. The crucial moves prove to be very height-
dependent, the tall will find it 5b and the short 6a.

Beady Eyed 6m VS 5a   (1993)
The diminutive arête on the left-hand side of the wall has two
'fun' moves, one to reach the horizontal break and one to stand
in it. The short leftwards-leaning corner to the left is **A Black
Ying** M (traditional).

Bumbler's Arête 7m M   (traditional)
The blunt nose-shaped arête to the left of the corner.

Fifteen metres left is another short wall split centrally by a
wide crack, this is:

PAL BUTTRESS

Kangaroo 7m VS 4c   (1993)
The right-hand arête of the wall has some pleasant moves.
Finish up the short flake crack. A short problem to the right is
Skippy VS 4c (1996) up the slabby right-hand face of the
buttress, first on its right, then centrally.

Pal Joey 7m VD   (1961-63)
Follow the thin crack to the right of the wide central fissure.

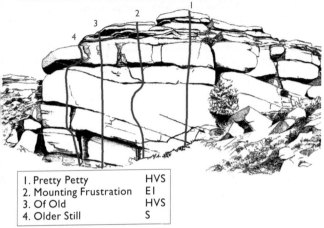

1. Pretty Petty	HVS
2. Mounting Frustration	E1
3. Of Old	HVS
4. Older Still	S

Palermo 7m VD   (1964-76)
Climb the wide central fissure.

Pal 7m S 5a   (1961-63)
Ascend the centre of the left-hand wall of the buttress.

Old Pals 7m VS 4b   (1984)
Climb directly, just to the right of the left-hand arête.

About 75 metres to the left, beyond a path that cuts through the edge, is a short buttress with a prominent hollybush growing at its lower right-hand edge and with a cutaway at its left-hand side.

Pretty Petty 6m HVS 5c   (1987)
A line up the wall just left of the hollybush past a couple of sketchy pulls and an easier finish.

Mounting Frustration 6m E1 6b ★   (1987)
The well-named centre of the wall has a baffling start, especially for the short.

Of Old 6m HVS 5b   (1983-89)
Climb the wall directly above the left-hand side of the cutaway using poor sloping holds to a slightly harrowing finish.

Older Still 6m S   (1996)
The short crack and left-hand edge of the wall is quite probably the original line used by Of Old.

Some 32 metres further to the left is a tall buttress, cleft centrally by a deep chimney and having a very healthy hollybush growing on a ledge on the right.

THE TWIN TOWERS

Accessory Wall 6m VS 4c (2001)
Climb the pleasant short wall right of the chimney with long reaches between good holds.

Accessory Chimney 13m D (1923-51)
Climb the chimney right of the hollybush directly to the platform behind the buttress.

The Groper 13m VS 4c ★ (1961-63)
On the right-hand tower climb the thin crack to the right of the holly and continue up the rib to a shelf. Move right to finish in an impressive position up a short crack in the nose.

The Unthinkable 13m E2 5b ★ (1984)
Climb The Groper as far as the shelf, step left and continue straight up the front of the overhanging tower finishing with a long reach; exposed.

Right Wall 13m S (1969)
The right-hand side of the central gully is too close to the opposite wall to be worthwhile.

The Watch-tower 13m HVS 5b ★ (1981)
Climb the right-hand arête of the left-hand tower to gain an undercut ledge, step left and climb directly over the rounded bulges to reach the top.

Tower Block 10m E3 6b (1985)
The left-hand arête of the left-hand tower has a short sharp initial section followed by an easier, but dirty, finish over a rounded bulge.

To the left of the The Twin Towers is a chimney containing a large, green, jammed block and then an area of shorter, slabby rock.

One Two Eight 8m HVS 5b (2000)
Start just right of the next route. Climb the slab and go over the overlap at its widest point. Move right to a small flake, use this to go over the bulge and teeter to the top.

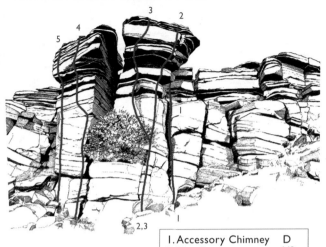

1. Accessory Chimney	D
2. The Groper	VS
3. The Unthinkable	E2
4. The Watch-tower	HVS
5. Tower Block	E3

Tumble Down 8m VS 4c (1992)
The slabby buttress has an overlap at half-height Climb to and over the left-hand side of this to finish up the short flake crack above.

Scoop and Corner 7m M (1961-63)
Climb the rib that forms the left-hand edge of the slabby buttress to finish up a right-trending scoop. The name Corner and Scoop would have been more logical.

Delirious 7m M (1992)
The crack just to the left is followed easily, passing a jammed triangular flake at two-thirds height.

Delovely 7m HS 4b (1992)
The slab to the left again is climbed initially up its centre and finishing by a thin flake near the left-hand edge.

Delicacy 6m HVD (2001)
Just left of Delovely are blocky steps leading to a flake/arête. Climb the arête with a delicate move to start.

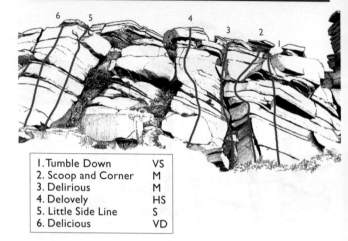

1. Tumble Down	VS
2. Scoop and Corner	M
3. Delirious	M
4. Delovely	HS
5. Little Side Line	S
6. Delicious	VD

Six metres farther left are twin slabs split centrally by an easy crack with a boulder at its base.

Little Side Line 7m S (1996)
Climb the right-hand side of the right-hand slab keeping just to the right of the blunt arête.

Delicious 8m VD (1992)
The centre of the right-hand slab.

Delightful 7m M (1992)
You've guessed it... the centre of the left-hand slab.

Thirty three metres further left is a seven metre-high buttress with a detached pillar immediately to its left.

Marmalade's Lost Start 7m E1 5c (1986)
Climb the centre of the small wall with tough, but well-protected moves, above half-height.

Jammy 8m HD (1992)
Climb the chimney-crack just left. Where this eases, step right and climb the wall to finish.

Pillar Arête 8m VD ★ (1961-63)
Immediately left of the chimney-crack is a short undercut arête; ascend this.

Greg's Retreat 8m HVS 5b (1989)
Climb the wall left of Pillar Arête, moving left at the top break
before finishing up the wall left of the small arête. Harder for
the short.

Pinch 10m HS 4b (1992)
The next arête to the left is climbed on its right-hand side.
Move right and finish over a small bulge.

Three metres to the left is the obviously named feature which
gives the next climb.

Chockstone Crack 8m S 4b (1961-63)
The chock-stoned flake-crack has a precarious layback start but
eases above.

Curving Buttress Corner 10m M (1961-63)
The deep right-angled gully immediately to the left is pleasant.

To the left things begin to improve again in the form of Curving
Buttress and then the superb Unconquerable cracks. The first
major piece of rock contains what is probably the most celebrated
route on Stanage, The Right Unconquerable. If ever one climb
stood for what Stanage has to offer, then it is this, big and bold,
with a perfect line and perfect protection and with an historical
pedigree to match.

From there, the edge twists and dips along for several hundred
metres and while never as continuous as the Popular End, passes
by a wealth of superb outcrops; Calvary Buttress, Namenlos,
Millsom's Buttress, Paradise Wall and Tower Face all stand out,
with endless challenges, many of them well-suited to the extreme
leader. The last word in this stretch is the Goliath's Groove area.
Four routes there, Goliath's Groove itself, Archangel, White Wand
and Ulysses, could stand alone as an example of all that's
inspirational about gritstone climbing. Purity of line is combined
with exquisite commitment (although Goliath's has now lost its
deadly reputation) to produce routes that could well be among
the boldest leads of many climber's lives.

CURVING BUTTRESS

Curving Buttress 16m E2 5b ★★ (1930s)
Climb the blunt arête right of Curving Chimney and make
committing moves up and rightwards to gain a good ledge in
the centre of the wall. Continue above to a narrow ledge and
pull over the final bulge to finish. Given Very Difficult in 1951,

HVS in 1964 and E2 in 1989, the grade appears to have stabilised for the time being. **Direct Finish** 1993, start as for the original route but don't make the move right to the good ledge, continue up the arête, this gives a more sustained outing at the same grade. **Direct Start** 6a 1983-1989, gains the ledge directly using undercuts and an extended reach, although it will require a leap for the short.

Curving Chimney 15m VD ★★ (1923-50)
Ascend or avoid the classic narrow chimney just to the left.

Curving Chimney Left Arête 17m E2 5b (1983-96)
It is possible to climb the narrow face to the left of the chimney.

Around to the left is a fine wall boasting the three impressive cracks of:

THE UNCONQUERABLES

As well as the classic cracks there are the inevitable more modern (and less worthwhile) variations.

The Vogon 30m E1 5b (1976-81)
Climb Curving Chimney (or more pleasantly Monday Blue) then traverse the break that cuts across the Unconquerable face at two-thirds height until it is possible to swing round the arête and finish up The Little Unconquerable.

Monday Blue 17m E2 5b ★ (1981)
Climb the slab on the right-hand side of the front face without recourse to the right-hand side of the arete. An awkward start is followed by precarious moves at half-height. Finish over the final overhang of The Right Unconquerable.

The Right Unconquerable 17m HVS 5a ★★★ (1949)
One of gritstone's greatest classics now beginning to show its age with the repeated insertion and removal of cams, which has damaged the flake. Start up the slippery crack in the centre of the face then stride right to gain the base of the flake. Attack this in spectacular fashion, passing the nose with difficulty, to reach easier but still strenuous climbing and, with luck, a rest below the capping roof. Purists will finish directly over this while others will traverse left to finish up a short wide crack. The obvious direct start is 6a (1964-76).

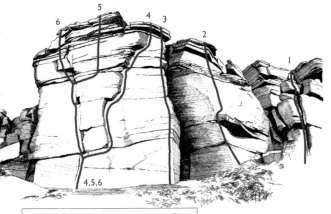

1. Chockstone Crack	S
2. Curving Buttress	E2
3. Monday Blue	E2
4. The Right Unconquerable	HVS
5. Vanquished	E5
6. The Left Unconquerable	E1

The Left Unconquerable 17m E1 5b ★★★   (1949)
Climb the slippery crack and continue in the same line to reach
the horizontal break that runs across the buttress. The next
moves up and left are the crux to reach easier ground and
monster buckets to the top.

For many years habitués wishing a change from the usual Left and
Right Unconquerables have started up one and finished up the
other. Starting up the Right Unconquerable and finishing up the
Left includes the cruxes of both routes and is E1 5b. Doing the
opposite avoids both crux sections and is HVS 5a.

Vanquished 17m E5 6b   (1988)
Follow The Left Unconquerable to the good break just below
its crux. Hand-traverse one metre rightwards and climb straight
up the wall past poor breaks and a small pocket.

The Little Unconquerable 12m HVS 5a ★   (1953)
The left-hand of the three cracks is a good test of jamming
proficiency. Start from the platform high on the left. Enter the
overhanging crack with difficulty and finish with urgency.
Thought by some to be the hardest of the trio.

147

7. Defying Destiny	E6
8. Calvary	E4
9. Calvary Direct	E5
10. Telli	E3

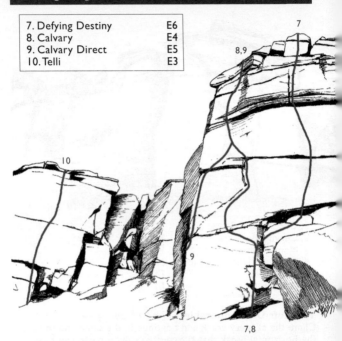

DESCENT ROUTE

The easy gully that runs down behind the left-hand side of The Unconquerables is the best descent for this immediate area.

Across the gully is a broad wall split vertically by three cracks and increasing in size towards its left-hand side.

Three Lanky Sassenachs and One Wee Jock
10m E1 5c   (1994)
The short crack below the right-hand arête of the wall is climbed to a ledge. Finish up the square arête above.

Ritornel   13m   HVS 5a   ★   (1972)
To the left is a thin crack in a rightwards-sloping groove. Follow this to a ledge at five metres. Move up and right to the centre of the wall and traverse right to the arête; finish straight up.

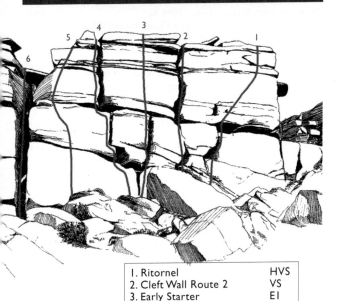

1. Ritornel	HVS
2. Cleft Wall Route 2	VS
3. Early Starter	E1
4. Cleft Wall Route 1	S
5. Plugging the Gaps	HVS
6. Chockstone Chimney	HVD

Lucky Strike   13m   E1 5b   (1986)
A short direct finish to Ritornel. Follow Ritornel to its traverse
and climb the face above to an awkward finish.

Cleft Wall Route 2   13m   VS 5a   ★   (1923-51)
Just to the left is a straight crack that runs the full height of this
part of the buttress; follow it throughout.

To the left is a crack that divides at two metres.

Early Starter   13m   E1 5b   (1988)
Start up the crack in the middle of the wall and continue up the
wide crack. Finish up the wall above on sloping holds.

Cleft Wall Route 1   13m   S   ★   (1923-51)
Start as for the previous climb, but move left at the first bulge
and follow the obvious zigzag crack to the top.

149

Plugging the Gaps 13m HVS 5a (1986)
From a small flake to the right of Chockstone Chimney climb
the wall leftwards to finish near the left-hand arête.

Chockstone Chimney 13m HVD 4c ★ (1923-51)
Ascend the chimney that splits the centre of the buttress in
classic fashion. A good line, though a bit of a grunt. Previously
graded Moderate.

To the left is an imposing face with a short crack in its centre.

Dark Reign 15m E5 6a ★ (1999)
The right-hand arête of the main section of the buttress is
followed throughout.

Defying Destiny 19m E6 6b ★★★ (1982)
A superb but serious direct line up the centre of the wall with
hard moves and worrying protection. Climb the initial crack to
a move right and gain the next break with difficulty. Dubious
cams in flared placements to the left protect the crucial pull, on
tiny brittle flakes, for the thin finishing crack. It is also possible
to climb the centre of the lower wall directly at 6b ★ (1982-
89). This is more popular as a 'highball' boulder problem.

Calvary 19m E4 6a ★★★ (1970/1976)
Another classic gritstone frightener and probably the best
route of its grade on the edge. Start up the steep, central crack
to the ledge. Hand-traverse left and make a difficult move to
gain a friable black flake. Go up this and move left to climb the
shallow scoop to a ledge near the arête. Place protection in the
break then summon all your courage and either climb up and
teeter right, or harder, move right and up the bulging headwall
directly. **Calvary Direct** E5 6a ★★ (1989) gains the arête to
the left of the normal start from a block on the left and makes
a couple of bald, reachy moves to gain the deep horizontal
break. Move right to join the regular route.

Nightsalt 15m E4 6c ★★ (1984)
The right-hand arête of the cleft to the left provides a
frustrating but excellent problem. It eases dramatically after the
first horizontal break is reached.

Rib Chimney 13m VD ★ (1923-51)
The black cleft on the left is entered and climbed to ledges and
the dividing rib a short distance from the top. Finish up its left-
hand side. The depths of the chimney can be explored to an
exit from a recess at the top of Chockstone Chimney to the
right.

1. Traversity	E1
2. Michelle My Belle	E3
3. Vision Set	E2

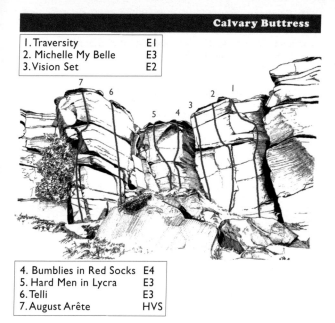

4. Bumblies in Red Socks	E4
5. Hard Men in Lycra	E3
6. Telli	E3
7. August Arête	HVS

To the left of the chimney are two short walls that are home to five routes which are rarely repeated and have generally been undergraded in previous guidebooks.

Traversity 12m E1 6a ★   (1959)
Start from an embedded block just left of the chimney and make hard, bouldery moves to reach flakes and then a horizontal crack just above mid-height. Step right to gain the ledge and take the final wall trending leftwards.

Michelle My Belle 10m E3 6a   (1984)
A hard start or a long reach gains the thin flake in the centre of the wall which leads to a break. Continue up the left-hand side of the blunt arête above.

Vision Set 11m E2 5b   (1984)
Swing in from the left and climb the wall passing a suspect flake, keeping just right of the left-hand arête.

To the left the two walls are split by a corner.

Bumblies in Red Socks 7m E4 5c   (1983)
Start up the blunt rib to the left then move rightwards up the

slab to a hard and usually green finish up the steepening rib. Originally graded a suicidal E2.

Hard Men in Lycra 7m E3 6a   (1997)
Start as for the previous climb but step left after the start and climb the rib by a decisive mantelshelf. Unfortunately the crux is avoidable by stepping further left.

DESCENT ROUTE
The blocky corner on the left is the usual descent route for this area.

To the left is an attractive slab climbed centrally by the neo-classic of Telli.

TELLI SLAB

Telli 10m E3 6a ★★   (1978)
Climb the centre of the bald, lower slab to gain a break. A tough sequence leads to a standing position and a difficult move up the centre of the final slab to reach small finishing holds. An inferior version of the route, **Telli Right-Hand** E2 5c (post-1978) takes the lower slab close to its right-hand edge to reach the horizontal break and continues up the upper slab close to its right-hand edge.

August Arête 14m HVS 5b ★★   (1959)
Just around to the left is an arête with a holly on its left-hand side. Climb the leftwards-slanting crack just right of the holly to a ledge. Move right and gain the arête by an awkward move. Continue up the arête with difficulty.

Groovy 12m E2 5c   (1999)
Start as for the previous climb but climb the flake and the groove above the holly throughout.

To the left is a taller buttress with a conspicuous shallow ramp running leftwards up its right-hand side. To the right of this is a holly tree growing in a short corner and three metres right of the tree is a slab with a diagonal crack rising across it from left-to-right. This is:

NAMENLOS BUTTRESS

Short Straw 7m VS 4c   (1992)
Climb to a small overlap and move rightwards over this to climb the arête on the right-hand side of the final slab.

Straw Crack 7m S   (1961-63)
Fight past the bush and ascend the right-hand crack.

Holly Crack 7m VD   (1961-63)
Do battle with the prickly horror and finish up the barely
independent left-hand crack above.

Memory Loss 13m HVS 5b   (1991)
Climb the steep wall to the right of the initial straight crack of
Namenlos using an extended reach to attain a good ledge. Step
left and climb the rounded rib to ledges, move left again to
climb the awkward scoop in the final tower.

Namenlos 13m E1 5a ★★   (1950-51)
A great route requiring a steady approach. Climb the steep thin
crack at the right-hand end of the buttress to a good ledge.
Move left and climb into a delicate and poorly-protected
shallow ramp-line. Ascend this delicately and finish carefully up
the chimney behind the large mushroom-shaped block.

Improbability Drive 12m E3 6b ★   (1978)
Start three metres to the left of Namenlos and climb a short
crack followed by thin flakes to a good horizontal break. The
crux involves gaining a standing position in this, using whatever
pebbles remain. Use the shallow flake above the small overhang
to join the previous route.

Direct Loss 6m E4 6a ★★   (1986)
Immediately to the left, a crack runs halfway up the cliff. Climb
this and continue up the much thinner crack-line above, before
moving rightwards to finish just left of the blunt arête. A hand-
placed blade-peg in a pocket to the right of the top of the thin
crack provides potential protection, though solid runners are
not too far below. Finish over the centre of the capstone.

Wall Buttress 12m VS 5a ★★   (1930)
Climb either the jamming crack in the centre of the face before
traversing leftwards to gain the fist-width crack in the upper
face, or take the rightward-slanting flakes to the left before
moving right to join the upper crack. Once established,
continue to an awkward exit or step left to an easier finish.

Walrus Butter 12m E4 6b   (1986)
Climb the wall between the two alternative starts to Wall
Buttress by a hard dynamic move from pebbles (low side-
runner). Finish up the previous route, or more in keeping, try
Direct Loss at the same grade and a couple of stars overall.

6. Wall Buttress	VS
7. Moribund	E3
8. Badly Bitten	E4
9. Boys Will Be Boys	E6

To the left is an overlap at three metres.

Moribund 10m E3 5c ★★ (1980)
Climb past the left-hand end of the overlap to reach a
horizontal break. Swing right into the centre of the face.
Harrowing moves past a poor pocket lead to another
horizontal break. A hard pull leads to an excellent flake on the
left and easier ground.

Badly Bitten 10m E4 6a ★ (1984)
Start as for the previous route but step left above the overlap
and climb the rib to reach an obvious 'Thank God' pebble.
Using this, gain the next break and finish up the centre of the
final wall.

Capstone Chimney 10m VD (traditional)
The obvious cleft, capped by a huge chockstone is a real
struggle. The escape inside the chockstone is only for the slim,
others will have to use the right-hand outside exit at VS 5a.

Boys Will Be Boys 8m E6 6c ★★★ (1986)
The imposing wall just to the left provides a steep and serious
route, which follows the 'obvious' line of non-holds just left of

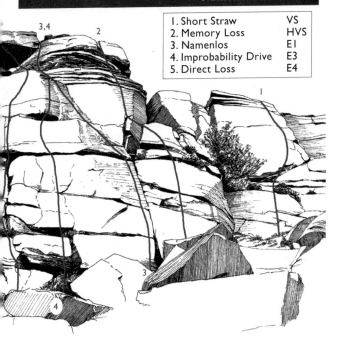

1. Short Straw	VS
2. Memory Loss	HVS
3. Namenlos	E1
4. Improbability Drive	E3
5. Direct Loss	E4

centre. Climb to a flat ledge and make increasingly difficult
moves up to a crucial stretch for a good pocket; easier climbing
remains.

O.D.G.'s Chimney 10m VD (1998)
The deep chimney to the left is entered awkwardly and
followed to the top of a large flake. The short easy corner to
the left leads to the top.

Men Only 10m E1 5c (1998)
The left-hand arête of the chimney is formed by a flake. Layback
awkwardly up this to its top. Step right and climb the upper
arête before moving round to the face on the right to a final
tricky move.

DESCENT ROUTE
To the left is an easy way down.

Sixty metres below the edge is a large lozenge-shaped boulder

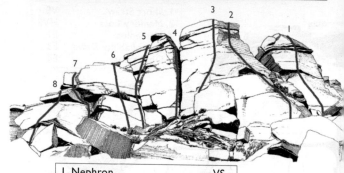

1. Nephron	VS
2. Symbiosis	HVS
3. Blue Fluff	E4
4. Straight Ahead	VS
5. Slanting Crack	HS
6. Billy B	HS
7. Cannon	D
8. Elephant in the Doghouse	E1

perched on a plinth with an impressively smooth valley face. There is one short route there and two shorter boulder problems. **Fear and Loathing** E3 5c ★ (1979) takes the centre of the roadward face after an awkward start from a block and feels bigger than it is. Left again is **Editor's Vaseline** HVS 5b (1979) starting up the left-hand edge of the undercut north face before moving out right to gain and climb the north-west arête. A direct start is E2 6a (post 1989).

Returning to the Edge, and after a ten metre gap, the next feature is a steep wall bounded on the left by a straight crack and on the right by two slabby ribs.

Nephron 8m VS 4c (1978)
The wall right of the next route is taken direct, passing a couple of small overlaps.

Symbiosis 10m HVS 4c ★ (1974)
The blunt sloping arête is climbed directly. Delicate and poorly protected where it matters.

Don't Fluff It 10m E4 5c ★ (1998)
Start just to the right of a tall block and climb thin cracks to a

bulge. Pull rightwards over this using a good jug to a step left. Balance up to indifferent holds and a harrowing final sequence.

Blue Fluff 10m E4 5c ★ (1990)
The thin crack that splits the steep wall to the left is gained from a block and leads to a bold, blunt rib above and to the right.

Straight Ahead 8m VS ★ (1961-63)
The widening cleft that splits the centre of the buttress has several chockstones providing threadable protection and a means of progress. As a long-standing Diff this may have been the most undergraded route on the cliff for many years. A technical grade was impossible to decide upon, try it and see why.

Slanting Crack 8m HS 4b ★ (1961-63)
Start up the slab to the left and enter the rightward-slanting crack, which is followed to the top.

Billy B 6m HS 4b (1990)
Climb the centre of the short slab to the left passing the midway heathery, horizontal break.

Turnbull's Trajectory 6m S 4a (1989)
The extreme left-hand edge of the slab is climbed via the arête, a short diagonal crack and the upper slab. A variation **Don't Tell Maurice** HS 4b (1992) ascends the right-hand wall of Cannon to the crack below the roof, pass this by a swing right round the arête to the parent route.

Cannon 8m D (1961-63)
Just round to the left at a lower level is a green crack in a corner with a tree on its right. Climb the crack and pass round the left-hand side of an overhang to finish up a short crack.

Elephant in the Doghouse 8m E1 5b (1990)
Three metres to the left of Cannon, climb the wall followed by a thin, brittle flake to reach an overlap. Tackle the final slab bearing slightly rightwards. The short flaky wall to the left, and beyond an easy chimney, is taken up its centre to give **Modesty** VS 4c (1992).

DESCENT ROUTE
To the left is an easy way down.

Mitch Pitch 7m El 5c ★ (1984)
Twelve metres up and to the left is an attractive short slab just
to the right of a gap in the edge. This route is the sketchy right-
hand line with a harrowing finish.

Tridymite Slab 7m VS 5a ★ (1961-63)
Use a short flake-crack to reach a ledge and a mantelshelf to
reach an easier finish.

DESCENT ROUTE
To the left is an easy way down.

Eighteen metres to the left the cliff starts to increase in height,
eventually developing into the impressive, rounded bulk of Billiard
Buttress and to its left the crack-riven Paradise Wall. Before these
are reached is a shorter wall.

Pool Wall 8m VS 4a (1961-63)
The short wall on the right has a steep start which is climbed
initially on its left-hand side and then on its right-hand side to
easier ground.

Between the Two 8m HVS 5b ★ (1976-82)
The steep wall four metres to the left is reachy. Start at an
excellent pocket in a blunt rib. Pull left on to the wall, which is
tricky to start but soon eases.

To the left are twin cracks that were originally described as one
route called Pool Cracks, D. They are now considered to be two
separate routes.

Right Pool Crack 8m D (1961-63)
This is the wider right-hand crack set in a corner.

Left Pool Crack 8m D (1961-63)
The slightly tougher left-hand crack is just sufficiently
independent to be recorded as a separate route.

Ten metres down and to the left is an impressive, rounded buttress
easily identified by a steeply sloping crack/ramp running up its
right-hand side. This is:

BILLIARD BUTTRESS

Help the Young 7m E5 6c ★★ (1996)
The short, hanging, pocketed arête to the right of Cue gives a

tough and technical 'highball' boulder problem but no sneaky bridging at the start.

New Balls Please 20m E1 5b   (1999)
Climb the rib on the right-hand side of the recess from which Cue starts. Make a long reach and a difficult mantelshelf to reach easier ground. Climb to the top of the tower, lean across and pull on to the wall just left of a nose and finish directly.

Cue 23m HVS 5a ★★   (1959)
A route that is good value at the grade. Climb the awkward slanting chimney at the right-hand side of the buttress with difficulty at the overlap. Follow the easy groove to a hand-traverse left below the overhang until a steep pull gains access to a thin hanging crack. An exciting variation **Cue Extension** HVS 5a (2001) continues the hand-traverse leftwards to join and finish up Millsom's Minion.

A Problem of Coagulation 22m E3 5c ★   (1982)
Climb over the first bulge of Cue on to a ramp and make a bold swing on to a flake on the face. Continue until just short of a blunt arête and continue up the flat wall.

Back in the Y.M.C.A. 17m E6 6c ★★   (1991)
Surmount the overlap and climb a fierce, pocketed wall to the left of the start of Cue to join Millsom's Minion just below its crux; finish up this.

The front face of the buttress is home to several excellent climbs, the exact starts of which have always been vaguely described in the past.

In-off 22m E3 5c ★★   (1988)
An excellent hybrid route which forms a good direct way up the face. Climb Millsom's Minion Direct to its deep horizontal break. Continue straight up the wall into the base of the scoop to the point where Millsom's Minion comes in from the right; finish easily.

Millsom's Minion 24m E1 5b ★★★   (1962)
No longer a serious lead with modern protection; a great route. Start up the leaning wall three metres to the right of the left-hand arête and climb rightwards to a flange. A tricky move reaches the major horizontal break cutting across the face which is traversed right for three metres. Move up delicately rightwards via a large shallow pocket and use this to gain a break above. Step left to enter a scoop that leads to easier

1. Cue	HVS
2. A Problem of Coagulation	E3
3. Back in the Y.M.C.A.	E6
4. Millsom's Minion	E1
5. Pot Black	E2
6. Billiard Buttres	HVS
7. Silica	E2
8. Sand Gully	D

rock. **Millsom's Minion Direct** E3 5c ★★ (1984) starts under the left-hand end of an overlap running along the right-hand side of the front face at three metres. Climb to the edge of the overlap, move rightwards over it on pockets and up to the horizontal break to join the parent route

Pot Black 22m E2 5b ★★ (1976)
Climb the leaning pocketed wall just right of the left-hand arête to a ledge. Ballance up the steep slab above continuing directly up a shallow groove to easier rock; bold.

Billiard Buttress 22m HVS 5a ★★ (1959)
A fine and varied line up the left-hand side of the buttress. Follow Pot Black to the horizontal break. Traverse left, climb the delicate arête and continue up the pleasant slab.

Cemetery Waits   E7 6c   (page 135)
Climber: Joe Brown   Photo: Jez Portman

Overhanging Crack **HVS 5a** (page 172)
Climber: Mick Carr Photo: David Simmonite

Gothic Armpit **E5 6b** (page 175)
Climber: Dave Thomas **Photo: Rich Heap**

Dreadnought E7 7a (page 178)
Climber: Mike Lea Photo: David Simmonite

Billiard Buttress Direct   20m   E2 5c   (1998)
The left-hand arête of the buttress can be climbed in its
entirety. The occasional pocket on the start of Pot Black may
prove useful and the crucial moves are an uncomfortable
distance off the ground.

Curved Crack   15m   VS 4c   ★   (1923-51)
Just to the left, the curving fissure has hidden delights. Gain the
crack awkwardly and follow it with 'interest'.

Sand Crack   11m   S   ★   (1951-56)
To the left is a crack in a corner. Climb this steeply passing the
hollybush and finishing up a sandy groove.

Silica   12m   E2 5c   ★★   (1977)
Left again is a thin-flake crack running up an undercut slab.
Climb easily up the wall and pull strenuously over the overhang
using the flake which is followed until its end. Continue
precariously using the right arête.

Quartz   14m   HVS 4c   (1992)
Climb the bottom wall of Silica until a step left on to the small
pinnacle standing in front of the face can be made. Move up to
the base of the right-hand crack in Sand Gully, step out right to
a shallow corner and climb directly to the top; poorly
protected.

Sand Gully   14m   D   ★   (traditional)
The gully-cum-corner immediately to the left. Start either side
of the small pinnacle and climb to a ledge. Continue up the
corner above using the two cracks.

American Gritfeati   14m   HVS 5b   (1982)
From partway up Sand Gully, muscle up on a jug to gain a ledge
on the left-hand wall. Traverse left to the arête and finish up
this. A poor route that could do with a direct start.

Round the arête to the left is a square wall. Near its right-hand
side a prominent crack containing a small hollybush is:

Paradise Crack   14m   VD   ★★   (1923-51)
Ascend the wide crack in the right-hand edge of the front face
of the buttress to a tricky finish.

The 'smooth' face to the left has two pocket-pulling eliminates
that are worth seeking out.

5. Comus	E4
6. Comet	E3
7. Paradise Wall	VS
8. Paradise Arête	VS

Comus 13m E4 6a ★★ (1979)

The right-hand line. Climb through an overlap at a block and head up the wall on blind, painful pockets, one of which contains a slot for a hand-placed peg. Once the horizontal break is reached the upper section of the climb can be savoured.

Comet 13m E3 5c (1985)

Climb the wall a metre to the right of the cracks of Paradise Wall via good but escapable moves. Finish up the delicate, open, upper wall in the same line. Often gritty and dirty.

1. Silica	E2
2. Sand Gully	D
3. American Gritfeati	HVS
4. Paradise Crack	VD

Milton's Meander 18m VS 4c ★★ (1961-63)
In the wall to the left are twin cracks which start from a ledge
and merge two-thirds of the way up the cliff. Climb these to
just below their confluence then traverse rightwards using
parallel horizontal breaks to a finish up the arête beside
Paradise Crack.

Paradise Wall 14m VS 4c ★★★ (1923-51)
A classic and compelling line up the centre of the buttress.

1. Flate	VS
2. Overhanging Wall	HVS
3. Crossover	E2
4. Flake Gully	D
5. Back to School	HVS
6. Pegasus Wall	VS

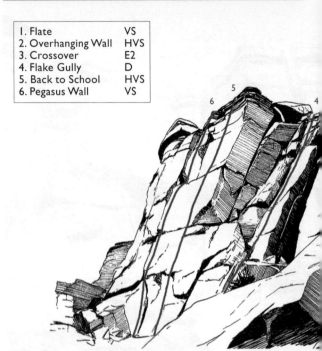

Climb the parallel cracks (as for Milton's Meander) until they merge and take the straight left-hand crack to the top.

Paradise Arête 13m VS 4c ★★ (1964-76)
Gain the flake crack that starts from a ledge two metres right of the arête and climb it until it fizzles out. Shuffle left to a small ledge and climb the arête directly to the top.

Parasite 13m HVS 5a ★ (1981)
Climb into and up the shallow square corner in the arête to join Paradise Arête. Step right and finish directly up the centre of the wall on an assortment of breaks and poor holds.

Paradise Lost 12m VD (1961-63)
On the left-hand side of the buttress is a crack starting from a recess. Climb this to a rock fang and follow the continuation crack above. Finish directly or more easily out to the right.

DESCENT ROUTE
To the left are several easy ways down.

Twenty five metres to the left is a short wall capped by a large block which protrudes over both the front face and the right-hand side of the wall.

Zero Point   7m   HVS 5a   (1979)
The wall near its right-hand side is climbed on 'reasonable' holds, finishing at the notch in the perched block.

Unpredictable   8m   HVS 5b   (1961-63)
Climb the wall directly below the left-hand tip of the overhanging block on a series of rounded diminishing holds.

To the left again is a taller buttress with a prominent overhanging nose at three-quarters height. The first route takes the face on its right-hand side.

Flate   7m   VS 5a   (1979)
The obvious, thin flake just to the right of the arête is followed
to finish up the wall on rounded holds.

Passover   8m   E2 5c   (1986)
The short, pocketed, right-hand rib of the buttress has a hard,
fingery start but an easier finish.

The front face of the buttress has two counter-diagonals, both of
which will test your rope work, as well as a more direct offering.

Crossover   12m   E2 5c   ★   (1951-56)
A counter-line to the original route, Overhanging Wall. Start
just right of the arête below the overhanging nose and gain the
obvious ledge. Climb the slabby right-hand rib of the buttress
and balance up this to the roof. Traverse left to a flange and
swing left around the corner to finish boldly up the shelving
wall, without sneaking off to the left. It is possible to finish up
Overhanging Wall at E2 5c which reduces the rope drag but
only gets you two 'half ticks'.

Overhanging Wall   12m   HVS 5b   ★★   (1950)
Start below the left-hand side of the overhang and climb a
difficult thin crack to a flake beneath the roof. Traverse right
below the overhang and swing round the corner before
finishing up the side-wall. **Flatlander** E2 5c (1995) climbs
Overhanging Wall to just below the flake under the roof to
finish directly up the wall above on rounded holds keeping to
the right of the finish of Crossover; little new climbing.

To the left, the open gully contains a large flake.

Flake Chimney   10m   S   (traditional)
Take the chimney up the right-hand side of the large flake to a
narrow exit.

Flake Gully   10m   D   (1923-51)
Ascend the well-scratched corner on the left-hand side of the
bay to a steep exit. The slabby crack just to the right provides
an alternative start at VD. The very narrow right-hand slab
surely has the accolade of being the most squeezed in route on
Stanage; **Flake Gully Slab** HS 4a (2001).

Round the arête to the left is an attractive wall with a straight
crack in its upper right-hand side and a prominent holly in the
base of another crack on the left. This is:

PEGASUS WALL

Pegasus Rib 13m HVS 5a ★ (1972-73)
To the left, start up the crack directly below the sharp angular
rib that forms the right-hand edge of the buttress. Climb the
flake crack to gain the arête and climb this on its left-hand side
by pleasantly exposed moves. **Flake Gully Crack** HS 4b
(2001) takes the same start but climbs the hand crack just right
of the arête in its entirety; unfortunately contrived and
escapable.

Back to School 12m HVS 5b (1989)
Climb directly up the centre of the narrow wall just to the left
of the arête, using a couple of pockets early on.

Pegasus Wall 10m VS 4c ★ (1923-51)
Just to the left several thin cracks trend slightly leftwards up
the wall. Reach these awkwardly and climb them pleasantly.

Valhalla 10m VS 5a ★★ (1948)
To the left is a prominent straight, smooth-sided crack set in a
shallow leftwards-facing corner. Reach this from the left via a
shorter crack and a heathery ledge.

Klingon 10m E6 7a ★★ † (2000)
In the centre of the smooth wall to the left of Valhalla, move up
to and use undercuts and a pebble to make hard moves before
a dyno gains a good break/pockets, gear and an easier finish.

Star Trek 10m E6 6b ★★ (1989/1991)
The smooth-looking wall left again is started from the block on
the left. Move right to the centre of the face and continue up
and right to reach a good handhold below the overlap. From
there shelving holds lead to the top. A side-runner in Taurus
Crack reduces the grade to E5 and converts a 'crater' into a
mere 'crash-landing', 6c for the short.

To the left is an obvious flake-crack which finishes just below the
cliff top.

Taurus Crack 11m HS 4c ★ (1923-51)
Climb the previously mentioned flake-crack. The holly that
guards access to the climb is a prickly pain and the crux moves
are where the crack isn't.

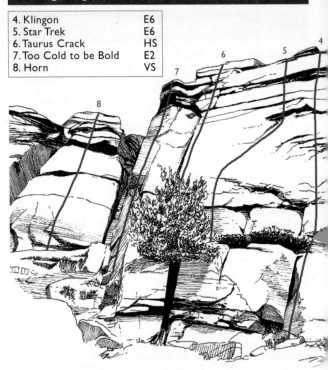

4. Klingon	E6
5. Star Trek	E6
6. Taurus Crack	HS
7. Too Cold to be Bold	E2
8. Horn	VS

Too Cold to be Bold 13m E2 6b (1987)
The technical arête left of Taurus Crack, which provides a side-runner.

Horn 9m VS 5a (1992)
On the short wall to the left, climb the flake just left of the centre and continue up the centre of the buttress passing a small overlap.

DESCENT ROUTE
There are several easy ways down over the next 60 metres before any significant rock reappears.

Twenty five metres down and left of the Pegasus Wall is a tall, pointed tower easily visible from afar. Long before routes were established there this was known as Budgie Rock because of its obvious beak and eye when viewed from the north. Although

1. Crossover	E2
2. Pegasus Wall	VS
3. Valhalla	VS

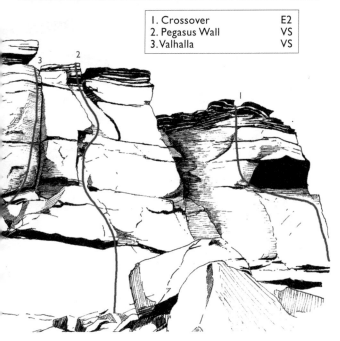

this is effectively just a big boulder, the four routes on it are excellent and certainly long enough to be considered as more than just boulder problems.

Savage 6m E3 6a   (1999)
The short arête on the block just up and right of Walking the Whippet and just before a wide crack has a couple of long reaches.

Walking the Whippet 8m E3 5b ★   (1984)
The right-hand arête of the wall facing the car park and the Plantation boulders proves to be worthwhile and scary. Unprotected where it matters.

Unfamiliar 9m E7 6c ★★★   (1992)
The front arête of the tower is sustained, precarious and fingery. It can be started directly by jumping for the first hold, or by leaning in from the left using a pile of rocks. One of the best, hard routes on Stanage and at the top end of the grade.

6. Hathersage Trip	E4
7. My Herald of Free Enterprise	E6
8. Mercury Crack	VD

Punishment 8m E5 6b ★★ (1986)
The north-east arête of the pinnacle can be climbed on its
right-hand side by a harrowing and sustained sequence above an
unpleasant landing.

Crime 6m E4 6a ★ (1986)
For a different view the slightly less worrying left-hand side of
the arête gives good climbing and a better landing.

Returning to the main edge, the next routes are 60 metres to the
left where the crag becomes a complicated series of walls and
slabs scattered around the slope. This is actually the right extremity
of the Tower Face Area, the main section of which lies about 100
metres to the left and at a lower level. The whole area is rather
confusing on first acquaintance. The first buttress to be described
is a slabby 'collapsed' face below the main cliff, split by a horizontal
overlap at two-thirds height. The first four routes are:

Margery Daw 14m HVS 5b (1972-73)
Halfway up the slab is a sloping ledge leading to an overlap.
Start on a large block to the left and swing right on to the

1. Margery Daw	HVS
2. Seesaw	VS
3. Fulcrum	HVS
4. Corner Crack	VS
5. Overhanging Crack	HVS

arête before climbing the slight depression passing the centre of the overlap. There is an easier but less worthwhile right-hand start.

Seesaw 14m VS 4c ★   (1960)
Start as for the previous climb but continue directly up the left-hand edge of the buttress. Finish up the final short arête.

Fulcrum 10m HVS 5a   (1976-82)
In the left-hand side-wall of the Seesaw slab is a thin crack. Climb this and swing right to gain the wide, upper crack.

Mr Twitch 7m E6 6b (1996)
Round to the left is a short steep slab. Climb up the centre of
this to finish on the ledge below Overhanging Crack.

Above the collapsed slab and forming the true upper edge of the
cliff is a steeper, flat wall split into thirds by two vertical cracks.

Big Bob's Bazzer 8m E1 5b (1982)
Climb the thin flake just left of the right-hand arête then
continue up the overhanging rib above.

National Breakdown 8m E3 6c ★ (1987)
Climb the bulge and pocketed wall to the left of the flake with
considerable difficulty.

Corner Crack 8m VS 4c (1960)
The undercut crack to the left is difficult to start but eases
once established above the initial overlap.

Overhanging Crack 10m HVS 5a ★ (1923-51)
The steep, wide crack in the centre of the wall is difficult to
enter, strenuous and not that easy to escape from.

The Hathersage Trip 10m E4 6a ★★ (1982)
A good, strenuous route to the left of Overhanging Crack. Start
on the right but move left to climb the centre of the wall.
Patience is needed to arrange the protection using camming
devices and small wires.

My Herald of Free Enterprise 10m E6 6c ★★ (1989)
The technical and serious arête to the left is gained from the
right. A poor Friend 1½ may well prove crucial.

Mercury Crack 11m VD (1923-51)
Start below the cave at the left-hand end of the buttress. Gain
the cave and after an awkward move to exit it, climb the easier
crack above.

To the left is a short slab which provides the upper section of The
Edale Trip (Beyond Hope). The start of this is reached by scrambling
down and left to a ledge which is situated below a green
rightwards-slanting shallow groove. The same place can be reached
by scrambling up and right from the foot of Hercules Crack.

The Edale Trip (Beyond Hope) 14m E3 6a ★ (1991)
A worthwhile climb with an exciting finale. Climb the slab
keeping between the shallow, green groove and a large block, to

1. My Herald of Free Enterprise	E6
2. Mercury Crack	VD
3. Squally Showers	VS
4. Shelf Life	E3
5. Hercules Crack	VD
6. Gripe Fruit Juice	HVS

reach a niche. Exit steeply from this to gain a good ledge. Step right and climb the precarious upper slab. Once committed the reason for the name becomes apparent.

Squally Showers 14m VS 4c   (1991)
Climb the aforementioned green groove then continue straight up leaning rock to gain a ledge. Finish up the pleasant arête.

Down and to the left is a prominent rightward-slanting flaky crack that splits the left-hand side of the buttress. This is Hercules Crack.

Fruitcake 12m VS 4c   (1997)
Climb the easy crack on the right-hand side of the buttress and traverse delicately leftwards along the shelf of the next route to a steeper finish up the left-hand arête.

Shelf Life 14m E3 5c ★   (1991)
Start just to the right of Hercules Crack and climb a tricky wall

173

to a bulge split by a thin crack. Head rightwards over this on sloping holds (or go directly at E4 6a) to gain a ledge before stepping back left and climbing the upper wall directly.

Mythology   15m   HVS 5a   (1997)
An odd combination of the three other routes. Start as for Shelf Life but at the bulges step left into a crack. Hand-traverse back to the right and gain a standing position. Finish up the right-hand side of the left-hand arête of the buttress.

Kinell   14m   VS 5a   (1996)
Climb Hercules Crack to a ledge. Move out right past an overlap to finish up the right-hand arête of the wall.

Hercules Crack   14m   VD   ★   (1923-51)
Climb the flake-crack to a ledge and continue up the wider crack above. 'The upper continuation of the crack is wide enough to effect an entrance, but the curving side-walls are smooth and need Herculean strength to overcome them'. (1951)

Gripe Fruit Juice   14m   HVS 5a   (1991)
Start at the lowest point of the buttress, just to the left of Hercules Crack and climb the blocky arête and crack to a good ledge. Climb the steeper arête to the left of the top crack of Hercules Crack with a final difficult move. A poor route.

Stacked Blocks   12m   VS 4b   (1992)
Around the corner to the left of Hercules Crack the side wall is made up of a series of stacked blocks. Climb these, trending leftwards, with escalating difficulty.

To the left the cliff is split into two tiers. The lower tier is blocky and sports a large oak tree growing on a ledge near its centre. The upper tier is more continuous and is bounded on the right by a huge block that appears to have tipped leftwards off its pedestal and now leans against the face to the left. The front face of this block is slabby.

Note: The whole of this Upper Tier (as far as the short rock wall above Tower Face) is described first before a return to the delights of the Lower Tier.

DESCENT ROUTE
The easiest way down from the cliff top is to scramble down the easy gully to the right of the undercut slab of Small Dreams,

1. Stacked Blocks	VS		6. Pizza Slab	S
2. Scorpion Slab	S		7. Gardener's Crack	D
3. Small Dreams	E2		8. Compost Corner	D
4. Gothic Armpit	E5		9. Gardener's Groove	HS
5. Poor Pizza	D		10. Sustenance	HVS

then to cut across below the base of the slab and reverse the
bottom section of Scorpion Slab.

Big Screams 14m E1 5c ★ (1991)
Start at the short steep wall to the left of the corner, directly
below the right-hand arête of the tilted block. Swing awkwardly
up and right to gain a pocket and continue more easily to the
overlap. Cross this and finish warily up the centre of the slab.

Scorpion Slab 11m S (1960)
Gain the midway ledge from the left and a move right to climb
the right-hand arête of the slab.

Small Dreams 11m E2 6a ★ (1978)
Start under the left-hand edge of the undercut slab and, after a
difficult move over the initial overhang, follow the delicate left-
hand arête to the top.

Gothic Armpit 10m E5 6b ★ (1998)
Gain the obscure bottomless alcove to the left by negotiating a
hanging, black blade of rock. Exit rapidly rightwards from there
until it is possible to escape around the arête to reach easy
ground; exciting stuff.

Paping About Like a Man With No Arms
8m VS 4c ★   (1989)
A great name for an unsavoury route. Squirm through the left-
hand of two narrow slits in the spacious chimney behind the
Small Dreams block; probably ungradable. The right-hand slit is
S 4a. Big persons need not apply.

Nasty Green Dwarf   8m   VS 4c   (1992)
The narrow, green slab immediately to the left is climbed
passing a small overlap and without recourse to the straight
crack to its left.

Poor Pizza   10m   D   (1992)
The short straight crack just left again is followed.

Cheapest Topping   10m   VS 4c   (1992)
Start at the cutaway under the right-hand corner of the slab.
Climb delicately up the slab to join the final moves of Poor
Pizza.

Pizza Slab   10m   S   (1961-63)
Starting from the foot of Gardener's Crack, climb the slab on
the right trending slightly right to finish up its centre.

Gardener's Crack   10m   D   ★   (1960)
This is the wide crack to the left starting one metre to the
right of a square-cut arête.

Percy's Prow   8m   S   (1976-82)
Step off a boulder to the left and climb the arête to the
junction with the upper section of Compost Corner up which
the route finishes.

Compost Corner   8m   D   (1976-82)
The green corner around to the left is climbed to a ledge.
Fortunately it is not quite the midden that the name suggests.

To the left is a smooth wall and beyond this a straight crack in a
shallow, leftwards-facing corner.

Gardener's Groove   10m   HS 4b   ★   (1960)
Struggle past the painfully-positioned hollybush and climb the
pleasant corner.

Sustenance   14m   HVS 5a   ★   (1996)
Start immediately to the left of Gardener's Groove and climb

the slab leftwards to below the centre of the roof. Make a long reach round this to finish more easily.

Slab and Crack   14m   VS 5a   ★   (1958)
Five metres to the left of Gardener's Groove, climb the cracked heathery slab to the overlap and a move right into the Z-shaped crack. Make strenuous moves over the bulges to reach the top.

Obstinance   14m   VS 4c   (1960)
Climb the previous route to the overlap. Go over this and make a long reach to gain the arête.

To the left is a short buttress with an overlap at three metres that runs out leftwards to form an undercut arête.

Anji   10m   VS 4c   ★   (1970)
Start three metres to the right of the arête and climb a short wall to the overlap, move up and left to finish just right of the arête.

Grooved Arête   8m   S   (1961-63)
Starting round to the left of the arête, move right and climb the nicely exposed arête to the top.

DESCENT ROUTE
The easiest way down from the cliff top is via the easy gully immediately to the left of Grooved Arête. Then either follow the ledge back rightwards (looking in) below Obstinance, or continue awkwardly down, zigzagging left then right, to arrive by the side of the small buttress containing Nuke the Midges.

Twenty metres to the left is a short wall split by two cracks, a curving, right-hand one and a straighter, wider, left-hand one. Below the right-hand fissure is what is possibly the oldest inscription on the edge, 1661 WG.

Foetus on the Eiger   10m   E1 6a   (1988)
Climb the centre of the technical wall just to the right of the curving crack of Crescent, which provides side-runners. Previously and incorrectly described in the past as climbing the very narrow wall between Crescent and The Mangler.

Crescent   10m   VS 5a   ★   (1959)
The curving crack. Climb this with an awkward layback move at half-height and good protection throughout.

6. Crescent	VS	10. Nuke the Midges	E1
7. Dreadnought	E7	11. Invisible Maniac	E3
8. Scapa Flow	E6	12. Scuppered	E4
9. Terrace Gully	S		

The Mangler 10m E1 5c ★   (1959)
Just to the left again is a wide undercut crack which can be
climbed by an awkward thrutch or an unlikely layback.

The undercut wall to the left is home to a couple of hard routes.

Dreadnought 10m E7 7a ★★ †   (1999)
In the centre of the wall, and with protection as for Scapa Flow,
make a desperate move over the undercut to stand on the large
foothold. Using pebbles gain the next break by extremely
frightening moves. The upper section relents somewhat.

Scapa Flow 10m E6 6c ★★   (1992)
The smooth wall to the left is approached from the left where
a way through the initial bulges can be found. Climb to the lip

178

1. Skidoo (2)	E6
2. Skidoo	E6
3. The Strangler	E4
4. Neutrons For Old	E2
5. Swooper	E5

(small cams) and make a long move to a small niche. Move right from this (crux) to gain a standing position in the centre of the wall, continue by trending rightwards with more difficulty and fierce pebble-pulling to a deep break and an easier finish.

The Chute 10m VS 4b   (1961-63)
Start at the left-hand corner of the terrace. Ascend the steep corner to a ledge and continue up the awkward wide fissure just to the right.

Terrace Gully 8m S   (1961-63)
Start as for The Chute but climb the steep, often wet, corner throughout.

Running out to the left is a narrow ledge that is actually the top of the Tower Face. Starting from this are several small but hard and worthwhile offerings in a relatively remote setting as well as one unidentified route: **Friction** XS 6c (1994) 'the slab at the top of Tower Face' which is likely to be one of the next few routes.

Scrittalacious 6m E4 6a   (1999)
The right-hand brushed line on the short wall, finishing directly
over a small roof.

The Descrittalizer 6m E5 6b   (1999)
The next line to the left via a pair of crimps.

Nihilistic Narl 6m E5 6b ★   (1984)
From the centre of the ledge climb the obvious brushed slab on
tiny edges. Reachy and scary despite its diminutive size.

Four Star, E10, 7b 6m E5 6c   (1999)
Climb the centre of the left-hand side of the slab trending
rightwards past a poor pocket.

Miserable Miracle 7m E2 5b ★   (1976)
The left-hand arête of the face from the ledge is fine and
features unprotected and highly exposed moves on slopers.

The next climbs are on the lower tier of rock below the tilted
block of Small Dreams. As mentioned earlier the first buttress
contains a large oak tree on its right-hand side and to the left of
this is a clean slab with a hanging arête on its left-hand side. The
first two routes are reached by scrambling onto a heathery ledge
from the left-hand extremity of the buttress.

Skidoo (2) 12m E6 6b ★   (1997)
Climb the right-hand line on the slab from right-to-left starting
at a cutaway and passing a constellation of three small pockets.
Climbed in mistake for the original Skidoo.

Skidoo 12m E6 6b ★★   (1985)
The slab, two metres right of the arête taken by The Strangler,
is climbed directly and provides a frightening challenge. A long
reach is very useful and a steady nerve essential.

The Strangler 12m E4 5c ★★★   (1977)
Climb the left-hand arête of the front face starting from a
heather ledge. At the lower end of the grade and an excellent
introduction to the edge's harder arête climbs.

Neutrons For Old 13m E2 5c ★   (1981)
From the lowest point of the side wall of the tower follow
cracks to the left-hand arête. Make committing moves
rightwards to finish up the right-hand arête.

Round to the left is an inconspicuous rectangular slab tackled by:

Swooper 6m E5 6b ★ (1984)
Start in the centre of the slab and climb up, trending leftwards,
to finish near the left-hand edge. A belay is advisable at the
start. The finish is often sandy and vegetated due to the gradual
collapse of the ledge above.

Hare and Graces 6m E4 6b † (1995)
Right of Swooper is a three metre long hanging green slab
gained via easy moves up the gully. From below the centre of
the slab step on to it with intrepidation and move up to a crimp
and sloping rib before dynoing for the smooth top.

To the left is a small attractive buttress standing to the right of
the impressive wall of Tower Face.

Nuke the Midges 10m E1 5c ★ (1977)
Start at the right-hand side up easy ledges. Traverse left on a
break for five metres (tricky for the short) to a hard move up
to gain a big flat jug. Mantelshelf on this to reach the top. It is
also possible to continue straight up above the easy ledges, but
this avoids the main point of the climb.

Invisible Maniac 8m E3 6b ★ (1996)
A direct line up the wall to arrive at the crux of Nuke the
Midges. A fearsome mantelshelf allows access to pockets and
eventually the break of Nuke the Midges and a common finish.

Scuppered 10m E4 6a ★ (1988)
From the end of the ledge to the left of Nuke the Midges, move
left along the break and climb the difficult blunt rib on its right-
hand side followed by the wall above.

Stretcher Case 11m E2 5c ★ (1981)
The crack in the right-hand wall of the gully to the right of
Tower Face is taken to the final break. Traverse rightwards
around the arête for three metres and lurch for the top; reachy.

To the left is a high rectangular wall, one of the highest on the
cliff. This is:

TOWER FACE

The lower half of the wall has the occasional hollow hold, whilst
the upper half is dominated by a superb vertical flake. There have
been several generations of routes and variations put up on this
face and for the first time they are all described together. All are
worthwhile.

181

1. Crescent	VS
2. Dreadnought	E7
3. Nuke the Midges	E1
4. Invisible Maniacs	E3
5. Scuppered	E4
6. Tower Face Original	HVS
7. Indian Summer	E6
8. Flight of Ideas	E7
9. Cinturato	E1
10. Additive Chimney	S
11. Centaur	E1

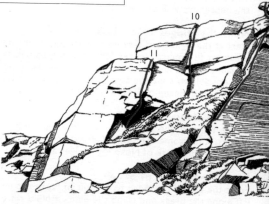

Tower Traverse 50m E1 4c, 5b, 5b ★   (1972)
Another of those girdle traverses which, although well worth
doing, has never proved popular probably because of all the
effort required to get the tick. Start up the easy corner on the
right-hand side of the face and traverse the obvious mid-height
horizontal break leftwards across Tower Face to finish round
the corner at a stance in Tower Chimney. Climb the Chimney
then hand-traverse the horizontal crack around into Tower
Crack and go up to a ledge and stance. Cross the Tower Gullies
and hand-traverse to Esso Extra, up which the route finishes.

Tower Face Indirect 25m VS 4c ★   (1930s)
A route with a rather trivial start but a grand finale. Climb the
easy chimney on the right-hand side of the face until it is
possible to step out to the left and make a short awkward
traverse leftwards to reach the base of the central flake-line.
Finish up this in a glorious position.

Scrole Not Dole   25m   E5 6b   (1984)
A thin route starting as for Tower Face Indirect (or perhaps
more in keeping, the Direct) but from halfway along the
leftwards traverse head directly up the steep wall to the right
of the upper flake-crack by sustained climbing. Finish up a short
crack.

Tower Face Original   25m   HVS 5a   ★★★   (1933)
Start below the centre of the face and climb to the second
horizontal break. Attain a standing position in the break and
make a difficult foot-traverse rightwards to a broken friable
flake just before the arête. (It is also possible to traverse

rightwards a couple of metres higher; better but harder.) Climb the flake, with care, to another break and pull up to join a traverse line. Follow this leftwards to gain the fine finishing flake. It is also possible to climb straight up to the base of the friable flake, but it is less well-protected.

Tower Face Direct   25m   E2 5b   ★★★   (1956)
An excellent route. The moves to reach the central flake are especially memorable due to the flight potential. Climb up to the sinuous crack in the centre of the face and move up and left to a shallow crease. An awkward move on this leads rightwards to better-than-expected holds, followed by a final harrowing pull to finish via the upper flake.

B P Super   28m   E3 5c   ★   (1956)
A devious and early attempt to climb the left-hand side of the face. The route is not without its moments and it was an impressive effort for its day. Start three metres to the right of the left-hand arête and climb over the rather crusty overlap at eight metres to reach a horizontal break. Swing left and up to a second break, which is traversed back rightwards to reach the upper flake. Finish up this more easily.

Indian Summer   25m   E6 6c   ★★★   (1986)
A superb direct line up the left-hand side of the face; the loss of crucial pebbles has elevated the route from E5 6b to its current grade. Start as for B P Super and follow it to the first horizontal break. Use sandy edges and what pebbles remain, to reach the upper break. Move slightly left and finish up the demanding and almost vertical wall above on minute holds.

Flight of Ideas   22m   E7 7a   ★★★   †   (1994)
Another great route, which is highly technical but has the luxury of good runners below the crucial upper arête. Start as for the previous two climbs. Follow B P Super to the arête and climb this to the deep horizontal break. The magnificent and holdless upper arête is climbed on its right-hand side and requires technique, imagination and considerable commitment.

Tower Chimney and Face   28m   VS 4c   ★   (1951-64)
A route that is perhaps best soloed by the competent unless you are ready for a nightmare of rope drag around its four right-angled corners. Start around the arête to the left of the main face and climb a steep blocky crack to a good stance in the obvious rift of the Chimney. Swing rightwards around the arête using the parallel breaks and scuttle right to the ever popular flake up which the route finishes.

Tower Chimney   20m   E1 5b   ★★★   (1933)
The obvious, shallow, flared chimney around the arête to the
left is a classic of its genre. Climb the easier lower section to
the bell-shaped upper part and gird your loins. This can be
squirmed, thrutched, back-and-footed, bridged or straddled,
take your pick. Good gear is available in the depths of the
recess. Perhaps the least popular three star route in the Peak.

Tower Crack   24m   HVS 5a   ★★   (1950-51)
To the left of Tower Chimney is a parallel fissure, in the form of
a beckoning hand-crack. An easy crack leads to a good ledge
below the real meat of the route. The leaning jamming crack
doesn't give up without a fight until a gritty ledge is reached.
Step right into a corner, move up to an overhang and traverse
right round the arête to finish on the ledge above Tower Face.
The contrasting delicate micro-route of Miserable Miracle
provides a way to the cliff top if you crave a summit
experience.

To the left is a wide and often green gully. There are two ways up
this.

Tower Gully   14m   VS 4b   ★   (1923-51)
This is the more spectacular, better and easier right-hand
branch, climbed initially up an awkward chimney/crack to ledges
and on up the impressively overhanging corner above. Make an
exposed exit left at the top.

Waterloo Branch   14m   VS 4c   ★   (1923-51)
The left-hand branch has a hard and steep exit where the
chimney closes.

Esso Extra   17m   E1 5b   ★   (1957)
Once a route only for the elite and now just another tough E1.
Climb up into the square-cut cave in the left-hand wall of the
gully, swing leftwards and into a cramped niche with difficulty. It
is possible, and easier, to swing further left and enter the niche
from the left but that is not really cricket. From the niche, jam
up the short, but strenuous, overhanging crack to the top.

Darkness Falling   15m   E6 6c   (1999)
The tasty scoop right of Grace and Danger. Start direct and
bridge up using the adjacent boulder until runners can be
placed in the horizontal break just on the right. Now move
leftwards into the scoop and climb it to an obvious sloper. A
final hard move leftwards leads to easier ground.

185

7. Additive Chimney	S
8. Centaur	E1
9. Hot and Bothered	E3
10. Fina	HVS

Grace and Danger 15m E6 6c ★★ (1986)
Excellent climbing up the blank wall below the cave of Esso Extra requires commitment and technique. If successful you will be left hanging from the base of Esso Exra's niche. Finish up the crack on the right or, more sensibly, escape out left on to the upper section of Cinturato.

Cinturato 14m E1 5b ★ (1967)
To the left of the previous routes is a slabby arête. Gain the base of this up a tricky step (or scramble around to the left) and move out right at the lowest possible level to climb up the left-hand side of the delicate arête. An enjoyable and exposed lead. It was traditional to position the belayer up the bank on the left effectively forming a side runner (HVS).

Stealth 12m VS 4c (1992)
Start as for Cinturato but trend left up the slab to a wide horizontal break and climb the narrow rib above finishing over a big block.

1. Flight of Ideas	E7
2. Tower Chimney	E1
3. Tower Crack	HVS
4. Esso Extra	E1
5. Grace and Danger	E6
6. Cinturato	E1

DESCENT ROUTE
To the left grassy ledges and short corners provide a way down.

Left again are lower walls and then a buttress with a thin crack springing from the roof of a cave. Above the right-hand side of this is a narrow rift.

Additive Chimney 10m S 4a   (1961-63)
Climb a steep corner to a ledge, step right and attack the short
parallel-sided chimney which proves to be an unprotected
tussle.

Louis the Loon 5m E2 6a   (1990)
Climb the right-hand side of the technical blunt rib on the left.
The route **Sky Bouldering** E3 6c (1999) climbs 'the blunt
arête to the right of Louis the Loon'.

A Day Without Pay 5m E6 6c ★   (1989)
To the left is a short wall above a block-filled gully. A bad
landing, no protection and highly technical climbing are not
features designed to make a popular route, but the climbing is
good.

Centaur 8m E1 5c ★   (1958)
From the cave get established, with difficulty, in the hanging
crack. Use a creaky flake on the right-hand wall to gain the
upper crack at which point the difficulties ease.

Hot and Bothered 9m E3 6b   (1989)
Start as for Centaur but at three metres make hard moves left
to a ledge on the left-hand arête. Finish up the arête. On the
first ascent a 'side-runner was placed (on lead) in the top of
Centaur'.

Fina 15m HVS 5b ★★   (1958)
Start up a thin crack on the left-hand side of the buttress and
after a couple of moves hand-traverse rightwards along the
lowest break. Climb the arête and face with difficulty. **Four
Star** E4 6b ★★ (1982) is the fine problem arête, climbed on its
left-hand side and finishing up the upper part of Fina.

Worth Travelling Four Hundred Miles For?
12m E1 5c/6c   (1996)
Start up the thin crack of Fina, swing right and ascend the
centre of the face above the horizontal break via some very
extending reaches. The first move above the break is
particularly hard for the short (6c).

Unleaded 9m S   (1992)
Climb the thin crack of Fina and bridge up the continuation
before moving right and climbing the right-hand side of the
upper arête.

Three Steps to Heaven 12m S (1996)
Ascend the buttress to the left of Fina's start, via a series of
awkward mantelshelves.

DESCENT ROUTE
To the left is a 20 metre gap in the edge which provides the
best easy way down in the immediate area.

The next section of rock is recognised by an undercut slab on the
right and a gradually widening central crack containing a couple
of prominent chockstones. This is:

PULLOVER BUTTRESS

Roll Neck 8m VS 5a ★ (1992)
From a block by the bottom right-hand side of the slab, pull
awkwardly leftwards on to it. Once established, climb directly
and pleasantly up the right-hand side edge.

Woolly Pully 8m HVS 6a (1991)
Start at the right-hand of a pair of jammed blocks/flakes under
a roof and go directly over the bulge to enter a shallow scoop.
Continue more easily.

Pullover 8m HVS 5b ★ (1958)
Just to the left is a second flake/block under the lip of the roof.
Use this to move up and leftwards to attain a standing position.
Follow the slab above via a large pocket and horizontal breaks.

Mark's Slab 10m VS 5a (1978)
From three metres up the chimney on the left, tiptoe out to the
right then ascend the slab just to the left of the central rib.

Marked Up 8m HVS 5b (1996)
Effectively a right-hand version of The Mark Devalued that
eschews all use of the arête. Start to the right of the fissure
that splits the buttress and climb the lower wall to a break.
Continue just right of the arête to the top.

The Mark Devalued 7m VS 4b (1992)
Take the left-hand arête of the slab, finishing directly.
Occasional use of the edge of the chimney to the left is difficult
to avoid at the grade, especially in the lower section.

Central Reservation 8m S (1996)
The block-filled chimney that splits the buttress, passing the
largest boulder on the left.

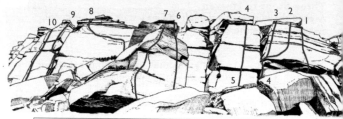

1. Pullover	HVS	6. Stirrup	HS
2. Mark's Slab	VS	7. Hot Spur	VS
3. The Mark Devalued	VS	8. Fairy Steps	VS
4. Living at the Speed	E1	9. Leaps and Bounds	E1
5. Satin	E3	10. White Wand	E5

Living at the Speed 9m E1 5b ★   (1979)
Go up the chimney to reach the obvious hand-traverse running
leftwards into the centre of the slab. Make a tricky move to
attain a standing position on the break and continue delicately
to the top.

Satin 8m E3 6b ★   (1984)
Effectively a direct start to Living at the Speed, over the overlap
and up the slab. A piece of technical wizardry where most
climbers seek in vain for something on which to pull. The
desperate slab just left is **Pressure Drop** E3 7a ★ (2000) and
joins Satin at the break.

To the left is a grassy chimney then a narrow slab tucked in behind
a huge fallen block.

Corduroy 8m VS 4c   (1992)
Climb the right-hand edge of the slab until a step rightwards
across the chimney, and level with a large jammed flake, can be
made. Finish up the left-hand arête of the upper slab of Living at
the Speed.

Ride Him Cowboy 14m VS 5a   (1991)
To the left climb the centre of the slab, behind the block, to
reach a thin overlap. Layback the right-hand arête to a ledge
and finish up a scoop in a tower.

The leaning block to the left has three routes and some worthwhile
boulder problems.

SPUR SLAB

Stirrup 11m HS 4b   (1992)
Take the centre of the right-hand wall of the leaning slab to
reach a short, wide crack. Continue upwards via thin moves to
the summit of the block and a finish up the wall behind.

Hot Spur 11m VS 4c ★   (1992)
Using a convenient block, step across to the nose on Spur Slab
and climb a blind groove and the arête above. A more direct
start is 5b.

Spur Slab 11m D ★   (1923-51)
Hop on to the easy-angled slab from the left and move up and
right to a ledge. Continue up the flaky corner to the top of the
block. **Spur Slab Left-Hand** HD (2001) starts in the same
place but continues up the left-hand side of the slab and
finishes up the wall left of the crack.

Two boulder problem starts are possible up the undercut front
face of Spur Slab.

Right Spur 6b (1976), rockover the lip assisted by thin vertical
flakes and traverse off left. **Left Spur** 6b (1986), uses the short
hanging edge to the left to pass the lip of the bulge; walk off. A
harder, sit-down start is also possible as well as an excellent
traverse under the roof from left to right to either finish.

DESCENT ROUTE
To the left of Spur Slab is an open grassy gully offering an easy
way down and the last for some distance.

To the left is the extensive and popular Wall End Area which
features some of the best lines and routes on the cliff. On the
right-hand side is the broad smooth wall crossed by Fairy Steps
and right of this is a short jutting buttress split into two tiers.

WALL END AREA

Double Act 12m HVS 5c   (1991)
Both tiers offer technical moves. Attaining a standing position
on the mid-way break proves to be the crux.

Fairy Steps 15m VS 4a ★★   (1961-63)
A great little route which follows a narrow ledge system, to

cross the vast wall to the left of the easy corner. Climb the blocky corner on the right followed by a tricky wall to reach the start of the ledge system. Make a delicate traverse left, moving away from the protection, until a line of better holds leads straight up to the top. A slightly easier but no safer alternative is to begin the traverse from higher up the right-hand bounding gully.

Gnome Man's Land   20m   E5 6b   ★   (1984)
A hard eliminate that crosses Fairy Steps. From a belay on the grassy ledge below the traverse of that route gain the obvious, prominent hold from the left and move up (crux) passing the centre of the Fairy Steps' ledge system and pressing on directly to the top. An excellent direct start can be made up the slanting arête to reach the grassy ledge at 6b ★ (1990s).

Holly Bush Gully Right   20m   D   ★★   (1890-1903)
The Puttrell-vintage gully to the left has a slab hidden in its deep recess. The gully is reached either by climbing the twin cracks (VD) or by a traverse from the blocks on the right.

The Wall End Traverse   70m   VS 4c   ★   (1946-51)
A rather tortuous girdle, with some interesting climbing and comfortable stances. Climb Holly Bush Gully Right to the base of the deep upper section and traverse leftwards along a ledge to a tricky move round the corner to a stance in Holly Bush Gully Left. Follow the ledge out leftwards and descend a short section of Doncaster's Route to the stance on Goliath's Groove. It is most logical to follow the break round the corner, but the historically correct route follows the groove to a point above the bulge and traverses round to gain the upper section of Helfenstein's Struggle. Descend the gully and move out leftwards to gain the upper end of a ramp which is descended to reach the base of Wall End Crack up which the route finishes.

Leaps and Bounds   20m   E1 5b   (1982)
Follow the left-hand of the twin cracks of Holly Bush Gully Right until is possible to step left on to the central ledge of White Wand. Continue delicately up the left-hand side of the arête overlooking the chimney.

Left again is the first of a series of superb arête climbs, all effectively unprotected and covering the grades from E3 to E6. The grades given asume that no bouldering mats are used.

Flight of Ideas   E7 7a   (page 184)
Climber: Simon Jones   Photo: David Simmonite

Deliverance 6c (page 205)
Climber: Sam Whittaker Photo: David Simmonite

Careless Torque E7 7a (page 208)
Climber: Malcolm Smith   Photo: Ray Wood

White Wand 23m E5 6a ★★★ (1975)
The prominent arête to the left is approached up easy rock.
Getting established on the sharp arête above is the crux and
above this 'panic point' a harrowing layback leads to the halfway
break. From there continue more easily up the front face of the
buttress using occasional good holds round to the left. As might
be expected, on the crucial section protection is non-existent
and the route has a nasty landing. Probably E6 for the short.

Holly Bush Gully Left 20m HS 4b ★★ (1912-14)
The steep corner around to the left has a tall flake standing in
it, cleft into four by three horizontal breaks. Start up the left-
hand crack passing the exposed chockstone to gain the easy
upper section of the gully. Either move left to the final short
crack of Doncaster's Route, squeeze through a skylight, or exit
rightwards as for Holly Bush Gully Right.

Ulysses 20m E6 6b ★★★ (1983)
The square-cut right-hand arête of the deep 'V' of Goliath's
Groove had achieved classic status even before it was first
climbed. The arête gets harder with each move until the
midway ledge on Goliath's Groove. Finish easily up the blunt rib
above. An audacious route requiring good technique, deft
footwork and total commitment.

Doncaster's Route 22m HVS 5a ★★ (1930s-40s)
An early attempt on Goliath's Groove escaped out rightwards
below the bulges. Ascend Goliath's Groove to the halfway ledge
(possible stance) and climb a short slab on the right to a larger
ledge. Finish up a thin crack in the centre of the back wall.

Goliath's Groove 21m HVS 5a ★★★ (1947)
The stunning, sinuous groove-line is a classic and one of
Britain's finest routes. The initial clean-cut corner is thrutched,
bridged or jammed elegantly to the halfway ledge and possible
stance. The upper bulging section of the groove can be
laybacked by the strong or bridged by the technical. If you use
the midway stance be careful of your ropes jamming in the
crack below.

The Archangel 20m E3 5b ★★★ (1972)
The immaculate arête on the left is climbed on its left side,
offering superb, sustained and committing climbing high in the
grade. Start from blocks on the left, take a deep breath, and
sprint for the midway break. Continue up the easier arête
above, still with interest. Pre-placed side runners in the left end
of the first horizontal break significantly reduce the grade and

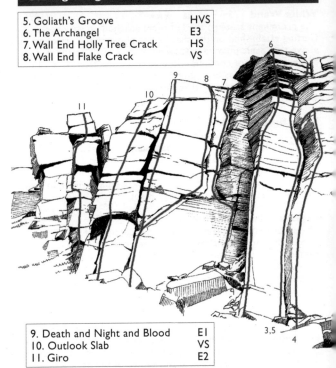

5. Goliath's Groove	HVS
6. The Archangel	E3
7. Wall End Holly Tree Crack	HS
8. Wall End Flake Crack	VS

9. Death and Night and Blood	E1
10. Outlook Slab	VS
11. Giro	E2

the experience. For a different and underrated view, climb the arête on its right-hand side throughout, **Don** E4 5c ★★ (1985).

Dark Angel 21m HVS 5b   (1986)
Start as for Helfenstein's Struggle but hand-traverse the horizontal break rightwards until one can gain a standing position using a small pocket. Gain the left-hand arête as soon as possible and follow it to the top; worthwhile.

Saul's Arête 22m VS 4b ★   (1965)
The original approach to the upper section of The Archangel provides devious access to the well-positioned final arête. Climb the chimney of Helfenstein's Struggle to the horizontal break and hand-traverse this out to the arête; finish pleasantly up this.

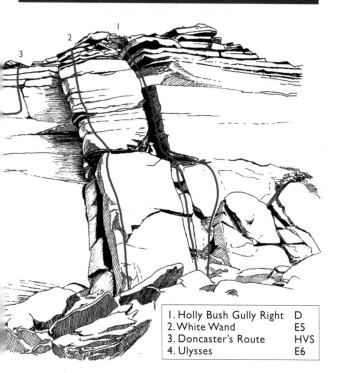

1. Holly Bush Gully Right	D
2. White Wand	E5
3. Doncaster's Route	HVS
4. Ulysses	E6

Helfenstein's Struggle 20m VD ★★ (1930s)
The classic wide rift on the left. Climb a short, polished corner
on the left to get into the lower section of the big gully and
climb easier rock to a position below the large boulder which
corks the rift. Either squeeze through the 'rat-hole' that gripped
Helfenstein like a vice, or ignore the historically correct
approach and make an exposed and eminently sensible, but
slightly harder, 'outside' exit on the right.

I Never Said It Was Any Good 18m E1 5b (1989)
Climb the short slippery crack in the left-hand wall of
Helfenstein's Struggle and continue up the wall directly above
on shelving holds. Try to avoid the temptation to bridge the last
few moves.

On the wall to the left of the chimney are two fine flake cracks that face each other. Unfortunately they are rather close together and a puritanical approach may be required.

Wall End Holly Tree Crack   18m   HS 4b   ★   (1923-57)
The right-hand of these two flakes can be reached by the thin, scratched crack in the left-hand wall of Helfenstein's Struggle and is then followed by pleasant jamming and bridging.

To the left and down the slope is a crack in a shallow corner which is used to start the next three routes.

Wall End Flake Crack   20m   VS 4c   ★★   (1919-23)
Climb the corner-crack until it is possible to traverse right up the sloping ramp to the foot of the two flakes. Climb the left-hand flake by well-protected laybacking and jamming.

Death and Night and Blood   18m   E1 5b   ★   (1978)
Start up the jamming crack as for Wall End Flake Crack. Step slightly right and climb the exposed and delicate arête, passing a rickety flake, to a final precarious section. A high side-runner in Wall End Crack reduces the grade to HVS. An excellent boulder problem start is possible up the slab to the right at 6a.

Wall End Crack   16m   S 4a   ★   (1919-23)
Start up the left corner to a ledge. Ascend the slab for a metre before stepping right to gain and follow the main crack-line. The upper crack can be approached via the short jamming crack used by the start of the previous two climbs at HS 4b ★★.

Outlook Slab   16m   VS 5a   ★   (1978)
The horizontally fissured slab to the left is ascended directly up its centre without using either of the arêtes. Start up a blunt rib and press on via escapable but pleasant climbing with a well-protected, though baffling, crux move where things steepen up.

The Coign   16m   VS 4b   ★★   (1958)
The left-hand arête of this section of the wall. Climb the short corner of Wall End Crack to a ledge and step up and left on to the main arête which is followed pleasantly to the top.

Slanting Chimney   10m   HS 4b   (1961-63)
Around the corner to the left is a blocky leftward-slanting crack-line. The lower section leads easily over the blocks and to where the deeper leaning upper section provides the fun and games.

Jammed Stone Chimney   8m   HD   (1961-63)
This route appears to have been misplaced in previous editions
of the guidebook, though the 1964 volume clearly describes 'a
short chimney with many jammed blocks' 60 feet right of Wall
End Slab. Now that it has been identified you can climb it via its
many jammed blocks.

P.O. Crack   8m   HS 4b   (1961-63)
The block-choked gully of Jammed Stone Chimney has a
widening crack in its left-hand wall. Climb to this passing over a
variety of obstacles to finish awkwardly over an overhang.

Giro   9m   E2 5c   ★   (1982)
The narrow buttress immediately to the left is climbed via a rib,
a short ramp and a swing rightwards below the final roof,
where an extended reach for the top provides the crux.

Frankie Ferocious   7m   E3 6a   (1999)
Climb the centre of the narrow wall between Giro and Cheque
to a break. Extend for the top and a very difficult finish.

Cheque   7m   VD   (1992)
The obvious short corner to the left may certainly have been
climbed in antiquity.

Mate   7m   E1 5b   (1992)
Start up the blunt rib two metres to the left and make long
reaches to a black hole and then a break. Swing rightwards
around the arête and step left to climb the final wall directly.

DESCENT ROUTE
To the left a narrow break in the cliff is an easy way down.

Several pleasant problems exist on a short, flat wall to the left of
the descent route. Beyond a V-shaped groove, with a perched block
on its right-hand edge, is a slightly taller wall with a hollybush at
its top left-hand corner.

Sittin' Here Drinkin'   7m   HVS 5b   (1993)
The left-hand arête of the V-shaped groove is short lived.

Standing Around Trying   7m   VS 5a   (1993)
The wall just left of the arête.

Narlavision   7m   HVS 5b   (1984)
Climb the wall left again passing immediately right of a holly
bush.

Impure, Grey and Mildly Threatening   6m   S 4b   (2001)
To the left of Narlavision, climb the crack and wall before
tackling the block above directly.

To the left a huge, slabby block lies slumped against the main
edge. This is home to a variety of climbs from a classic VS to an E4
frightener and is:

WALL END SLAB

Pure, White and Deadly   14m   E2 5c   (1982)
A delicate, unprotected and uninspiring route up the right-hand
arête of the slab. Start below the bottom right-hand side of the
lower slab and climb its right edge. Continue trending delicately
rightwards and keeping close to the edge to eventually join the
easy upper section of Wall End Slab.

Wall End Slab Direct   15m   E2 5b   ★★   (1930)
An astonishing effort for 1930. Climb the lower slab right of
centre to a ledge and then go up to a horizontal break. Move
right and balance up the slab using an undercut flake to a
mantelshelf a worrying distance above any gear. If successful,
climb to the next break and move right to ascend the easy
upper arête on its right-hand side. The bold **Wall End Slab
Direct Finish**, E3 5c ★★ (1983), follows the parent route to
where it goes off right and then teeters directly up the scoop in
the steepening final wall.

Wall End Slab Super Duper Direct
14m   E4 5c   ★   (1991)
Climb the centre of the lower slab and then continue over the
middle of the bulge above on pleasantly surprising pockets. The
final broad rib is the main challenge of the route. A nut in the
crack to the left reduces the grade to a less harrowing E2.

Wall End Slab   22m   VS 5a   ★★★   (1919-23)
A devious but venerable classic. The polished first three metres
to the good ledge can be ascended in several places; the easiest
way, though still forming the crux, is on the right via a pocket.
The central and left-hand lines are nearer to 5b/c. If all else
fails, it is possible to traverse the break from the slope on the
right reducing the grade of the climb to VS 4b. From the first
ledge, climb over the bulge just to the right of the left-hand
arête to reach a triangular ledge. Step down and traverse
rightwards across the slab to reach its right-hand arête. Follow
the right-hand side of the arete to the top.

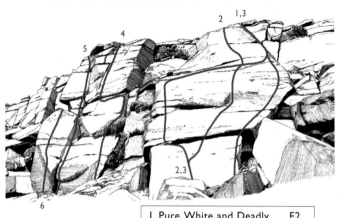

1. Pure, White and Deadly	E2
2. Wall End Slab Direct Finish	E3
3. Wall End Slab	VS
4. Fern Groove	E2
5. Fern Crack	HVS
6. Silk	E5

Bridge's Variation 14m VS 5a ★   (1930s)
Follow the regular route to its triangular ledge and then climb
the crack that rises from the back of this to the top of the slab.
Stride across the gap to the main face and finish up this.

Virginia Calling 14m HVS 5a   (1995)
The left-hand arête of the slab is climbed throughout with the
final rounded section providing the crux.

Toothcomb 12m VS 4c   (1988)
The heavily overgrown buttress to the left has two grass fields,
a small (rock) bulge and a battle with a hollybush to finish.

To the left is a gully with an obstinate hollybush sprouting from
its base.

Smash Your Glasses 9m E5 6b ★★   (1988)
Climb the slab just left of the gully to reach a grass ledge and
step right to follow the arête as on its left-hand side to the top.
Runners protect the crucial moves over the bulge above the
horizontal break but above this the arête gives a frightening
lead with a crater potential. Gaining the arête from the gully to

the right and climbing it on its right-hand side gives a poor route, **Spartaciad** E1 5b (1981).

Fern Groove 17m E2 5c ★★ (1961-63)
The upper part of the buttress to the right of the straight fissure of Fern Crack is split by a fine hanging groove. Follow Smash Your Glasses to the grass ledge. Step up and move round the corner to the right to gain the horizontal break in the centre of the buttress. Swing leftwards along this and enter the groove by a tricky layback. Once established, climb the incipient crack with difficulty and at the point where the crack ends, so do the difficulties. High in the grade.

A boulder problem direct start to the centre of the grass ledge is possible for technically-minded climbers with the ability to 'stick' to blank rock, **Help the Aged** 6c (1985).

Fern Crack 16m HVS 5a ★★ (1923-51)
This long crack, the major feature of the buttress, is awkward to start. Climb the steep, slippery crack to a ledge. Make a tricky move to enter the wider upper crack and follow this and another awkward section until a step left gains a shelf. Finish up the easy scoop.

Silk 16m E5 6c ★★ (1984)
A bold, technical solution to a long-standing problem up the slabby face to the left of Fern Crack. Start just left of the base of the crack and mantelshelf over the bulge with great difficulty. Desperate and committing faith-and-friction moves lead intricately leftwards up to parallel breaks. The halfway ledge of the buttress is gained using a variety of poor pockets. From the ledge walk off leftwards or finish up Argus.

Dijon Dip 6m E2 6b (1989)
Below and to the left of Silk and just above the path is this short route, or 'highball' boulder problem, depending on your view. Climb the squat wall and the centre of the overhanging block.

The next climbs start from ledges up and left of Fern Crack, where there is a series of shorter walls that offer pleasant routes that are almost always devoid of crowds.

AMPHITHEATRE FACE AREA

Argus 8m E2 5b ★ (1977)
This route takes the upper half of the left-hand arête of the

1. Argus	E2
2. Tears and Guts	E2
3. Ladder Cracks	VD
4. Amphitheatre Face	VS
5. Bastille	E1
6. Flaky Wall	HVS
7. Tales of Yankee Power	E1

Fern Crack buttress. Starting from a ledge on the left, layback the arête in a somewhat dramatic fashion on its left-hand side.

Whimper 7m S 4a (1992)
The open corner-crack to the left is bridged to a finishing crack, which is awkward to gain but followed more easily.

Tears and Guts 8m E2 6a (1990)
Climb the narrow undercut wall to the right of Ladder Corner pulling over the initial roof. Continue via two breaks to finish, with difficulty, directly over the final overhanging nose.

Ladder Corner 8m M (1961-63)
The straightforward corner that bounds the left-hand edge of the buttress.

DESCENT ROUTE
The previous climb can be used as an awkward descent route.

Ladder Cracks 8m VD (1912-14)
Climb the parallel ladder-like cracks in the wall immediately to the left of the corner. They prove to be pleasant if rather awkward.

Amphitheatre Face 8m VS 5a/c (1923-51)
To the left is a green wall and left again is a squat pillar. This
route gains the ledge on the wall by a thin move and long reach
from the left, or more usually and more directly, by a short hop
for the tall or a massive leap for the short. Continue more
easily up the pleasant jamming crack. Originally graded Diff.

Shaky Gully 8m S (1992)
The corner on the left-hand side of the green face leads to an
awkward wide section and then on to the top of the pillar.
Finish up the short crack just to the left.

To the left a projecting, square block stands in front of the face.

Bastille 10m E1 5b (1992)
Make an awkward move to get on to a block under the right-
hand arête of the face and continue up the left-hand side of the
arête above.

Flaky Wall 10m HVS 5b ★ (1964-76)
Climb to creaky flakes just right of the centre of the block and
use these to move left. Move up via a long reach for the top.

Tales of Yankee Power 10m E1 5c (1984)
Climb the centre of the wall to the left of the flakes passing a
thin horizontal break with difficulty.

Around the corner to the left is a flake that leans against the wall.
The front face of this is home to two short but pleasant routes.

Splinter 7m HVS 5c ★ (1985)
Balance rightwards up a blunt rib in the centre of the wall to a
small ledge and finish with difficulty or a long reach.

Shard 7m HVS 5b (1997)
Starting in the same place as the previous route climb straight
up the delicate slab to a horizontal break to finish with a
mantelshelf.

Lookout Flake 7m S ★ (1961-63)
Three metres to the left of the previous climb ascend an
undercut flake which is difficult to start but soon eases.

I Didn't Get Where I Am Today 8m E3 5c ★★ (1984)
From the base of Outlook Chimney climb the front face of the
hanging buttress, swing rightwards and ascend the centre of the

1. Splinter	HVS
2. Lookout Flake	S
3. I Didn't Get Where I Am Today	E3
4. Outlook Chimney	VS
5. Outlook Crack	VS
6. Weather Report	E6
7. Look Before You Leap	E1
8. The Introvert	E2

wall passing a shallow pocket to a rounded exit. Graded for ignoring the tempting side-runner in Lookout Flake.

Outlook Chimney 7m VS 5a (1961-63)
The steep undercut chimney two metres further left has an awkward entry and a difficult exit.

DESCENT ROUTE
To the left is an awkward scrambling descent (though a much better one lies 20 metres left).

Beyond the descent route is a smooth wall split by an fine crack.

Outlook Crack 8m VS 4c ★ (1961-63)
The best reasonably graded route hereabouts. Approach the crack from the right and follow it pleasantly.

Nordes with Attitude 9m E4 6c (1989)
From a runner in Outlook Crack foot-traverse a horizontal break leftwards for two metres, enter a scoop and reach the top by a desperate undercut move.

Weather Report 9m E6 6b ★★   (1984)
A technically intriguing route that follows a shallow groove and
the centre of the wall to the left of the straight crack. It uses a
paltry set of holds and has minimal protection. Traversing in
from the right at half-height reduces the grade but misses the
point.

A Thousand Natural Shocks 6m HVS 5c   (1984)
Climbs the small arête forming the left-hand edge of the
buttress. It is started from the flat ledge at the base of Outlook
Layback.

Outlook Layback 7m S 4b ★   (1923-51)
To the left is an obvious corner crack starting from the back of
the flat ledge.

Look Before You Leap 8m E1 5c/6c   (1983)
The centre of the face of the buttress is ascended via a
perfectly-protected, height-dependent, 'flying-leap' from
undercuts at half-height. Pebble pulling and other technical
chicanery doesn't seem to help.

Tying the Knot 9m E3 6a   (1990)
Start just to the left of the blunt arête of the buttress below a
flake. Use the flake to gain the traverse line of Outlook
Buttress and continue up the steep wall using large slopers.

Outlook Buttress 8m HVS 5b ★   (1964-76)
Start on the north-facing wall of the buttress and traverse the
wide, rounded break to reach an arête which is climbed to the
top in a pleasantly exposed position.

The Introvert 8m E2 5c   (1984)
Quietly sneak around the corner and starting as for Outlook
Buttress climb the centre of the left-hand wall of the buttress

DESCENT ROUTE
To the left of Outlook Buttress is a major break in the edge
used by the slabbed path that runs from the Plantation car park,
up through the Plantation and across the moor to Stanage Pole
before descending towards Sheffield. This is thought to be an
ancient pack-horse route used for bringing salt from Cheshire
and entering the city along what is now Psalter Lane.

THE PLANTATION BOULDERS

Below the Unconquerable Cracks is a fine plantation of deciduous and evergreen trees, always a beautiful spot to pause in while going to or from the crag. This Plantation in turn gives its name to the boulder field which extends from its south-western edge as far as the bottom of Goliath's Groove and this area is home to many of the finest, hardest and most famous boulder problems in the country.

It is not hard to see why. Massive blocks of perfect rock have stopped on their roll down from the main edge and are ideally formed to allow climbing on their every face, usually with very friendly landings. Of the two main areas, the collection closer to the Plantation has a higher number of problems scattered on every face and arête of these blocks, ranging from the not-too-hard to the hard-as-they-come. The Pebble boulder, Jerry's Block and the Green Traverse are the landmarks and there's usually someone around to point you in the right direction. The other main area, the Not To Be Taken Away area (the Grand Hotel boulder) lies below Goliath's Groove. While there are less problems there, this is easily made up for by the stature and nobility of those that there are. Many of the best lines require a steady head as much as strong arms and have long been established as classic micro-routes. That said, however, you will still need strong arms to get up them.

The area is invariably extremely popular and, unfortunately, it is suffering from both erosion and litter. No attempt is made here to describe the myriad of problems, though the best of these are listed, as has long been the tradition. The easiest approach is from the Plantation car park. From the swing gate at the exit from the Plantation the main boulders can be seen up and right for the area around The Pebble and straight ahead for the area containing the Grand Hotel boulder. On the far right-hand side of the first area, below Millsom's Minion, is the obvious cubic block of:

THE PEBBLE

Deliverance 6c ★★★   (1987)
The centre of the south face of the block is approached by a delicate traverse from the left to the obvious blind flake in the centre of the wall. The top is reached by a flying leap, (or more rarely, statically) and strong legs are an asset.

The Pebble Arête 5c ★★   (traditional)
The south-west arête, which is usually started from the right,
has a slightly harrowing finish. Can also be climbed on the left,
at roughly 5c/6a.

Up and right (north-west) of The Pebble is a boulder with a hanging
beak and, usually, a pair of chalked holds.

The Ace 7b ★★   (2001)
A desperate problem which keeps having more moves added
to it. At this standard, start in the hanging break, gain the
two well-brushed edges and go for the top of the block.
Possibly the hardest problem on Stanage and one of the
hardest on gritstone. Originally started life as **The Joker** 7a
★★ by hanging the two edges from a convenient boulder and
leaping for the top. It was also one of the shortest problems
around.

Up to the left (north-east) of The Pebble is a flat block underneath
the trees. Usually featuring a heavily-chalked traverse, this is the
well-named:

GREEN BLOCK

The Green Traverse 6c ★★★   (1980s)
Start on the sloping right-hand end of the block and traverse
left around the front face, until better holds lead to the rock-
over onto the slab on the left-hand side of the block. The
classic boulder traverse with a boulderer nearly always *in situ*.

Back down the slope towards the car park and beyond The Pebble
is a boulder with an array of poor sloping holds on its west face.
This is:

THE FACE OF BUSINESS

Rose and the Self-Employed Business Man 6c ★
                                             (1980s)
The high traverse from the ledge on the right of the front face,
moving leftwards just below the top of the block, until the
'Rose' move (the clue's in the name) leads to the big flakes and
easier ground.

Jerry's Traverse with Ben's Extension 7b ★★ (1990s)
Traverse the whole face starting around to the right and
keeping low. The original 'Jerry's Traverse' starts on the ledges
on the right of the front face and goes left at a low level to gain

ramps on the front face and then finishes straight up. Extra kudos is gained from doing 'Ben's Extension', starting further right and dropping onto the ledge from a high sloping 'pod' on the right wall.

Farther along the flagged path from the swing gate is the second main area of large boulders directly below Goliath's Groove, which is home to many excellent boulder problems and micro-routes. On the right-hand side of this section is a huge elongated horizontal block on a plinth, with an undercut right-hand arête.

The Photograph   7m   E3 5c   (1982)
From the plinth step up and traverse rightwards to the right arête passing a thin slot. Surprisingly exposed. A direct finish from the thin slot is possible, **Snap Shot** E3 5c (1992).

Lichen Alive   7m   E5 6a   †   (2001)
Between Snap Shot and Video Nasty is a vague flake; climb it directly. A tied down 'spotter' is said to be helpful as the landing is nasty and the route is unprotected.

Video Nasty   6m   E1 6a   (1986)
The centre of the face of the block is more technical but less scary than The Photograph.

Adults Only   4m   E1 6b   (1990s)
The left-hand arête of the block is taxing.

At the back of the boulder is a hidden pit, usually with someone *in situ* attempting what is one of the hardest problems at Stanage.

Brad Pit   7a   ★★★   (1995)
The obvious well-brushed faint groove on the back of the boulder — the only line of 'weakness' on this part of the block. At this grade the start is from the horizontal edges. A 'bendy' sequence leads to the layaways and the obvious jug below the top. Was first climbed dynamically at 'baby' 7b. A sitting start followed by the dynamic approach gives a very hard 7b † (2000).

On the same wall to the left and at a slightly higher level is a pleasant little 6b dyno from a sloping break; some light relief for those of us who can't do the 'big brother' problem. Just left again is **Overexposed** E5 6b † (2000). From the arête traverse left for a few rather scary moves until you reach the arête of The Photograph.

Looking down the slope and to the right, the largest boulder near the footpath is the:

GRAND HOTEL

On the front face of the boulder is a diagonal ramp-line that rises from right to left.

Rotor 5m HVS 6a   (1970/80s?)
The fragile flakes on the right side of the face are climbed to a perplexing final move. Easy for the tall, a jump if you are short.

Not To Be Taken Away 7m E2 6a ★★★   (1976)
Simply the best problem of its grade on Stanage. The leftwards rising ramp-line up the front of the Grand Hotel block is climbed in its entirety. Essentially a 'highball' problem, with the crux being the first move to gain the ramp, but a steady approach is needed. An exciting alternative is **To Be or Not To Be** E3 6c ★★ (1997) after gaining the ramp at the start of the parent route continue direct via crimps and throw a dyno for the top.

Careless Torque 7m E7 7a ★★★   (1987)
The undercut left-hand arête of the block proves almost impossible to attain and even harder to climb. The first acensionist used to 'practise' the fall from the arête by jumping off from increasing height, prior to the first ascent. A superb addition and well ahead of its time.

To the left again (looking towards the edge) and even closer to the path, is an obvious and attractive curved arete. To the right of this are some short problems ranging from 5b to 6c, but the main attraction is:

Crescent Arête 7m E1 5b ★★★   (1976)
This classic arête is climbed on its left-hand side and is delightfully technical. The definitive Stanage 'highball' problem. It is not unusual to see good climbers unused to gritstone arêtes retreat from this.

Behind, and up to the right of the Crescent Arête boulder, are two more large blocks (the larger one dubbed The Mental Block) with an uninviting 'crevasse' between them and an attractive hanging left arête.

Deadline 7m E5 6c ★   (1999)
Traverse the left-hand wall of the boulder to a prominent

pocket then make a very hard move to reach the final hold on Beneath the Breadline. Quite a high 'highball'.

Beneath the Breadline 7m E5 6c ★★ (1999)
The left arête of the block is followed from ground level to the top. A serious but a delightful solution to a long-standing problem. It was originally started by stepping off the adjacent block to gain the arête halfway up, **Breadline** E4 6b ★ (1984).

Big Air 4m E6 6b ★ (1987)
An unusual and highly dangerous problem. Leap the crevasse to the prominent square pocket and continue up the wall above, trending slightly right. Once you have summoned up the courage to make the leap, the pocket is actually quite good.
Unfortunately, the wall above is harder than you would like.

The problems listed here are merely the tip of the iceberg. Literally hundreds of problems litter this section of the crag. These are covered in much more detail in dedicated bouldering guides. The problems mentioned are the most obvious classics and may encourage the reader to explore this area further.

Back to the main edge and beyond the major break, 80 metres from Outlook Buttress, is a broad, tiered buttress reached by a short diagonal descent. This is Two Tier Buttress and the left-hand side of it is indeed split conspicuously into two tiers.

MOTHER'S DAY AREA

Waffti 11m VD (1984)
The oddly-named right arête of the wall proves short and quite pleasant. Start on the left and finish around to the right.

Olly Wall 10m S 4a (1999)
Start just to the right of the holly and climb the wall via flakes to an awkward move onto a ledge just below the top.

Zero Zero Sputnik 11m E2 5c (1984)
To the left is a hollybush in a corner and beyond this is a short blunt arête. Follow the arête starting on its left and finishing around to the right with a long reach.

Moments of Inertia 10m E2 5b (1999)
Climb delicately up the centre of the steep slab to a long reach.

Afterthought 11m S 4a (1961)
To the left are twin, parallel cracks that start from ledges

reached by an easy scramble. Climb the left-hand crack until it becomes very thin, transfer to the right-hand fissure and follow this to an awkward heathery exit. An alternative is to climb the right-hand crack for two metres, before stepping left and up the left-hand crack, **Forethought** HS 4b (1999).

Warlock 12m   HVS 5b   (1976)
Start below the upper series of overhangs at a heathery finger-crack. Climb the crack to ledges and continue up a series of short walls to a larger ledge. Move left to the arête and climb to a bulge which blocks upward progress. A hand-traverse leads out right to a short crack which is used to pass the bulge. Finish up the middle of the headwall.

To the left the upper tier of the buttress is split by a square recess and beyond this the lower tier has a wide overhang which runs across its full width and is split centrally by the prominent bulging crack of Surprise.

1. Warlock	HVS
2. Mother's Day	VS
3. Surprise	HVS
4. Feminist's Breakfast	E4
5. Ma's Retreat	E1
6. Hard Head	HVS
7. Stumpy	E1
8. Dot's Slab	D
9. Tom-cat Slab	E1
10. Basil Half-Tail	E1

Mother's Day   11m   VS 4c   ★   (1957)
The crack, of awkward width, on the right-hand edge of the
upper wall is approached via a grassy groove directly below and
proves to be rather strenuous, especially on the crux bulge.

The centre of the slab to the left is climbed by the direct start to
the next route.

Surprise   16m   HVS 5b   ★★   (1959)
A disjointed route offering excellent climbing. Overcome the
thin bulging crack on the left-hand edge of the lower tier, move
right and jam the short steep crack to exit on to the final slab.
A **Direct Start** 6b ★ (1970s) can be made to the right by
mantelshelving fiercely onto a couple of reasonable holds in the
centre of the slab directly below the crack in the upper wall.

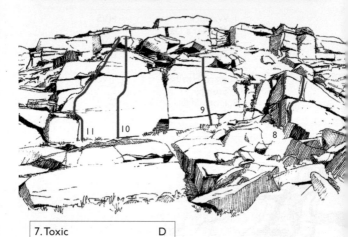

7. Toxic	D
8. Marmite	VS
9. Sithee	E1
10. D.I.Y.	E3
11. Black and Decker	E2

Feminist's Breakfast 16m E4 6b ★   (1985)
A worthwhile line up the wall left of the upper crack of
Surprise. Start as for the Surprise Direct Start and pull through
the bulge on the left with some difficulty and increasing fear,
moving rapidly left to finish up the right-hand side of the arête.

The next routes are reached by a short scramble up the gully to
the left of the lower slab, to gain an area of ledges below a corner
with slabby rock to its left and steeper terrain to its right.

Boobagram 9m E1 6a   (1983)
This short route climbs the undercut right-hand arête of the
bay on its left-hand side with a side runner in the crack to the
left. Alternatively the upper half of the arête can be reached
from a thin crack in the wall to the left, **Ma's Retreat** E1 6a
(1977).

Tram Eaters 9m E2 6a ★   (1983)
Start up the thin crack of Ma's Retreat but continue directly up
the short wall via a very long stretch. The anagram is much
easier to unravel than are the crucial moves.

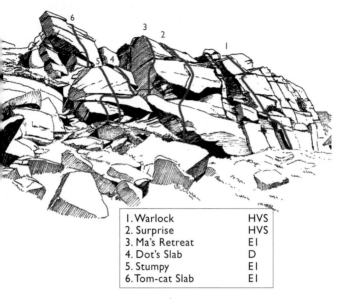

1. Warlock	HVS
2. Surprise	HVS
3. Ma's Retreat	E1
4. Dot's Slab	D
5. Stumpy	E1
6. Tom-cat Slab	E1

To the left, the main angle of the bay is formed by two diverging cracks.

Flute Chimney 8m HD   (1961-63)
The right-hand crack widens gradually and forms a narrow chimney in its upper section; awkward but well-protected.

Dry Crack 6m D   (1961-63)
Strangely enough the crack in the main angle of the corner is often wet.

Non-toxic 9m VS 4c   (1984)
The wall and blunt arête to the left of Dry Crack.

Short Crack 8m M   (1961-63)
The left-hand crack to the left of the main angle is, er... short.

DESCENT ROUTE
The V-shaped groove of Short Crack gives an easy way down leading into the back of the bay.

Skin Grafter   9m   E3 5c   ★   (1982)
A delicate climb up the unprotected, right-hand edge and arête
of Tom-cat Slab has a particularly precarious finish.

Tom-cat Slab   9m   E1 5b   ★★   (1961-63)
The centre of the steep slab to the left gives another scary
pitch. From just left of centre, loose flaky holds lead to a
difficult move at mid-height and a delicate finish up the middle
of the final wall.

Basil Half-tail   9m   E1 5c   (1988)
Pull over the undercut at the left-hand side of the slab, trend
left to finish out on the pleasantly exposed arête.

The descriptions now return to the lower tier. To the left of the
gully, used to gain access to the previous climbs, is a slab with an
undercut right-hand corner.

Hard Head   8m   HVS 5b   ★   (1994)
Pull over the undercut left-hand side of the right-hand arête of
the slab, (5c for the short) or if all else fails start around to the
right of the arête at 4a, then climb the delicate slab keeping just
left of the arête.

Stumpy   8m   E1 5a   ★   (1994)
Starting at a cutaway beneath the centre of the slab, climb
directly up middle of the slab by delicate and poorly protected
climbing.

Dot's Slab   10m   D   ★   (1959)
Climb the left-hand side of the slab via a series of steps to
reach a ledge running across the face. Traverse rightwards along
this and step round the arête to finish up a short corner-
crack. The shelving left-hand edge of the slab is **Old Slob** VD
(1994).

DESCENT ROUTE
The gully to the left of the slab is the easiest way down in this
area. Some scrambling is required near the bottom.

To the left, the crag is split into two tiers. The upper tier is generally
short but the lower one consists of a series of low walls, mostly
in the form of steep slabs and is home to a series of short but
worthwhile routes on excellent rock; another good place to escape
the crowds. The first route is situated 20 metres to the left of
Dot's Slab and starts to the right of a crack formed by a left-
facing flake leaning against the wall. This is:

D.I.Y. AREA

Cixot 6m VS 5a   (1997)
Start on a ledge one metre right of the leaning flake and make a
couple of awkward moves to reach its crest. Step left and climb
the short-lived upper arête.

Toxic 6m D ★   (1961-63)
Climb the sharp flake, which rests on the wall, to its top and
then move right to reach twin cracks and a pleasant finish. The
awkward wide crack in the side wall around to the left is
Marmite VS 4c (1981).

DESCENT ROUTE
The short corner just to the left of the crack of Marmite offers
an awkward descent.

To the left is a broad wall split centrally by the obvious straight
crack of Grime.

Sithee 8m E1 5b ★   (1977)
Start just to the right of the centre of the right-hand section of
the wall and climb on to a flake. Lean leftwards and swing
across to reach good pockets in the centre of the face. From
these, gain a horizontal break and finish directly up the centre
of the upper wall.

Sithee Direct 8m E1 6b ★★   (1981)
A good technical problem taking the true line up the wall. Start
from a small flat block embedded in the ground and make hard
moves on undercuts, pebbles and pockets to join the previous
route at its pockets. Finish directly up the wall. The lurking
block-filled hole in the ground adds spice to the crucial moves.

Grime 8m HS 4b   (1961-63)
Jam the thin undercut crack to enter the wider upper section.

Torture Garden 10m E3 6b ★★   (1985)
The section of the wall immediately to the left of the crack is
climbed directly, initially reaching the prominent slot via a huge
reach and passing it with difficulty. At this grade, the short may
need to start the route by leaning in from the crack on the
right.

D.I.Y. 10m E3 6a ★★   (1981)
The centre of the left-hand section of the wall is climbed via a

vague shallow groove. This has a tough start leading to insecure climbing. An ingenious crux move is required to pass the one good flake hold at mid-height.

Black and Decker   9m   E2 6b   ★   (1985)
The left-hand side of the wall is climbed with great difficulty to reach a sloping ledge. Step left and finish up the easy arête.

Leave Heather Alone   10m   HS 5a   (1976-80)
Climb the short finger-crack on the left-hand side of the face past a useful heather clump. Continue up the easy arête above.

Bell Heather   10m   VS 5a   (1997)
Climb the open groove on the left-hand side of the wall and the square yellow arête above to an awkward final move; poor.

Hairless Art   20m   E1 5c   ★   (1987)
The wall can be traversed at half-height in either direction, to give an admirable excursion.

Five metres to the left and at a slightly lower level is a short face with a shallow ramp running rightwards up it. This provides three problems: **The Amazing Harry Greystoke II** HVS 5b ★ (1986) up the centre of the face using a prominent pocket, **Edgar Rice Burroughs** S (2001), the arête to the right and **Feeding the Pony** S 4a (1994), the left-hand arête of the wall.

The next routes are located on a slabby wall which has a shallow diagonal crease, rising from right-to-left. This is taken by Setsquare. The previous guide listed a route, **Preston's Wall** HVS 5b (1986) that was situated 'up the centre of the buttress 12 metres right of Setsquare'. As there is no buttress of anything like this height to the right it is possible that this may have been a slightly more direct version of Protractor.

Setsquare   8m   S 4a   ★   (1959)
Start on the right-hand side of the slab and tiptoe halfway along the leftward-slanting crease. Go straight up the wall on sharp edges and pockets to a mantelshelf right of the capping block. Exit to the left for an exposed finish.

Protractor   8m   HVS 5b   ★   (1976)
Balance up the shallow scoop to the upper end of the diagonal crease. Move up to the overlap, go left and surmount its left-hand edge to finish on a broad ledge.

Sharpener 8m HVS 5a   (1992)
Start three metres right of the left-hand arête. Climb directly,
passing a heathery break, to reach a large platform by a final
awkward move. The face on which Kitcat lies is directly above
and forms a logical extension.

Kitcat 6m HVS 5a   (1976-82)
The centre of the square, tilted wall above and left of the last
three routes is climbed centrally passing a pocket or two.

Have a Break 7m E3 6a   (1988)
The leaning arête left of Kitcat is technical and serious despite
its diminutive size.

DESCENT ROUTE
To the left is an easy break that offers a way down.

Down and to the left is a buttress characterised by a central crack
with a holly tree growing on a ledge immediately to its left. The
wall to the right of the crack has been mistakenly climbed as an
undergraded Kitcat since 1989. Consulting the previous edition
of the guide revealed the true whereabouts of this elusive route.
This face is actually tackled by:

The Anomalous Snail 9m HVS 5c ★   (1984)
A hard start on sloping holds leads to easier climbing up
horizontal breaks.

Have a Nice Day 9m VS 5a ★   (1991)
The right-hand arête of the wide, central, corner-crack is
followed throughout; pleasant.

Canton 9m D   (1961-63)
The aforementioned crack leads to the holly ledge and the
continuation finishing corner.

The next climbs are located up and left, where a low wall runs
leftwards to eventually form a tall rectangular buttress with a
conspicuous cave below its centre. All of this is:

COUNT'S BUTTRESS AREA

On the right-hand edge of this section of rock is a small, square
tower with an obvious horizontal break cutting across it at half-
height.

Amoeba on the Edge of Time 6m VS 5b (1984)
A pleasant micro-route following the right-hand arête of the tower.

Bon Ami 6m VS 5a ★ (1981)
Take the central, open groove then follow flakes up the left-hand side of the front face of the small tower. The more direct version up the centre of the tower is 5c.

To the left is a corner with a suitcase-shaped pedestal of rock standing in it. Left again is a slabby wall with a blunt central arête where a diagonal crack and an overlap form a large 'V'. A short flake crack descends from this 'V'.

The Stretcher 9m VS 4c (1973/1996)
Start one metre to the right of the flake crack in the centre of the buttress. Climb delicately up and right to enter the base of the right-trending overlap/groove. Follow this rightwards and make a tough pull over its fading right-hand end.

Flaked Traverse 10m S (1961-63)
Start in the centre of the buttress and climb the flake to the overlap. Traverse delicately rightwards to finish up a thin crack in the blunt arête on the far right-hand side of the buttress.

The Trickledown Fairy 10m E5 6b ★ (1988)
The hanging slab above the initial crack of Flaked Traverse looks innocuous enough, though in reality its upper slab requires a slick approach and the 'bottle' to run it out.

Flaked Crack 10m HS 4b (1961-63)
The left-slanting crack just to the left of the arête is reached via the central flake and is marginally easier than it looks. If the short diversion on to the ledge on the left is avoided it is VS 4c.

DESCENT ROUTE
To the left is a corner that offers an awkward way down.

Left again, and beyond the descent route, is a steep slab that is often well-chalked, at least in its lower section.

Shock Horror Slab 9m E2 6b ★★ (1980)
Scratch and smear desperately up pebbles and slopers below and right of a slight rib on the right-hand side of the bulging wall to reach a delicate finish. Stepping in from the boulder on the right is not allowed.

Shirley's Shining Temple   9m   E5 6c   ★★★   (1984)
An excellent and tenuous route taking the blank slab to the left.
Start at a small overlap in the centre and get established on the
slab with difficulty. More hard moves up and slightly left allow a
direct ascent of the final section of the slab. A committing and
technically superb route high in the grade.

Prickly Crack   9m   VD   (1961-63)
The twin cracks in the shallow corner to the left are followed
pleasantly to a hollybush and unpleasantly thereafter.

To the left is another steep slab, crossed at both one-third and
two-thirds height by heathery breaks.

Lino   12m   VS 5a   (1959)
Start just left of the right-hand arete of the face. Go up to a
block and move left to a vegetated ledge. Finish directly or
traverse leftwards to finish up Scraped Crack.

Mop Up   9m   E1 5c   ★   (1994)
Climb thinly up the centre of the slab passing through a gap in
the vegetation early on and finishing over the centre of the
capping bulge with care.

Basil Brush   9m   HVS 5b   ★   (1984)
Climb straight up the steep precarious slab just right of the
corner with sketchy moves to reach the ledge system. Finish
easily over the overhang at the top.

Scraped Crack   8m   D   (1912-14)
The somewhat scruffy right-angled corner just to the left.

Dracula   9m   HVS 5b   ★   (1967)
The prominent sharp arête to the left is approached via a tough
initial bulge and climbed on its left-hand side by well-protected
laybacking.

Anxiety Attack 2   9m   E2 6a   (1984)
A direct ascent of the narrow slab between the arête and the
corner has a hard start to reach the first ledge. Highly technical
climbing leads to the break and easier final moves.

B Crack   9m   S 4a   ★★   (1912-14)
The smooth, right-angled corner bounding the right-hand side
of the main bulk of Count's Buttress provides a sustained
route.

To the left of the deep angle is the protruding square bulk of:

COUNT'S BUTTRESS

Count's Crack 12m VS 4c ★★   (1932-33)
In the right-hand side wall of the main buttress is a steep,
straight crack. This is usually approached from the right by a
short traverse from the corner via a horizontal break and once
entered provides classic jamming, leading to a steep juggy finish.
The steep left-hand crack at a higher level gives **Count's**

1. Shock Horror Slab	E2
2. Shirley's Shining Temple	E5
3. Lino	VS
4. Mop Up	E1
5. Basil Brush	HVS
6. Dracula	HVS
7. Anxiety Attack	E2
8. B Crack	S
9. The Count	E2

Crack Left-Hand Finish HVS 5a ★★ (1976-83) starting up the regular route. The base of the parent crack can also be reached directly by a fierce pull on fist jams aided by an *à cheval* up the hanging left-hand arête at HVS 5c.

The front face of the buttress is home to 11 closely packed routes. On first acquaintance these appear to be rather too close for real independence, but once embarked upon they all prove to be quite separate enough to ensure that there is no chance of straying on to another climb.

The short buttress situated under the right-hand side of the face

1. Dracula	HVS
2. Count's Buttress	E2
3. Abacus	E2
4. Counterblast	E3
5. Count's Wall	HVS
6. The Cool Curl	E6
7. Out For the Count	E4
8. Sleepwalker	E2
9. Daydreamer	E2
10. Nightmare Slab	E1

offers **Countdown** 5a (1960s), a pleasant problem up the centre of the buttress to reach the main ledge below the face.

The Count 14m E2 5c ★★   (1976)
A good route, with a worrying start, that follows the right-hand arête of the buttress throughout. Start from blocks under the right-hand side of the arête and climb to a suspect flake under the roof. Use this to reach the break over the lip. Make a fierce move up to reach a small ledge on the arête and climb this to horizontal jams below the bulge. Go over this to follow a short flake and the final arête.

222

Count's Buttress 16mm E2 5c ★★★ (1955)

The original route (probably) of the buttress provides the easiest way up it, following a devious but logical line. Start to the right of the edge of the cave and climb the unprotected, blunt arête on side-pulls to gain a ledge below the steep slab. Make an awkward traverse right to reach another small ledge on the arête. Stretch up delicately for the horizontal break above, before traversing back left to a short final crack. The route may also be finished by traversing rightwards from the horizontal break, round the arête to gain the crack of Count's Buttress, **Right-Hand Finish** E2 5c ★★ (1964-76). Although covering virtually no new ground this is a worthwhile outing, though with potential for rope drag.

223

Count Me Out   15m   E2 6a   ★   (1985)
Follow the original Count's Buttress to the ledge above the
initial overhang and ascend the slab just to the right, on a trio
of small pockets, with a very long reach to the centre of the
horizontal break. Finish straight up the steep wall above via a
good pocket.

Count's Buttress Direct   14m   E3 6a   ★   (1932-33, 1959)
Follow the original route to the first ledge then make a delicate
step up using a two-finger pocket for the right hand to reach a
higher ledge, before climbing with great difficulty straight up the
left edge of the green streak that issues from the final crack.
Finish much more easily up this.

Abacus   16m   E2 5c   ★★   (1976)
Climb the right-hand edge of the cave (one and a half metres
left of the original start) and gain the ledge above by a difficult
move on sloping holds. From the ledge step left and climb
straight up the poorly protected wall, directly above the right-
hand edge of the cave, using spaced holds and a pocket, to
reach a horizontal break. Continue in the same line to the top
with a long reach followed by easier climbing.

Counterblast   16m   E3 5c   ★   (1981)
Follow the previous route to the ledge then step left again to a
point directly above the centre of the cave. Climb the slab via a
pocket and a small vertical crease. Continue straight up the wall
above passing a small bulge en route via a long reach.

Count's Wall   17m   HVS 5b   ★★   (1959/1976)
The left-hand arête of the cave is climbed to reach ledges.
Above, follow the delicate thin crack until a reachy exit gives
access to the easier final wall.

Counterfeit   14m   E2 5b   ★   (1997)
The pleasant right-hand arête of the deep chimney is climbed
on its right-hand side throughout. The 'blank' section at half-
height provides the fun. Side runners in the previous route
reduce the grade to HVS.

Count's Chimney   14m   D   ★   (1890-1903)
The classic fissure splitting the left side of the cliff is of true
Puttrell character and a route that started the 'counting game'.

The narrower buttress to the left of the chimney contains three
routes.

Crescent Arête E1 5b (page 208)
Climber: Stefan Glowacz Photo: David Simmonite

Big Air   **E6 6b**   (page 209)
Climber: Martin Veale   Photo: Ian Smith

Shirley's Shining Temple   E5 6c   (page 219)
Climber: John Allen   Photo: Paul Williams

Titanic VS 4c (page 246)
Climber: Victoria Hulme Photo: Ian Smith

Touched 14m HVS 5c (1981)
Climb the right arête of the lower wall to the first ledge.
Continue up the steep left-hand arête of Count's Chimney to
reach easier climbing; a poor route.

The Cool Curl 15m E6 6b ★★ (1984/1987)
The best and hardest of the trio. Ascend the lower buttress just
left of its right edge to the first ledge. Step up and left to make
a precarious pull and crucial high step to get established on the
central slab. Above this things ease dramatically.

Out for the Count 13m E4 6a ★ (1977)
The left-hand arête of the buttress is worthwhile and has a
potential deck-out move just below the midway bulge. Start
from the ledge beneath Nightride Corner and climb the lower
arête on its left side until it is possible to pull around to the
right. With runners on the right, go over the difficult overhang
and head up the final arête.

Nightride Corner 6m VD (1912-1914)
The short corner-crack on the left.

To the left is a steep, rectangular slab, or easy-angled wall,
depending on your view. It is home to a series of routes to delight
technicians and frustrate thugs. A drop below the ledge that runs
across the base of the routes means that they are best treated as
short routes, rather than just boulder problems; don't jump off
without a 'spotter'.

NIGHTMARE SLAB

Sleepwalker 8m E2 6a ★ (1977)
Two metres left of the corner climb the steep slab passing a
couple of tiny overlaps early on.

Nightrider 9m E3 6b (1980)
An eliminate, up the green streak and line of pebbles just right
of the line of Daydreamer. Nicely sustained and not to be used
as a left-hand start to Sleepwalker.

Daydreamer 9m E2 6b ★★ (1960)
Start in the centre of the slab at well-buffed footholds and a
short vertical flake. Make intricate crux moves near to the limit
of adhesion to gain an obvious but sloping ledge, then continue
direct; very frustrating.

Dream Boat   9m   E3 6b   (1986)
The technical, sustained slab midway between the polished start
of Daydreamer and the left-hand edge of the slab.

Nightmare Slab   9m   E1 5c   ★   (1959)
Gain and follow the left-hand edge of the slab to a precarious
and unprotected high step to reach a good horizontal break.
Pass the bulge above by a long reach followed by either a stride
out right to reach a ledge above the difficult section of
Daydreamer and finish easily or, slightly harder, continue
directly. The slab can be traversed in either direction,
Insomniac E1 5c (1986). Simply keep repeating the moves until
you finally drop off.

Eden Arête   6m   S 4a   (1961-63)
Ascend the sharp left-hand arête of the open, flared chimney
bounding the left edge of the slab.

DESCENT ROUTE
There are a variety of easy ways down to the left of the cliff.

Fifty metres to the left beyond a section of grassy slabs is a short
tower set atop a slabby arête. This is taken by:

Conundrum   7m   E4 6a   (1997)
Climb the lower slab to a ledge and finish enigmatically up the
short arête. The top edge is gained by a dynamic move.

To the left of the Count's Buttress Area is one of the main breaks
in the Edge which is used by 'the Long Causeway', an old roadway
that links the Hope Valley with western Sheffield. Although
sometimes called 'the Roman Road' it does not date from that
period but is a more recent construction. From the parking area
near the right-angled bend by the cattle-grid at Dennis Knoll (SK
227 844), the Causeway gives the most convenient access to all
of the rock between Count's Buttress and Crow Chin. With the
exception of the ever popular High Neb region the whole of this
area rarely sees much in the way of 'traffic' (apart from thoughtless
drivers of four-wheel-drive urban assault vehicles) and is well
worth a visit if you want to 'get away from it all'.

Above the Causeway, at the right-hand edge of this section, there
is a series of short slabs and walls that are home to pleasant,
though often green, boulder problems. To the left of these is a
short undercut arête.

Beaky 7m   VS 5a   (1992)
Climb a corner on the right until it is possible to step left on to
a large hold on the arête which is followed to the top. The large
hold can be reached direct at 6a.

Six metres to the left is a buttress with a slabby left-hand side
and a steep right-hand face, not unlike a smaller version of
Centurion's Slab, which lies 20 metres farther left again.

Mini Motor Mile 7m   VS 4b   (1992)
Go up a groove on the right-hand side of the buttress to a
hand-traverse horizontally left across the side wall using a
break to the front face. Finish up the left-hand side of the
slabby arête.

Motor Mile 7m   HVS 5c   (1981)
The right-hand arête of the front face is gained by a taxing
series of moves.

Trench Deadlock 7m   HVS 4c   (1981)
The slabby front face of the buttress is poorly protected.

Twenty metres left is a larger and rather more impressive slab,
again with a steep right-hand wall.

Jude 8m   VS 4c   (1992)
An obscure route up the right-hand edge of the wall above the
start of the next climb to join it just below the top.

Duchess 10m   HVS 5b   (1981)
Gain and climb the right-hand edge of the slabby face of the
buttress via a difficult swing from the deep corner on the right-
hand side of the buttress.

Limitsville 8m   E3 5c   (1994)
The centre of the steep, well-brushed, right-hand wall of the
buttress is climbed direct above a small, ancient, carved cross.
The difficulties ease and the protection improves as height is
gained.

Centurion's Dexter 10m   HVD   (traditional)
Pull round the left-hand side of the overhang on to the front
face of the buttress and continue to the top.

Centurion's Slab 10m   D   ★   (traditional)
The route-march straight up the centre of the slab is pleasant.

1. Small Reward	HVS
2. Small Change	VD
3. Impostor	S

Left again are two short, projecting buttresses which have been ignored in the past because of their diminutive size. They are home to:

Small Reward 6m HVS 5a   (1997)
The right-hand arête of the right-hand buttress is the best of the trio.

7. Time and Tide	HVS
8. Waiting For M.I.B.	E2
9. Meninblack II	E2

Small Change 6m VD (1997)
The wall to the left is climbed passing a pocket and an overlap.

Impostor 8m S (1997)
Four metres left again is the second buttress. Climb a scrappy
lower section to a tricky step left and continue up the slab above.

To the left is an area of broken ground followed by three buttresses
separated by two recessed slabs, all set above a steep grassy slope.
To aid identification, the right-hand buttress has a diagonal right-to-
left overlap forming its left edge.

The Big C 7m VS 5a (1992)
Start up the narrow pillar below the centre of the buttress and
make an awkward step left on to the upper slab. Follow this more
easily to the top. **The Big C Left-Hand** VS 5a (1997) follows the
regular line until established above the overlap. Trend left pulling
around the left-hand side of the nose and on over a second
overlap to finish.

Set below the main line of buttresses is a short two-tiered slab taken
by **Interlude** VS 5b(1997) which climbs over the undercut and up
the split slab.

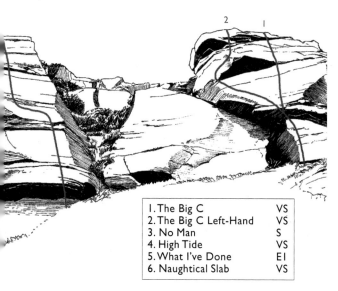

1. The Big C	VS
2. The Big C Left-Hand	VS
3. No Man	S
4. High Tide	VS
5. What I've Done	E1
6. Naughtical Slab	VS

Above and left again is a short slab bounded on its left by a grassy gully. This is followed by a projecting buttress which is undercut across its base by a long, narrow overhang.

No Man 8m S 4b ★ (1992)
Start up the right-hand arête of the buttress then, where the angle drops back, step left and continue up the delicate scoop in the centre.

High Tide 7m VS 5a (1992)
Starting from the left, step on to the left-hand arête of the buttress and follow it without deviation.

Just left is a steep recessed slab that has two short problems. **What I've Done** E1 5b (1993) climbs straight up the centre of the small slab via sketchy moves. **Naughtical Slab** VS 4c (1992) starts as for the previous problem but trends left to climb the pleasant left-hand arête of the slab.

The steeper left-hand buttress of the trio has three climbs, all of which are steep and not too well-protected.

Time and Tide 6m HVS 5b ★ (1983)
The right arête is gained over a couple of bulges and is best climbed quickly.

Waiting for M.I.B. 8m E2 5b ★ (1981)
Starts at a small overlap in the centre of the buttress to reach ledges with a strenuous pull. The remainder of the route trends slightly leftwards, is precarious, unprotected and has distant finishing holds.

Meninblack II 7m E2 5b ★ (1981)
A poorly-protected route up the leaning left-hand arête of the block. Start from the ledge on the left and climb the front face to ledges and an indifferent runner placement. Step left to a delicate final move. The short overhanging crack in the side-wall is **For Ever and Ever** VS 5a (1984).

Thirty five metres left is a short buttress with a central undercut 'nose' which projects from the hillside.

Whacky Attack 6m VS 4c (1997)
Start on the right-hand side of the central arête and follow it throughout.

1. Whacky Attack	VS
2. Black Attack	E3

Black Attack 7m E3 6a (1990)
Climb the left-hand side of the buttress starting at a blind
groove and passing small overlaps to the top.

The next feature along the edge is the once fenced-off rocks of
the Enclosure Buttress. This is 75 metres left of Black Attack and
has a large, impressive, overhang marking the upper right-hand
edge of the area. Another identifying feature is a very healthy
holly tree growing at the base of the centre of the cliff. The right-
hand arête of the buttress used to be formed by the 12-ton block
that now resides on the Causeway directly below the cliff.
Fortunately, there was no route up the arête, as the block was
very precariously perched on a sloping shelf. On its way downward
the block flattened most of the iron fencing that originally gave
the area its name.

ENCLOSURE BUTTRESS

Block Buster 10m VS 4c (1997)
Start at the toe of the buttress and climb slabby rock to a ledge
where the aforementioned block used to reside. Continue up
the arête on its right-hand side to ledges. Climb to the
capstone and step left to finish.

Turnover 9m S (1959)
Climb the grassy corner below the left-hand edge of the roof

231

1. Turnover	S	7. Slanting Chimney	HVD
2. Block Buster	VS	8. Four Winds; Eight Directions	E4
3. Europa	E4	9. Haze	HVS
4. Letter-box	VD	10. The Graduate	E1
5. Arsenic Poisoning	HVS	11. Centrepiece	VS
6. Keith's Crack	HS		

to a traverse below the overhangs. Step right round the arête
to finish up the side wall using good but suspect flakes.

Europa 8m E4 5c (1978)
Begin as for Turnover and take the overhang at its centre,
starting with a swift swing on a creaking, pointed flake. The real
difficulties now begin. The final reach up and right is the crux
and proves to be both strenuous and poorly protected.

Letter-box 6m VD (1959)
Climb the corner to below the roof of Turnover to reach a slot
in its left-hand side and make awkward moves leftwards across
the wall before finishing up a short continuation crack.

To the left a triangular overhang cuts across the right-hand side
of the next buttress at half-height.

Head Over Heels 8m E3 6a (1985)
Climb the lower slabby wall and then the difficult roof to the
left of the undercut arête. The name gives an indication of the
problem associated with getting all of your body over the lip of
the overhang.

232

Arsenic Poisoning   8m   HVS 5b   (1981)
Haul over the centre of the roof using suspect flakes to reach
easier slabs and a short easy flake-crack, up which the route
finishes.

Keith's Crack   9m   HS 4b   (1959)
The narrow left-hand side of the overhang is split by a thin
crack, which proves deceptively strenuous.

To the left is a grass-filled gully then a large buttress with double
overhangs on its right-hand arête. On the rightwards-facing wall
of this is a widening crack-line that rises to the right.

Slanting Chimney   11m   HVD   ★   (1959)
From the grassy gully climb the wall and cracks to enter a
shallow continuation chimney. Finish awkwardly on sloping
holds; satisfyingly steep.

Zit   12m   VS 5a   (1988)
Start up a slanting crack in the side wall of the buttress
(effectively a direct start to Slanting Chimney) then go
leftwards almost to the arête. Move back right to finish directly
up the wall.

Four Winds; Eight Directions   15m   E4 6a   ★★   (1981)
A worthwhile route attacking the overhangs in the nose of the
buttress. Climb the right-hand edge of the buttress, trending
leftwards over the initial overhang to reach a prominent flake
below and left of the nose. Stretch leftwards for the break
before swinging back right and breezing up the right-hand arête.
A long reach pays dividends.

Haze   13m   HVS 4c   (1981)
Start to the right of a holly and ascend directly to the slanting
crack in the centre of this section of the face. Continue, with
care, straight up on sloping holds and an occasional brittle flake.

Countess Buttress   14m   VS 4b   ★★   (1960)
Start to the left of the holly at a short crack and climb
diagonally rightwards behind the holly to reach the slanting
crack in the centre of face. Step up and traverse right to finish
airily up the pleasantly positioned right-hand arête.

The Graduate   13m   E1 5c   ★   (1977)
Start as for the previous route but climb straight up to an
overlap. Make a precarious high step up into a shallow scoop
above to reach a slot. Finish directly over two small bulges.

1. Countess Buttress	VS	5. Central Buttress	VS
2. Haze	HVS	6. Direct Start	
3. The Graduate	E1	7. Mantelpiece	VS
4. Centrepiece	VS	8. Bolt Buttress	VS

To the left again the face is split by an easy blocky gully and to the left of this is Central Buttress. The next route starts up the left-hand wall of the gully.

Centrepiece   15m   VS 4c   (1981)
Step up leftwards from the gully to gain the right-hand edge of the buttress, then follow its left-hand side to the top.

Central Buttress   18m   VS 4c   ★★   (1959)
A good and varied climb. From the chimney on the left, traverse right just above the overhang to midway across the buttress. Climb a steep wall by a strenuous move up and leftwards to finish up the centre of the contrasting top slab. The **Direct Start** 6b ★ (1981) is a superbly athletic problem going over the initial roof to the right. The obvious flake on the lip is gained direct and progressing from it is desperate.

Central Chimney   16m   M   (1959)
Amble up a grassy cleft that splits the buttress. Passing the closure at the top proves to be awkward.

Mantelpiece   12m   VS 4c   (1972)
Starting on its left, climb the stepped buttress by three mantelshelves of increasing difficulty. A little disjointed.

Enclosure Crack   12m   D   ★★   (1959)
Just to the left, climb a steepening corner before turning the
final roof on the right.

Warm September   10m   VS 4c   (1992)
From a boulder three metres to the left of Enclosure Crack,
climb the slab directly, tackling its final section by its left-hand
edge.

To the left is a short buttress with possibly the only bolt in the
whole of Stanage, but don't burst a blood vessel as it was placed
years ago by the landowner to hold up his fence.

Bolt Buttress   6m   VS 4c   (1992)
Climb the blunt arête above the 'thing' (no use as a runner)
before moving left to climb the final wall. **Spring Plum** E1 5c
(1997) starts as for Bolt Buttress but trends left to climb the
awkward, undercut arête.

To the left is a very substantial stone wall which delineates the
northern edge of Enclosure Buttress. Just beyond this is a small
buttress of quality rock and this is home to three short problems.
Cock o' the Rock 6c (1990s) is the highly technical, blunt arête
above the wall. **Historical Arête** 5c (1980s) starts on the right
and slants leftward to finish up the arête. Finally, **Historical Crack**
5a (1980s) takes the crack to the left of the centre of the buttress.

One hundred metres to the left is a long easy-angled slab which
offers:

Heather Slab   20m   VD   (1923-51)
The slab is broken into three steps, the top one of which is
vertical and awkward. Becoming overgrown.

Three routes have been climbed either side of Heather Slab:

Cinerea   10m   HVD   (2001)
Ascend the slight rib bounding the right-hand side of the slab
and mainly on the right arête.

Tetralix   8m   D   (2001)
In the gully to the right of Heather Slab is a problem arête.
Climb this and the wall in the slot above.

Vulgaris   10m   HVD 4a   (2001)
Climb the rib just left of Heather Slab following the clean rock.

1. Prowler	HVS	4. Blow Out	HVS
2. Full Blown Finish	E2	5. Blown Away	E2
3. Blown Drie	E1		

Twenty metres further left the rocks become more continuous again. There are a couple of smaller buttresses high on the right and then a piece of rock taking the form of a tall buttress split by vertical cracks. This is the:

BROKEN BUTTRESS AREA

Prowler 5m HVS 5a   (1981)
On the right-hand edge of the area, and set at a higher level, is a short buttress with a prominent prow. This squat route requires a strenuous pull up the flakes on the overhanging right-hand face of the buttress.

To the left and at the same level is a short, square slab set above a tree and this is home to a tiny pitch that can be used as an extension to the three longer routes that start down and to the left.

Full Blown Finish 4m E2 5b   (1995)
Start on the left and step down and right to reach a small ledge at the foot of the slab. Balance warily up this; exposed.

Down and left (and immediately left of the tree) is a barrel-shaped buttress split at two-thirds height by a horizontal break that forms a small roof on the left-hand side; there are four routes.

Blown Drie 12m E1 5c   (1997)
Start to the right of the toe of the buttress and climb its right-hand side via a short flake until it is possible to move delicately up and right. Finish via a precarious mantelshelf.

236

Blow Out 15m HVS 5b   (1983)
Start at the centre of the rounded buttress and climb it
trending slightly rightwards. The start requires technical ability,
a very long reach, or a jump.

Blown Away 15m E2 5c   (1997)
Start at the lowest point of the buttress and climb directly up
the centre of the left-hand wall passing left of a prominent
nose.

Jenny Wren 8m VD   (1997)
Start at a cutaway to the left and follow the easiest line up the
bottom wall and finish up the slabby top wall as for Blown
Away.

Twelve metres to the left is the main section of Broken Buttress,
characterised by many vertical cracks and a rowan tree growing
in front of its left-hand side. The first route here follows the
rightmost crack system which starts off as a right-facing corner.

Broken Groove 14m S 4a ★   (1961-63)
From grassy ledges, jam the initial short corner-crack. Continue
up a groove and crack system above.

Broken In 15m HS 4b   (1992)
Climb the heathery V-shaped groove to the left of the previous
climb until it is possible to gain a ledge on the left. Finish
directly up the centre of the wall above.

1. Blow Out	HVS	4. Pertinacious	E2
2. Blown Away	E2	5. Persuader	VS
3. Broken In	HS	6. Dissuader	HS

Broken Buttress 18m VD ★★ (1923-51)
Start immediately to the right of the rowan tree and climb an
awkward wide crack. Follow its blocky continuation on good
holds to below the final steepening which gives a well-
protected and pleasant finale.

Pertinacious 18m E2 5b ★ (1964-76)
The blunt arête immediately left of the tree is climbed directly.
The precarious lower half is unprotected though the crux,
which involves attaining a standing position on the sloping ledge
near the top; does have (low) runners.

Burgess Crack 18m D (1923-51)
Just left of the tree is a deep chimney containing three big
chockstones. Climb over the first one, then thread a way behind
the two larger ones, to emerge in a block-filled funnel;
scrambling remains. Alternatively, **Outside Exit** HS 4b (1998)
passes the second and third chockstones on the outside.

Persuader 16m VS 4c (1972)
Climb the face to the left of the cleft, initially following shallow
cracks, to reach an overlap. Unfortunately it is difficult to avoid
using the block in the chimney both for protection and as a
foothold when passing the overlap. Finish just to the right of a
large, insecure-looking block. Quite tough for the grade.

Darthuader 16m E1 6a (1997)
A technical eliminate up the wall just just to the left again,
featuring good moves and an easy escape if required.

Dissuader 15m HS 4b (1992)
Climb a green corner-crack on the left-hand side of the
buttress to a ledge, then finish up a continuation crack above.

Broken Arête 12m VS 5a (1997)
The projecting arête at the left-hand edge of the wall leads to a
heathery ledge. Above this, finish up the wall, passing another
heathery ledge en route to the top; poor.

Twenty five metres to the left, across a heathery gully, is a pair of
short, projecting buttresses.

Meaty Bugs 7m HS 4b (1997)
Bridge up a blocky cleft on the right-hand side of the buttress
to an awkward landing on a ledge. Continue up a crack in the
side wall of the buttress.

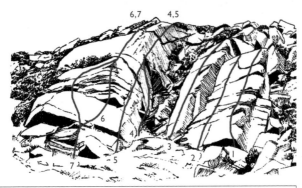

1. Creepy Crawly	HS	5. Cracked Wall Direct	HVS
2. Crawly	VD	6. Dope Test	E3
3. Creepy	S	7. Wall and Slab	HS
4. Cracked Wall	HS		

Creepy Crawly 8m HS 4b (1984)
Follow the right-hand arête of the right-hand buttress with
either a difficult undercut start (height dependant 5b) or more
normally step in from the right, when a delicate move at half
height provides the crux.

Crawly 8m VD ★ (1961-63)
Ledgy holds lead up the centre of the face to a short leftwards
curving crack.

Cringe 8m VS 4c (1979)
Ascend the left-hand edge of the right-hand slab with one
tricky move just below its top.

Creepy 12m S 4a ★ (1962)
The narrow, recessed slab to the left is climbed pleasantly,
though with little protection, to a finish by its right-hand edge.

Cracked Wall 11m HS 4c (1961-63)
Start in a gully between the two buttresses. Awkwardly gain and
follow a steep leaning Y-shaped crack to a finish up the arête. A
direct start, HVS 5a (1976-83), may be made up the thin cracks
just to the right of the arête followed by an extended reach to
join the normal route.

Dope Test 10m E3 6a (1990)
The undercut arête of the buttress has a taxing, central section
and a rounded exit.

Wall and Slab 12m HS 5a (1964-76)
Start under the nose of the buttress and attain a ledge up and to
the left by a long reach, alternatively sneak on from the block on
the left. Pull awkwardly over an overlap to gain an easier slab
above and climb this trending rightwards then leftwards; was VDiff.

To the left the edge breaks down into a series of small buttresses
and isolated blocks. In the past these have been ignored because of
their diminutive size. Closer inspection revealed a pleasant collection
of short climbs that are worth a visit if you want to escape the
crowds and experience the cliff as it used to be. The first buttress of
note has an overhang running across it at two-thirds height and a
sturdy oak tree growing against its left edge.

Squat 7m VS 5a (1997)
Climb the right-hand arête of the buttress to ledges and pull
through the bulges with difficulty using a black flake.

Teeter 7m S 4b (1997)
Ascend the left-hand arête of the buttress to gain a good ledge by
delicate moves. Step right to finish.

Up and to the left is a thin crack, **Grunt** VS 5a (1997), with a wider
central section, set in a steep wall.

To the left an attractive arête emerges from between two very healthy
holly bushes.

Fun in the Sun 8m VS 4c ★ (1997)
Use a large fallen block to gain a projecting ledge on the right,
crux. Step left and follow the pleasantly delicate left-hand side of
the arête throughout. Up the slope to the left of the holly is a
short white slab, **Short and Sweet** S 4a (1997).

Across the gully to the left is another projecting buttress.

Deal 6m HVS 5c (1997)
Layback up a short flake in the nose to start, then continue
straight up a wall via nice moves to finish up a vague groove.

Shuffle 6m S 4a (1997)
Layback up the short flake in the nose, as for Deal, but shuffle
around to the left to gain the front face. Continue up an arête.

Down and to the left is the tallest of the buttresses, consisting of a flat wall with a large holly tree growing in the corner on the right.

Reach for the Sky 8m HVS 5b ★   (1997)
Start from a block and climb the delicate, unprotected lower wall to reach parallel, thin cracks which lead to an upper arête.

Heather Heaven 8m HS 4c   (1997)
Climb a wide, awkward, heathery crack on the left to reach a heather ledge and finish up a thin seam in the upper slab. A route that improves with height.

To the left are shorter buttresses, the best of which features a conspicuous, perched flake with a wide crack on its right-hand side.

Flaked Out 6m HD   (1997)
Climb on to the heathery ledge cutting across the bottom of the face, then step right and follow the flake-crack to the top.

Hold Your Breath 6m S 4b   (1997)
Gain the heathery ledge and continue up the centre of the front face of the detached flake to the midway ledge. Make a delicate step up and climb the right-hand arête.

Thirty metres to the left is a wall with a quarried look about it, riven vertically by three thin cracks.

| 1. Self-Propelled | VS | 3. Genesis | HVS |
| 2. Magazine | VS | 4. Petazutte | VS |

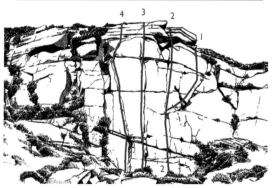

1. Grain of Truth	E4	4. Parallel Cracks	VS
2. Anniversary Arête	E1	5. 49th Parallel	HS
3. Beast of Endcliffe	E2		

Self-Propelled 8m VS 5a (1994)
Start up the right-hand crack in the wall and where it splits make a tricky move rightwards to follow the heathery right-hand branch until it is possible to climb directly to the top.

Magazine 7m VS 4c ★ (1979)
Follow the thin right-hand cracks to a finish at a notch.

Genesis 8m HVS 5a ★ (1959)
Use small, spaced holds to climb the centre of the cracked wall.

Petazautte 7m VS 5a (1994)
The left-hand crack is followed until it is possible to a step right into a groove to reach a slabby finish.

Fifteen metres to the left, across a grassy gully backed by a short rock wall is a projecting buttress that is home to Anniversary Arête. The first route described gains (or attempts to gain) a shallow hanging corner in the right-hand side of the face. There is a rumour, but no solid information, of an unnamed 6a up the wall to the right.

Grain of Truth 8m E4 6b ★★ (1981)
The base of the hanging groove is easy to reach though its main section is almost impossible to enter.

Anniversary Arête 11m E1 5b ★★ (1959)
Fine climbing directly up the blunt arête to the left leads to
thought-provoking moves to gain entry to a scoop near the top. A
solitary gem.

Beast of Endcliffe 9m E2 6a ★ (1997)
Climb a short crack to the left, then continue directly up the wall
making a long reach to a poor break. Climb the upper wall on
small holds and a mono-doigt, with good runners to the right.

Parallel Cracks 9m VS 4b ★ (1959)
To the left are twin cracks. Climb these starting up the left-hand
crack.

49th Parallel 9m HS 4c (1972)
From the foot of the twin cracks make awkward (or hard) moves
up and leftwards to reach the right-hand edge of a heathery ledge.
Continue up the thin crack.

Sixty five metres to the left, a buttress projects from the sea of
heather. It has a prominent central arête with an angular corner and
a lesser arête to its right.

Right 8m HS 4b (1985)
The arête right of the central corner-crack is pleasant.

Corner Crack 8m VD (1989)
The corner-crack to the left of Right and right of Left.

1. Right	HS
2. Corner Crack	VD
3. Nice One	VD
4. The Wide Crack	D
5. Sinister	VS

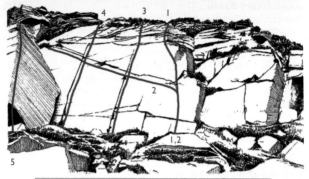

1. Scraps	VS
2. Scavenger	VS
3. Prairie Dog	HVS
4. Sneaking Sally Through the Alley	VS
5. Headbanger	E1

Left 10m VD ★ (1985)
The arête left of the central corner is the best route hereabouts.

Nice One 10m VD (1992)
The centre of the narrow slab to the left of the arête is escapable but nice enough.

The Wide Crack 10m D (traditional)
The central feature of the left-hand side of the buttress is obvious and must have been done 'years ago'.

Sinister 8m VS 4b (1992)
The centre of the left-hand side of the slab has a good finish.

Forty metres farther to the left is a broad series of quite complex buttresses, with perhaps the most prominent feature being a five-metre tall flake. To the right of this is a flat wall with a prominent diagonal crack rising across it from right to left.

Scraps 8m VS 5a (1985)
The right-hand arête of the wall is climbed starting up a water streak and finishing delicately.

Sneaking Sally Through the Alley 10m VS 4c ★ (1985)
Start as for Scraps and follow the leftward-rising break crossing Scavenger and finish up the left-bounding corner of the face.

Scavenger   8m   VS 4c   (1977)
The thin crack in the middle of the wall leads to a delicate
finish.

Prairie Dog   6m   HVS 5b   (1992)
The thin crack at the left-hand side of the face.

Headbanger   7m   E1 5c   ★   (1985)
Just to the left is a thin projecting flake/block. Difficult moves
over its undercut base enable its right-hand arête to be gained
and followed airily. Short but sharp.

To the left of the flake is a square-fronted buttress, with each
arête providing worthwhile climbs.

Blockhead Direct   8m   HVS 5b   ★   (1959)
Mantelshelf on to a ledge and climb the right-hand arête of the
block by a satisfying combination of layaways on the arete and
holds on the face.

Sinew Stretch   8m   HVS 5b   ★   (1978)
The left-hand arête has a technical start to reach a good hold
where easy ground is only a long heave away.

Angus   9m   S   (1959)
The undercut and narrowing chimney between the block and
the face.

1. Prairie Dog	HVS
2. Headbanger	E1
3. Blockhead Direct	HVS
4. Sinew Stretch	HVS
5. Mr Universe	E3
6. Titanic	VS
7. Titanic Direct	HVS

Mr Universe   9m   E3 6a   (1979)
Climb the centre of the face to the left, starting up a faint rib, to
reach a thin, horizontal break. Sketchy moves lead to better holds.

Miss World   9m   HS 4b   (1985)
The blunt left-hand arête of the face leads to heathery ledges.

Ten metres to the left is another projecting buttress with an
obvious set of overhangs above its right edge. This is:

TITANIC BUTTRESS

Titanic Direct   12m   HVS 5a   ★   (1967/1979)
Ascend the delicate right-hand edge of a slab to gain a slanting
crack on the left. Finish straight over the spectacular neb.

Gypsy Moth   12m   E1 5b   ★   (1997)
Tackle the centre of the smooth slab to the left of the arête
using a pocket. Cross the diagonal crack of Titanic Direct and
climb leftwards across a bulging wall to finish at the top of QE2.

Titanic   14m   VS 4c   ★★   (1958)
A worthwhile route which takes the curving central groove to a
position just below the overhang. Move rightwards to the arête
and climb the right-hand wall followed by the rightward-slanting
crack.

Q.E.2   12m   VS 5a   ★   (1972)
Enter the right-angled groove from the arête on the left-hand
side of the face. Leave it by tricky moves to finish steeply above,
taking care with loose rock.

Lusitania   12m   S   (1958)
The rather gloomy angular corner to the left leads to a short
bulging crack. At the top of this a somewhat friable finish is
climbed trending out to the right. The direct finish is HS 4a
(1964-76) and climbs direct over the bulges on shelving holds,
not all of which are completely solid.

Marie Celeste   15m   E1 5b   (1984)
Climb a slabby wall in the centre of the bay to the left. Passing
the blank section at half-height provides the crux. Finish over
the bulges above.

Gnat's Slab Arête   12m   HS 4c   (1983-89)
A direct ascent of the arête to the left has a couple of sketchy
moves to reach a heathery ledge, above which things ease.

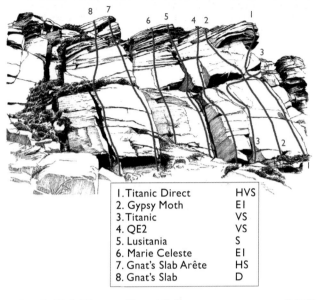

1. Titanic Direct	HVS
2. Gypsy Moth	E1
3. Titanic	VS
4. QE2	VS
5. Lusitania	S
6. Marie Celeste	E1
7. Gnat's Slab Arête	HS
8. Gnat's Slab	D

Gnat's Slab Direct 12m HS 4b (1989)
The centre of the slab is followed throughout.

Gnat's Slab 12m D (1959)
The left-hand side of the slab is climbed by a bent crack to
reach ledges. Move right and continue up the edge.

Barmy Brian's Flake Crack 8m VS 5a (1996)
Up the slope to the left is an awkward flake-crack that leads to
an even more awkward entry to the final, wide section; finish
leftwards.

Thirty metres farther left is a short, clean buttress with a slabby
right-hand side.

Midge 12m D (1986)
Start at the nose and ascend the right-hand side of the slab to
reach vegetated ledges. A chimney-crack on the buttress above
provides the way out.

Clegg 8m HVD (1986)
Start by standing in a letter-box in the centre of the slab and

247

climb to a large hold. Move left and up to heathery ledges. Scramble off leftwards or finish as for the previous climb. May also be started directly at either 4c or 5c (1997), depending on one's height, by scratching a way up the steep left-hand side of the buttress to join the regular route after four metres.

Thirty metres to the left lurks one of Stanage's best kept secrets. The heather-covered slabs should delight any horticulturists who specialise in rock gardens. The 1964 Stanage guide listed three routes on this section of cliff but was relatively imprecise as to their exact whereabouts. Three 'new' lines have recently been claimed up the cleanest sections of rock though these may well coincide with the earlier offerings.

On the right-hand side of the area are two short problems on a clean four metre-high block. **Flecky Wall** HVS 5c (1997) takes the centre of the wall with a couple of technical moves and **Flecky Wall Arête** VS 5b (1997) is on the left-hand side of the wall and is climbed using the arête as required.

On the right-hand side of the main, heathery slab are two clean ribs, the right-hand of which passes the left-hand edge of a large overhang near the top of the cliff.

Serapis 8m M   (traditional/1997)
The clean, right-hand rib is followed pleasantly.

Osiris 10m VD   (traditional/1997)
The clean, left-hand rib is better still.

The three heather-filled cracks that are the main feature of the centre of the slab may have been the three original routes of the slab, but surely no-one was ever really that desperate.

Apis 10m S   (traditional/1997)
On the left-hand edge of the slab is a square rib leading to a clean tower at the top of the cliff. Follow this directly.

One hundred and fifty metres farther left and one hundred and twenty metres before the more blatant delights of High Neb is a solitary, undercut buttress.

White Hare 8m HVS 5c   (1997)
Climb the undercut base and continue up easier rock. The short rib may (or may not) be a red herring.

The High Neb Area is one of the jewels in the crown of Stanage Edge, a kind of Popular End for the connoisseur. It was one of the first areas to be developed by the pioneers of Stanage, Ivar Berg's ascent of High Neb Buttress being a milestone in British climbing, and it is not hard to see what attracted them. A controlled angularity of form and a very high quality of rock are combined with a stately setting, being both high up in comparison to its surroundings and with a wilder aspect than its northern counterpart, all mean that High Neb is a very special place to climb.

And the climbs hereabouts are equal to their settings. Apart from High Neb Buttress itself, Kelly's Overhang, Quietus, Old Friends and The Crypt Trip, amongst others, were all worthy challenges for their respective generations, in fact, most still are. The list of first ascensionists, Berg, Morley Wood, Joe Brown, John Allen and Ron Fawcett, shows the calibre of suitor that these lines attracted. Besides these routes, lots of high quality passages exist in the area, from the lower to middle grades, and for those after a high concentration of classic routes and who are tired of the crowds at the Popular End, then High Neb is the place to be.

This continuous line of jutting buttresses is delightfully situated close to the highest point of the edge and in a commanding position above the surrounding moorland. High Neb offers climbing of every type and difficulty and, compared to the more accessible sections of Stanage, is usually less crowded except for sunny summer weekends. The area is best approached from the parking area by the right-angled bend at Dennis Knoll (SK 227844). The Causeway is followed until one of two stiles on the left (the second is drier in wet weather) provides a way over the iron fence and an uphill ascent (taking 10 minutes or so) leads to the base of the rocks.

On the right-hand side of the face is a buttress capped by a large overhang at its top left-hand corner and to the right of this is a large, slumped buttress resting against the face. Scrambling around to the right of this gains the base of a short south-facing wall split by a deep, horizontal break two metres from the cliff top. Starting along this is one of Stanage's better known girdle traverses.

High Neb Girdle Traverse c110m HS 4b ★ (1915/1921)
A pleasant route with one very exposed and quite strenuous portion. The route is perhaps rather too close to the top of the cliff at times to be a real classic but it is still worth doing.

249

Belays can be taken at intervals and are generally obvious, though at busy times the route is probably best done solo. Start by traversing the large rounded break (crux) at the right-hand side of the cliff, to reach the arête before passing below the roof of Jeepers Creepers to reach the angular corner of Ami. Use the highest continuous break to cross the exposed south face of High Neb Buttress, then continue at a slightly lower level (hands on the large ledges) to reach the deep angle of Neb Corner. From the recess of 'The Lair' traverse the steep wall to the left until it is possible to drop down on to the large ledge of Norse Corner Climb. Continue left, beneath the roofs of Quietus and Kelly's Overhang to a finish up a couple of shallow creases in the wall to the left of the top section of Twisting Crack.

Teenage Lobotomy 9m E1 5b   (1981)
The centre of the wall just right of the wide crack of Cave Buttress Right-Hand start is climbed passing a good ledge and using rounded holds and wide breaks.

Caved In 12m VS 4c   (1996)
Start on top of the 'cave block' and climb the wall just right of the arête to reach a short crack, then continue up the steeper wall above to an awkward finish.

Cave Buttress 15m S ★ ~~5~~ ~~Nancy~~ _L Gareth_   (1914-23)
A devious but worthwhile route. Start just to the left of the cave formed by the fallen blocks and after a tricky undercut start, climb the buttress front passing large, perched flakes with care to a point directly below the large overhang. Move right around the corner and finish awkwardly up the juggy face directly above the zigzag crack taken by the variation start, **Cave Buttress Right-Hand** VD (1914-23). The original route is more devious but offers better climbing.

Jeepers Creepers 15m E1 5b ★   (1958)
Follow the previous route to the overhang and attack the crack that splits the right-hand edge of the roof. Cheats will bale out on to the right wall at the earliest opportunity at HVS while true masochists will jam on to the bitter end.

High and Wild 15m E3 5c ★ †   (1985)
Follow Cave Buttress to below the overhangs and tackle these centrally, initially by a monstrous reach and then by a 'jug fest'. A hold may have come off this recently making it much harder.

To the left is a wide recess that provides an easy scramble and, beyond this, is a small, square-fronted buttress, on which lies:

Typical Grit 10m HS (1914-23)
Climb the smooth narrow slab and continue up easier rock above; poorly protected. If the finger flake near the right-hand edge of the blankest part of the slab is avoided (the way it was described in antiquity), the grade increases to an insecure E1 5b. The chimney just to the right is **Grit in the Eyes** D (2001).

Little Slab 14m D (1992)
The rather grassy, recessed slab just to the left.

To the left is a slab that forms the right-hand side of the corner of Ami, the left-hand side of which is the smooth and impressive wall of Old Friends. The right-hand arête of the slab is:

Sneezy 12m HS 4c (1996)
Follow the arête throughout. Passing the nose is the only ticklish manoeuvre.

It's a Cracker 12m S 4b ★ (traditional)
Go up the centre of the slabby face with an awkward, but well-protected, move to get established in the thin crack. Finish in the same line up steeper but juggy rock.

Mantelshelf Climb 14m D ★ _L Gareth_ _S Nancy_ (1919-23)
Go up the slabby face one metre to the right of the corner by a line of obvious ledges. Finish up a shallow right-facing corner.

Ami 14m M (traditional)
The awkward slabby corner is slightly spoilt by easily avoidable loose blocks in the final open gully.

The jutting buttress to the left is one of the edge's most recognisable features, with a sheer, south-facing, right wall and a slabby, west-facing, frontage. This is:

HIGH NEB BUTTRESS

The Dalesman 22m HVS 5a ★ (1983)
Climb Ami until it is possible to hand-traverse leftwards along the prominent horizontal break to a finish up the left-hand side of the far arête.

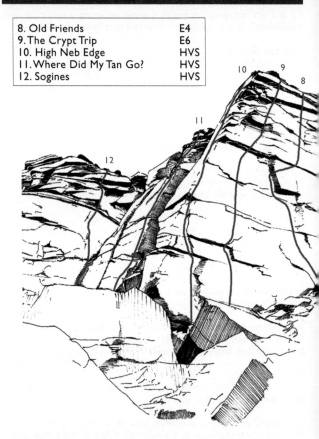

Old Friends 19m E4 6a ★★★ (1973)
'The east face seems to be impossible' 1951. One of Stanage's greatest classics, an audacious and still much sought after climb. From the bottom right-hand corner of the wall, make a tricky move left to gain finger holds in a tiny groove which lead up and left to the obvious central hanging groove. Ascend the groove with a harrowing, critical stretch to reach the horizontal break. Step back right and finish up the easier upper wall. Originally a 'tour de force', this remains an intimidating route with scant protection.

252

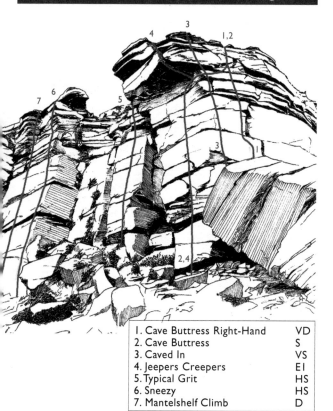

1. Cave Buttress Right-Hand	VD
2. Cave Buttress	S
3. Caved In	VS
4. Jeepers Creepers	E1
5. Typical Grit	HS
6. Sneezy	HS
7. Mantelshelf Climb	D

The Modest Carpenter 22m E4 6b   (1983)
A bizarre route that looks for, and finds, considerable difficulty.
Start as for Old Friends but continue the traverse left below its
crux to finish up the left-hand arête of the wall. The last move
is the crux.

The Crypt Trip 19m E6 6b ★★★   (1983)
The magnificent wall left of Old Friends is an arduous and
excellent route. Start under the right edge of a thin overlap in
the centre of the face. Climb up and left through the notch in
the overlap to gain the first proper break. More difficult, though
protectable, moves lead past a pocket to the main horizontal
break and an easier finish up the wall above

7. Sogines	HVS
8. The Logic Book	E3
9. King Kong	E3
10. Kelly's Variation	S
11. Norse Corner Climb	VS
12. Quietus Right-Hand	E4
13. Quietus	E2
14. Inaccessible Crack	VS

High Neb Edge   20m   HVS 5b   ★   (1970s)
Start up the shallow groove one metre right of the left-hand
end of the steep side-wall to reach a horizontal break on the
left, followed by the obvious flake. Continue on the right-hand
side of the arête until it is becomes imperative to move round
on to the front face, which is followed on the right edge to the
top.

The front face of **HIGH NEB BUTTRESS** is home to one of
the cliff's most venerable outings, first climbed way back in 1915.
Over the years several variations on the original route have been

1. High Neb Edge	HVS
2. High Neb Buttress	VS
3. Where did my Tan Go?	HVS
4. Tango Buttress	HS
5. Lost Soul	S
6. Limbo	S

found. For clarity and historical correctness the two main lines are described separately.

High Neb Buttress 20m VS 4c ★★★   (1915)
A classic climb and a bold route for its day. Start by a projecting rib under the centre of the buttress and gain the narrow ledge above. Continue to a good ledge which cuts across the buttress, good runners, then move right and climb the centre of the slab by a crucial mantelshelf. Finish more easily in a fine position.

High Neb Buttress Variation
20m VS 5a ★★   (traditional)
A good route though with a tough start. The upper section has

often been climbed in mistake for the true High Neb Buttress, probably because this is where the best runners are. Start near the right edge of the buttress at a thin crack and climb awkwardly up this, to the first break. Continue in the same line to a standing position on a good ledge, below the crux of the original route, and traverse left to runner slots. Make a tricky mantelshelf to reach better holds and finish up the left-hand side of the face above.

High Neb Gully 18m E (1900s)
The deep, block-choked gully just to the left is often used as a way down.

Where did my Tan Go? 14m HVS 5a ★ (1989)
The left-hand arête of High Neb Gully. Start at the base of the gully and climb a tricky wall to the first break. Move rightwards and climb the arête passing a flake at seven metres. Has a poorly-protected crux and is hard for the short.

Tango Buttress 14m HS 5a ★★ (1919-23)
The clean slab to the left has sketchy starting moves (crux). Continue up the centre of the fine face to a delicate section which leads to a curving finishing flake. The final section is not well-protected.

Tango Crack 14m VD ★ (1912-14)
The straight, wide crack has an awkward initial section. Continue up the easier cracks above.

Lost Soul 14m S (1992)
Start just to the left of Tango Crack. Climb the technical lower slab and then the easier narrow continuation.

Limbo 14m S (1978)
Climb the slab midway between Tango Crack and the diagonal break to the left by a series of steps. Cross the main diagonal break and finish up the final slab in the same line utilising a small ramp near the top.

DESCENT ROUTE
The diagonal break running across the slab, and linking Boyd's Crack and Tango Crack, can be used as a way down by the experienced. The less confident should use High Neb Gully to the right, or walk across to the right-hand edge of the cliff.

Following On 12m VS 5a (1993)
Climb the slab, parallel to and a metre or so to the right of, the

Quietus Right-Hand   E4 6a   (page 259)
Climber: Andy Cave   Photo: Ian Smith

Impossible Slab E3 6a   (page 260)
Climber: Rob Grundy   Photo: Ray Wood

Eric's Eliminate   S   (page 261)
Climber: Joanne Tagg   Photo: David Simmonite

Slap 'n Spittle   **E4 6a**   (page 286)
Climber: Dave Musgrove   Photo:Viv Durrant

straight rift of Boyd's Crack avoiding drifting rightwards towards the top. Delicate and rather dirty.

Boyd's Crack 12m D ★ (1912-14)
The next cleft to the left (and the first from the corner on the left) is climbed directly. The crack eases as height is gained.

Cent 12m E1 5b (1978)
The cramped slab immediately right of the corner is delicate and has an unprotected crux past the small overlap near the top.

Neb Corner 11m D (1912-14)
The deep angular corner bounding the left-hand edge of the slabby wall is climbed on good holds.

Sogines 11m HVS 5b ★ (1961-63)
Reach the thin flakes in the wall just to the left of the corner from directly below and strenuously follow them to a steep finish up the bulging rib to the left of the shallow cave.

The Logic Book 11m E3 6a ★ (1981)
A tough and well-protected eliminate up a slight rib just to the left. Climb directly up the rib keeping left of a white streak. The route proves to be horrendous for the short (E4 6b).

King Kong 12m E3 6a ★ (1978)
Start just to the left and bridge up a shallow scoop leading up to an overhang. Reach over this for a good hold on the upper wall. Progress from there is by means of a decisive and monstrous mantelshelf. In direct contrast to the previous route this one is harder for the tall (6b). A bit of justice after all.

Norse Corner Climb 15m VS 5a ★★ (1912-14)
A technical test-piece from yesteryear. Set in the arête to the left, and just right of the start of Quietus, is a rightward-slanting slab guarded by a steep wall. Pull desperately on to the slab using a large pocket or the crack to the right (crux), then follow it rightwards under the overhang to a large ledge; finish up the corner.

Kelly's Variation 14m S 4a ★ (1914-21)
Another way to reach the ledge. Start to the right and under the shallow scoop of King Kong and climb up diagonally left, via a shallow groove, to the ledge. Finish as for the previous route. A worthwhile variation.

7. Inaccessible Crack	VS
8. Kelly's Overhang	HVS
9. Mouthpiece	E2
10. Twisting Crack	S
11. Eric's Eliminate	S
12. Gunter	VS

Silence 14m HVS 5b (1979)
Start up Norse Corner Climb until an overgrown break can be followed back leftwards over the bulges to a pull back rightwards on to the ledge of Norse Corner Climb. The best finish is up the bulging right-hand wall of the final corner.

To the left is the great jutting prow that is one of the most recognisable silhouettes on grit, the great block overhang of Quietus.

Quietus 14m E2 5c ★★★ (1954)
Start directly under the centre of the great roof and climb a shallow curving groove directly to ledges below the huge overhang. Cross it using using good flakes and, before power or confidence ebbs away, make crux moves to get established on the vertical headwall using the cracks which split it. Quite simply one of the great gritstone roof climbs and high in the grade.

258

1. Cent	E1
2. King Kong	E3
3. Kelly's Variation	S
4. Norse Corner Climb	VS
5. Quietus	E2
6. Impossible Slab	E3

Quietus Right-Hand 14m E4 6a ★★ (1981)

Follow Silence or Norse Corner Climb, to the large ledge. Up and to the left is a beckoning hand-traverse line leading out through space and almost reaching a prominent fluting on the arête. Reach the start of the hand-traverse with difficulty and swing boldly out to the arête. A fierce pull is made to reach the fluting; finish with a flourish.

The previous guide suggested that a route had been reported through the roof to the right of Quietus at E5 6c though nothing else has been heard of this claim. It may well have corresponded with the following:

259

Quietus Middle Leg 15m E3 6a ★ (1980s)
A hybrid, recommended if only for its spectacular positions.
Climb Quietus to its flake under the lip, then hand-traverse
wildly rightwards to the arête. Finish with some alacrity as for
the previous route.

Eckhard's Chimney 14m VD ★ (1912-14)
Squirm up the overhanging chimney to the left, passing the
narrowing close to the outside edge. Once past the protruding
blocks the upper section is easier.

Eckhard's Arête 14m HS 4a (1919-23)
The left-hand arête of the chimney has a stubborn start. As
height is gained things ease, though avoiding the opposite wall
of the chimney is not easy.

Impossible Slab 14m E3 6a ★★ (1961-63)
The steep wall and slab left of the chimney may prove aptly
named for the short, though it is a test of commitment for all.
Start up the short crack one metre to the left of the arête and
where it ends make a couple of taxing moves to reach easier
ground. Continue to ledges, then balance up the final slab
leaving the runners far below. Side runners in the chimney to
the right reduce the grade.

Inaccessible Crack 16m VS 4c ★★ (1915)
To the left is a flat-roofed recess at the foot of the cliff. Follow
a crack rising from the right-hand edge of the recess to its end
and move left to below a prominent corner-crack. Climb the
corner passing a jutting snout with difficulty. May be started
directly at VS 4c up the arête and crack rising from the left-
hand edge of the recess. A logical line providing fine climbing.

The Beautician 14m E4 5c ★★ (1984)
Start as for Inaccessible Crack but make a precarious step out
left above the cutaway and climb a slab to the break. Climb a
difficult wall and a right-trending scoop above by a harrowing
sequence of committing and delicate moves.

Overflow 20m E1 5b ★ (1983)
Climb the direct start to Inaccessible Crack to a position below
its final bulge. Place a side runner and hand-traverse out left
above the lip of the overhang to finish in a fine position up the
exposed arête.

Inaccessible Slab 7m HS 5a ★ (1912-14)
To the left is a huge, square roof and directly below it is a slab

split by a horizontal break. Climb the slab with a hard move to attain a standing position in the horizontal break (not bad for 1912). From the top of the slab there are several alternatives. Moving rightwards into Inaccessible Crack is the most obvious whilst finishing up Mouthpiece is the hardest and most direct. Descending the green corner just to the left is the best escape route; V Diff in 1951.

Mouthpiece 15m E2 5c ★   (1973)
Climb Inaccessible Slab to the roof (or the green corner to the left), stretch out leftwards and swing boldly across to get established on a block at the lip (junction with Kelly's Overhang). Make difficult moves to finish straight up the wall above.

Kelly's Overhang 15m HVS 5b ★★★   (1926)
An amazing ascent for its day and held in awe for years. Despite the HVS tag, there are still plenty of climbers today who swear that the route is harder than Quietus. Climb Twisting Crack and make a gymnastic struggle out rightwards to the protruding block beneath the left side of the large overhang. Traverse rightwards along the lip and make a hard move up and right to reach good holds on the wall above. Finish up the face above.

Twisting Crack 14m S ★★   (1915)
A fine climb that is steep and intimidating, but on good holds and with excellent protection. Climb the deep corner-crack that twists up to the left edge of the overhang. Step leftwards on to the exposed arête and make a hard pull to gain and climb the excellent cracks above. A variation start is possible at HVS 5b ★ (1983-9) up the arête to the left.

Eric's Eliminate 14m S ★   (1923-51)
Ascend a short crack in the face round the arête from Twisting Crack. Continue directly to finish up the vertical crack just to the left of the final section of that climb.

Straight Crack 12m S 4b ★   (1923-51)
Start to the left of the previous route and follow the straight crack as it gradually widens. Difficulties escalate gradually to an awkward exit.

Gunter 10m VS 5a   (1966)
The thin, dog-legged crack up the slope from Straight Crack reserves its bite for the upper section.

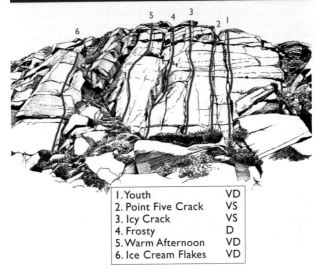

1. Youth	VD
2. Point Five Crack	VS
3. Icy Crack	VS
4. Frosty	D
5. Warm Afternoon	VD
6. Ice Cream Flakes	VD

Way Fruitsome Experience 6m HVS 5c   (1986)
The centre of the disappearing wall left of Gunter.

Continuing northwards for 300 metres from the left-hand end of
the ever popular High Neb Area is a series of interesting slabs
and walls that offer many fine routes well away from the crowds.
Most (though not all) of the buttresses are quite short, but as
ever the rock is impeccable and the situations are amongst the
best on the Edge, with an outlook over the broad back of Bamford
Moor and beyond to far-flung Kinder Scout. The first buttress
takes the form of an oval slab split by a series of four vertical
cracks of varying definition. This is 30 metres to the north of the
left-hand section of High Neb.

Old Man 6m D   (2000)
Climbs the wall right of Youth. A mantel leads to a ramp and a
finish on a good hidden hold. A slightly harder optional start can
be made on the front of the block below.

Youth 8m VD ★   (1961-63)
The thin right-hand crack matures towards the top.

Point Five Crack 9m VS 5a   (1989)
The converging cracks just to the left give a pleasant, if myopic,
pitch.

Icy Crack   9m   VS 4c   ★   (1978)
Another slightly artificial line following a thin crack and blunt
arête two metres to the right of the deep groove of Frosty.

Frosty   9m   D   (traditional)
Climb an open peapod-shaped groove in the left-hand side of
the face followed by the V-shaped groove above.

Warm Afternoon   9m   VD   (1992)
Start up the left-hand arête of the face, then step rightwards
and climb the centre of the narrow pillar to the left of the open
groove of Frosty.

To the left is a narrow pillar that leans back against the hillside,
this gives two short routes.

Ice Cream Flakes   8m   VD   (1992)
Climb the right-hand arête of the tower and follow the
rightward-slanting flakes above.

Side Plate   8m   S   (1992)
Climb the left-hand arête of the tower, starting over a small
nose and continue up the enjoyable, blunt arête above.

Twenty metres to the left is another slab similar to the last one in
that it is riven vertically by an assortment of crack systems. It also
has a rather smoother section to the left of centre. The first route
tackles the narrow south-facing wall of the flake that forms the right-
hand edge of the buttress.

Side-wall   7m   VS 4c   (1995)
The right-hand side face is climbed centrally to a steeper finish.

Staircase Rib   9m   D   (1992)
The obviously-named projecting rib is climbed directly up its front
face, or with slightly more difficulty, by a left-facing layback.

The line of pockets that neatly bisects the centre of the slab offers
the possibility of two closely linked girdle traverses. Both of which
start up Staircase rib. **Hands** 15m VS 4c (1993) traverses the slab
with your hands in the pockets and **Feet** 15m VS 5a (1993) is as for
Hands but with your feet in the pockets.

Solo Slab   9m   HVS 5b   (1992)
The narrow slab just to the left is climbed, avoiding the arête
on the right and the crack on the left to a finish up the short,
dog-legged crack.

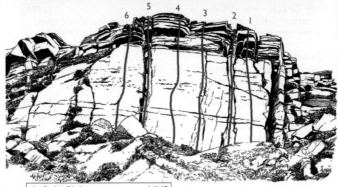

1. Solo Slab	HVS
2. Duo Crack Climb	HD
3. Rinty	VS
4. Fate	E1
5. Uno Crack	D
6. Ono	S

Duo Crack Climb 9m HD ★ (1921)
Ascend the pleasant parallel cracks just to the left and finish up a narrow blocky chimney.

Rinty 9m VS 5a ★ (1961)
Follow the thin shallow seams one metre left again with a couple of testing moves at mid-height. Keep off the easier parallel cracks on the right.

Fate 9m E1 5c ★ (1978)
The slab immediately to the right of the deep fissure of Uno Crack is climbed directly, with difficult initial moves, to reach the central line of pockets and serious final moves for the short. HVS with a runner in Uno Crack at half-height.

Uno Crack 9m D ★ (traditional)
Climb the wide crack towards the left-hand side of the slab.

Ono 8m S ★ (1976)
Go directly up the slab immediately to the left of the crack and finish through a juggy bulge.

Pleasant Slab 6m D (1993)
The 'slight' slab immediately left again leads to a heathery ledge and a juggy steepening below the top.

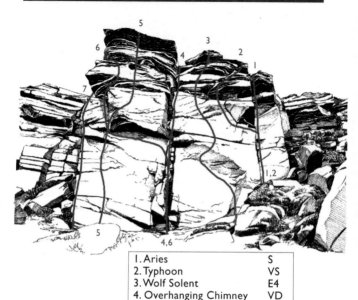

1. Aries	S
2. Typhoon	VS
3. Wolf Solent	E4
4. Overhanging Chimney	VD
5. Youth Meat	E4
6. The Blurter	HVS
7. Meddle	E2

The next routes are situated on a tall buttress 25 metres to the left and are characterised by a deep and narrow central chimney with a fine, tall buttress to its left, crossed at half-height by a band of overhangs. This is:

BLURTER BUTTRESS

The right-hand side of the buttress has an angular groove set in it. The arête to the right is:

Three Calm Men 10m E1 5b (1997)
The right-hand arête of the corner is climbed to a juggy bulging exit. Runners in the corner to the left reduce the grade to HVS.

Aries 10m S ★ (1957)
Climb the well-protected square-cut groove just left of the arête to a bulging exit.

Typhoon 12m VS 4c ★ (1959)

As for Aries to half-height but step left round the arête to follow a curving crack to a sloping ledge. Rounded rock leads directly to the top. A direct start E3 6a (1982) climbs just to the left of the arête from a block at the foot of a shallow leftward-rising scoop to join the regular route where it appears from around the arête.

Wolf Solent 16m E4 5c ★★ (1978)

An elegant, but bold solution to the attractive slabby buttress to the right of the central chimney. Start in the same place as for the direct start to Typhoon and teeter leftwards up the slab under the overlap to a position just to the right of the chimney. Pull over the overlap, first rightwards then leftwards, with difficulty and a poor pocket. Continue warily up the slab to a large ledge and an easier finish. The centre of the initial slab can be climbed directly at 6a (1981). **Andrea** E4 6a (1995) appears to follow similar ground to the direct start up the slab and then the bulge using a flake and a pocket.

Overhanging Chimney 16m VD ★★ (1915)

The central chimney is attractive in appearance but a bit of a beast to climb. Easy climbing on a series of jammed chockstones leads to a constricted struggle in the central portion, before things ease off again.

The Blurter 21m HVS 5b ★★★ (1959)

An excellent but devious climb, which in 1964 was regarded as one of the finest routes on Stanage. With the devious nature of the climb it requires careful rope work to avoid excessive drag. Start up the chimney until it is possible to make an awkward traverse leftwards below the overhang. This leads to a rest on large holds below a hanging groove. Enter this with difficulty and climb it to a small ledge. Step right and pull over a bulge before trending leftwards round the arête and go up the steep north wall to a juggy finish.

Enigma 18m E2 5c (1981)

An uncomfortable eliminate line which weaves its devious way up the front face of Blurter Buttress. Follow the regular route until established in the groove then swing rightwards from this on to the face above the roof and continue right of the arête to finish directly over the capping overhangs. Largely superseded by Wakamono which is, however, harder.

Youth Meat 18m E4 6b (1984)

An extended boulder problem that leads into the base of the

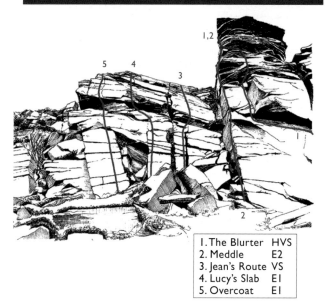

1. The Blurter	HVS
2. Meddle	E2
3. Jean's Route	VS
4. Lucy's Slab	E1
5. Overcoat	E1

groove of The Blurter. Start directly below the groove where a couple of easy moves lead to the crux, which involves using a poor pocket for the left hand, to enter the groove. Climbing the initial wall one metre left of the pocket is 5c and laybacking the arête just left again is even easier. Finish up The Blurter.

Wakamono 20m E4 6b   (1980s)
The bulge above the initial traverse of The Blurter gives a taxing couple of moves. Follow Youth Meat (hard, but in keeping with the rest of the climb) to the base of the groove on The Blurter then step right and pull over the roof with difficulty to join and finish as for Enigma. The crucial moves can also be approached via the start of The Blurter at a much easier grade.

Meddle 18m E2 5c ★   (1976)
A good climb with a couple of reckless-feeling layback moves forming its crux. Climb the left-hand arête of the buttress on its right-hand side, until level with the bottom of The Blurter groove. Swing leftwards around the arête and continue via a disconcerting barn-door move to reach a large ledge. Finish directly. Unfortunately the crux moves can be avoided by climbing the arête on its right-hand side, reducing the grade to

E1 5b. It is also possible to climb the less satisfying left-hand side of the arête throughout.

One-third of the way up the blocky gully that bounds the left-hand edge of the buttress is a boulder. Starting from this is:

Shout it Out 10m VS 4c   (1991)
Step right on to the wall and steeply climb it following the line of least resistance.

To the left is an area of slabby rock with three squat pillars standing in front of it. Between the first two pillars a continuous crack system runs the height of the cliff, **Stairway Crack** M. On the right-hand side of this is:

Jean's Route 10m VS 4c   (1978)
Climb a crack to ledges. Pull over an overlap and continue up the pleasantly green upper slab, keeping just right of Stairway Crack.

Lucy's Slab 12m E1 5b   (1978)
Just left of Stairway Crack is a second small pillar. Climb the left-hand edge of this to its top. Step left and cross the overlap (crux) at an obvious scoop to finish up the slab above.

Overcoat 12m E1 5b   (1981)
Five metres to the left of Stairway Crack a third pillar leans against the rock. Climb the centre of this to reach a large ledge below an overhang. Pull over this with difficulty, using one or both of the two parallel flakes.

Undercoat 15m S   (1997)
Climb the left-hand arête of the Overcoat pillar then a short wall to reach the large ledge. Traverse leftwards round the corner and then go up the centre of the side-wall.

Fifty metres to the left is a broad buttress, the most conspicuous feature of which is a deep chimney to the left of centre with a large block overhang halfway up its right-hand arête.

Pure Gossip 8m HS 4b   (1979)
Start one metre to the left of a perched block at the right-hand edge of the face and climb the wall, initially trending slightly rightwards, and then directly.

Hearsay Crack 10m E1 5a ★   (1957-60)
Despite rumours to the contrary this climb follows the well-

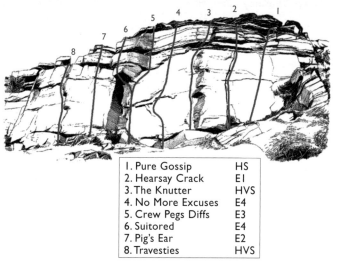

1. Pure Gossip	HS
2. Hearsay Crack	E1
3. The Knutter	HVS
4. No More Excuses	E4
5. Crew Pegs Diffs	E3
6. Suitored	E4
7. Pig's Ear	E2
8. Travesties	HVS

protected rightward-slanting crack to its end; continue directly
up the poorly-protected bulging wall above.

The Knutter 10m HVS 5b ★★   (1962)
The blunt central arête of the wall has a shallow flake-crack
running up it. Thin moves are required to grasp the elusive jug,
above which the climbing gradually eases.

No More Excuses 10m E4 6b ★★★   (1982)
The centre of the superb wall to the left is a taxing pitch, that
can be protected by a hand-placed peg in a unique hole just
above the obvious half-height pocket.

Crew Pegs Diffs 8m E3 6a ★   (1977)
Start below an overhang just right of the chimney. Move up the
arête, then step rightwards using a small flake. Another hard
move gains entry into a hanging groove. Gibber up this on
better holds to reach a wide, horizontal break and finish up a
short wall.

Suitored 8m E4 6a   (1987)
Start up Crew Pegs Diffs, but pull straight over the roof using a
wafer-thin flake and continue by laying away from the left-hand
arête.

Deep Chimney   7m   HD   (traditional)
Ascend the wide cleft that splits the left-hand side of the
highest part of the wall by a series of textbook chimneying
techniques, passing the bulge awkwardly.

The steep, square slab to the left of the chimney is home to two
thin face routes (as well as the arête), though it might be argued
that there is only really room for one.

Pig's Ear   7m   E2 6a   ★   (1978)
A worthwhile and technical climb using a series of tiny edges up
the 'non-line' just right of the centre of the face. An eliminate
up the right arête is **Lamb's Tail** E2 6a (1991).

Timothy Twinkletoes   7m   E2 6a   (1984)
Make a sequence of thin pulls directly up the left-hand side of
the square face to the left of Pig's Ear and immediately right of
the shallow groove of Travesties.

Travesties   7m   HVS 5b   ★★   (1976)
Excellent moves lead into and up a shallow left-slanting groove
in the centre of the wall. Not to be confused with The Knutter.

Flipside   6m   E2 5c   (1984)
An extending problem up the wall to the left of Travesties, with
an uncomfortably high crux to reach a horizontal break.

Heather Crack   6m   HVD   (1958)
Follow a thin crack as it slants leftwards, then use a flake to pull
over a bulge near the top.

Lamia Antics   6m   HVS 5b   (1990)
Start one metre to the left of the flake of Heather Crack. Climb
the slabby face to reach a tricky finish via a slight ramp. The
shallow groove of **Erica Micra** S (1992) is just to the right of
the left-hand arête of the wall, using the arête as required.

DESCENT ROUTE
To the left is a flake that gives an awkward descent route.

The Long and the Short   7m   VS 5b   (1996)
To the left of the easy flake-crack is a short wall. A baffling
couple of moves lead to easier ground and a ledge with a holly
tree. Finish via the short hanging crack just to the right.

Little Things   4m   HVS 6a   ★   (1970s)
The conspicuous hanging roof-crack up to the left above a

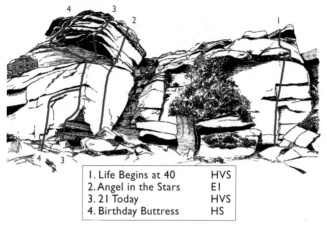

1. Life Begins at 40	HVS
2. Angel in the Stars	E1
3. 21 Today	HVS
4. Birthday Buttress	HS

ledge is best led because of the big drop below it. Much harder, if at all possible, for the short.

Across the gully is a short, rounded buttress with a hearty holly growing on its left side.

Life Begins at 40   6m   HVS 5a   (1987)
Climb the arête to the right of the holly and move rightwards at the bulge to finish up the arête.

To the left is a rounded buttress with a ledge and roof at its top right-hand corner. This is:

BIRTHDAY BUTTRESS

Angel in the Stars   7m   E1 5c   (1997)
The side-wall of the buttress is climbed with a sneaky rest on the midway ledge if required.

21 Today   7m   HVS 5c   (1983)
The right-hand arête of the buttress, climbed on its left-hand side, has a difficult start, a good rest on the midway ledge, and a rounded finish.

Birthday Buttress   10m   HS 4b   (1959)
From the centre of the buttress, hand-traverse rightwards to an arête. Ascend this to a large ledge, return leftwards, then go up to finish around the left-hand edge of the overhang.

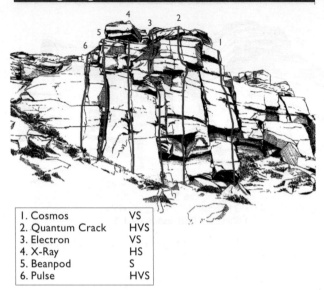

1. Cosmos	VS
2. Quantum Crack	HVS
3. Electron	VS
4. X-Ray	HS
5. Beanpod	S
6. Pulse	HVS

Going Grey 7m HVS 5a   (1996)
Start as for Birthday Buttress, but continue directly to the
ledge. Finish over the left-hand side of the bulges above, right of
the finish of Birthday Buttress. A similar line **Newborn** climbs
the top bulge further right at HVS 5b (1997).

Twenty metres to the left the next section of rock is recognised
by having a stepped series of overhangs crowning its right-hand
side and a triangular roof at two metres in the centre of the
buttress.

COSMIC BUTTRESS

Cosmos 8m VS 4b   (1989)
The right-hand arête of the buttress is started on its right-hand
side by a strenuous pull or judicious use of a nearby block and
is followed more delicately. An alternative start up Cosmic
Crack is possible.

Hale-Bopp 9m E1 6a   (1997)
Pull on to an undercut slab with difficulty and climb the
steepening wall to a finish at its top right-hand edge using a
hidden jug.

Cosmic Crack 9m VS 4c ★★   (1959)
Superb climbing on widely spaced holds up the undercut crack
right of Quantum Crack.

Quantum Crack 9m HVS 5a ★   (1964)
This route takes the face between two crack-lines via a couple
of niches. Swing round the initial triangular overhang with
difficulty to gain the slab above. Follow this to below an
overhang where an ungraceful traverse leftwards leads to a
ledge and an easy finish.

Electron 8m VS 5a ★   (1964)
The poorly protected crack rising from the left-hand side of the
triangular roof, features some awkward bridging to pass the
final roof and a tough move to reach easy ground.

X-Ray 7m HS 4b ★   (1961)
The continuous thin crack to the left requires slim fingers for a
couple of moves.

Beanpod 6m S 4a   (1959)
The appropiately named wide crack to the left. Climb into the
small sentry-box at half-height and finish up the thinner crack.

Pulse 6m HVS 5a   (1992)
The thin crack immediately to the left.

Fifteen metres to the left is a short buttress split in two by a
shallow chimney with protruding chockstones and a ledge system
at two-thirds height.

1. Ginger Tom	HVS
2. Lucky	VS
3. Kitten	VS
4. Puss	HVS
5. Pup	HVS
6. Sudoxe	HVS

Ginger Tom 7m HVS 5c (1997)
Starting one metre to the right of the chimney climb the right-hand wall up bulging rock.

Lucky 7m VS 5b (1991)
The right-hand arête of the left-hand section of the wall.

Kitten 8m VS 5b ★ (1959)
Start in the centre of the left-hand wall and move slightly right, then go straight up with less difficulty to finish.

Puss 8m HVS 5c ★ (1974)
A short problem with an entertaining couple of moves. Climb the centre of the wall just to the left.

Pup 8m HVS 6a (1964-76)
Start directly below a small flake in the left-hand arête. Gain the flake and use it to climb the arête past another flake. An easier start moves in from the left to reach the second flake, HVS 5b.

Jam Good 8m VD (1992)
The clean-cut crack just to the left is followed by the short corner above.

Ten metres to the left is a small rectangular tower, detached from the cliff and to the left of this is a steep crack-ridden wall. This is:

EXODUS BUTTRESS

Radox 7m S (1992)
Climb the shallow groove just to the left of the right-hand arête of the tower to finish up the pleasant arête above.

Sudoxe 8m HVS 5b ★ (1961-63)
Good technical climbing up the centre of the tower using a series of small iron rugosities. Most teams trend rightwards towards the top, whereas the more direct finish is E1 5b.

Treatment 6m VS 5a (1979)
Climb the left-hand arête of the tower with the occasional long stretch between good jugs.

The steep wall to the left has six discernible crack systems. Unfortunately they are so close together that there are in fact only four worthwhile routes, though with blinkers it would be possible to squeeze more routes out of the wall. All the routes are tough for their respective grades.

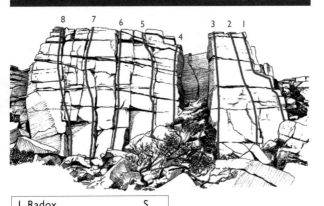

1. Radox	S
2. Sudoxe	HVS
3. Treatment	VS
4. E.M.F.	HVS
5. Missing Numbers	HVS
6. Leviticus	HVS
7. Deuteronomy	HVS
8. Exodus	HVS

E.M.F. 7m HVS 5a ★ (1979)
Although small, the right-hand arête of the cracked wall has good moves on positive holds.

Missing Numbers 8m HVS 5b (1981)
The first thin crack, on the right-hand side of the wall, saves its crux for the final moves.

Leviticus 10m HVS 5b ★ (1961-63)
The next two cracks are gained from a block, then followed in tandem, though mostly using the better defined left-hand one.

Deuteronomy 10m HVS 5b ★★ (1974)
Start at the lowest point of the wall and climb the left-slanting crack. Step left and climb the thin crack that springs from the lip of the roof.

The Cracks Between 10m E1 5b (1976-81)
With considerable self-discipline it is possible to start up Exodus, then climb the thin crack that splits the bulge and continue up the wall above without touching the routes on either side.

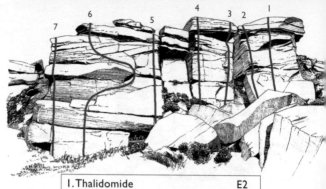

1. Thalidomide	E2
2. Side Effect	VS
3. Spectacle	S
4. Bandits in the Woods	HVS
5. Lepton	HS
6. Meson	VD
7. Ventured Point	HS

Exodus 10m HVS 5a ★ (1959)
The left-hand crack emerging from the left-hand edge of the
roof is entered awkwardly and followed religiously to its end.

Cheeky Little Number 9m E2 5b (1982)
The left-hand arête of the wall is gained via an awkward blunt
rib, then followed more easily.

Forty metres to the left, past lesser rocks, is a short buttress that
has an undercut slab topped by a short, overhanging wall on its
left-hand side and a protruding, square buttress on its right.

The Other Effect 7m E1 5c (1997)
Climb the right-hand arête of the buttress to gain a scoop and
finish directly above this.

Thalidomide 8m E2 5c (1983)
Climb up to and over the bulges in the centre of the buttress.
Poor cams protect.

Side Effect 9m VS 4c (1978)
Pleasantly follow the left-hand arête of the buttress and finish
awkwardly over the narrow, capping roof.

To the left is a deep corner with a wide crack in its back leading to an overhang.

Spectacle 8m S 5a   (1992)
Climb the slab on the left to enter an awkward chimney. Finish either by swinging out to the right-hand side of the crowning chockstone or by grovelling under it.

Bandits in the Woods 8m HVS 5a   (1983)
The slab and thin crack just to the left lead to a finish over an overhang which caps the wall.

To the left is a square roofed-in recess with an arête to its left.

Lepton 8m HS 4b   (1989)
Step from a block on to a slab and pad up this to climb the arête and the short crack that springs from the top left-hand corner of the recess.

Meson 9m VD ★   (1960)
From the centre of the buttress gain the first ledge and trend rightwards to reach a second ledge just above. Climb leftwards across the wall to a juggy exit.

Quark 10m VS 5a   (1983)
Start at the left-hand arête of the buttress and mantelshelf on to the initial ledge. Climb a short, leaning wall and mantelshelf on to a second ledge. Move right, crossing Meson, and finish up the right-hand edge of the wall as for Lepton.

Ventured Point 9m HS 4b   (1983)
Climb the left-hand edge of the buttress, via a good ledge, and continue up the right-hand side of the arête.

Ten metres to the left is prominent, projecting beak and starting below this is:

Th'ickle Buttress 6m E1 5c   (1997)
Begin at large holds in the centre of the front face and climb the right arête with difficulty, to a finish up the side-wall of the beak. HVS 5a for the tall.

Five metres to the left is the square arête of Hardly Hyperkeratosis. This is the right edge of Twin Buttress. The crack in the right-hand face of the buttress provides pleasant jamming, **Twin Set** D (1999).

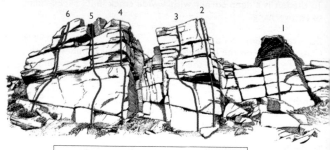

1. Th'ickle Buttress	E1
2. Hardly Hyperaktosis	E2
3. Seranata	E1
4. Certainly Parakeratosis	E1
5. Bottomless Crack	HVS
6. Undercut Crack	VS

TWIN BUTTRESS

Quadrille 6m HS 4b ★   (1964-76)
Skip up a short arête then follow a bottomless groove on the right-hand side of the buttress. The wall and crack to the right is **Quadrangle** HD (1990s).

Hardly Hyperkeratosis 7m E2 5c ★   (1982)
Climb the right-hand arête of the buttress keeping on its left-hand side throughout. Passing the projecting nose provides most of the fun.

Seranata 7m E1 5b ★   (1958)
From the centre of the right-hand buttress move up and left to gain a good flake. Continue up past a pocket to finish with a long reach for rounded holds.

Frank Sinatra 7m HS 4c   (1999)
The cracks on the right-hand side of the central recess of the buttress are entered steeply and lead to ledges. From there step out right on to the front face for the final move.

Bow Crack 7m VD ★   (1964-76)
The pleasantly steep cracks in the left-hand side of the chimney recess that divides the buttresses are approached by a tricky lower corner.

The front face of the left-hand section of Twin Buttress contains a wide central crack which does not reach the ground and a pair of cracks further to the left which do, albeit as a single entity.

Certainly Parakeratosis 8m E1 5b ★   (1982)
The right-hand arête of the left-hand Twin Buttress is taken initially on its left-hand side to a finish up a leaning crack on the right-hand side of the nose.

Lysteria Hysteria 9m E3 6a   (1990)
From two metres up Certainly Parakeratosis, break out left to a position below a good pocket. Use this to continue directly up the wall.

Bottomless Crack 8m HVS 6a ★   (1972)
A frustrating move leads to a small ledge below and to the right of a hanging crack in the centre of the wall, which is reached by another awkward move. Once gained this leads relatively easily to the top. The crack is more easily reached by a strenuous swinging hand-traverse from the left at HVS 5a.

Undercut Crack 8m VS 5a   (1972)
Climb the left-hand crack, step right and follow the extension by a hard pull on narrow jams. Alternatively continue up the easier left-hand crack, **Straight Variation** VS 4b (1993).

Pull and Step 6m VD 4b   (1993)
A difficult pull gains a ledge on the wall to the left of the crack. Once established, the left-hand arête above is followed.

Three hundred and fifty metres to the north, past a couple of inconsequential outcrops, is Crow Chin, an isolated face with a small cave at the right-hand side, also known traditionally as Kelly's Wall. Most of the climbs are in the lower grades and are worthwhile.

CROW CHIN

Bright Eyed 9m VS 4b   (1985)
Climb the centre of the black slab up to the right of the cave.

Twilight 10m HS   (1998)
Start in the small niche to the right of the cave, pull over the overhang and continue up a crack above.

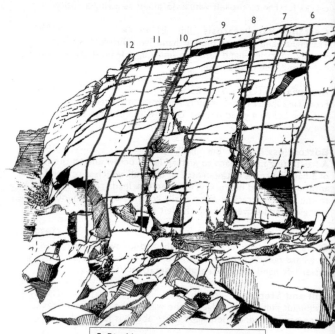

5. Big Al	HVS
6. October Slab	HS
7. May Crack	VS
8. October Crack	D
9. Kelly's Eliminate	HS
10. Kelly's Crack	HS
11. Feathered Friends	VS
12. Perforation	HVS

Autumn Gold 10m HS   (1983)
Climb a flat wall right of the main cave to a ledge and finish up
a crack.

The Marmoset 6m VS 4c   (1915-21)
Deemed 'Difficult' in the 1920s and 'impossible' in 1957. Climb
over the centre of the roof of the cave, using jammed blocks
with care. If successful scramble easily up the narrow chimney.

1. Bright Eyed	VS
2. Autumn Gold	HS
3. The Marmoset	VS
4. New Year's Eve	HS

New Year's Eve 10m HS 4b   (1989)
Climb the awkward left-hand arête to the left of The Marmoset
cave, then step right and climb the flat wall to ledges. Step left
to finish up a crack system.

Clare L   6.6.04

Bent Crack 10m VD ★ *Nancy S*   (1915-21)
Around to the left of the cave is a leftward-facing corner. Climb
the corner-crack to ledges and follow an easier corner to
below a capping roof. Traverse out left to finish up a small
corner.

Big Al 10m HVS 5a   (1993)
The centre of a steep slab to the left of Bent Crack is followed
delicately. Start just left of the corner and climb leftwards, and
then back rightwards, on small holds to enter a shallow groove.
Finish directly up the slab.

October Slab 10m HS 4b ★★   (1923-51)
Ascend the right-hand arête of a triangular niche and follow the
thin seam above, finishing over a stepped overlap; excellent
climbing.

May Crack 10m VS 5a   (1985)
Climb above the left-hand edge of the triangular niche and
continue up a thin crack above the overlap.

October Crack 10m D ★★ Nancy L   6.6.04   (1923-51)
                                  Claus
Ascend the obvious wide crack splitting the centre of the face.

Just to the left is a clean, attractive buttress.

Spring Sunshine 10m VS 4c   (1993)
Start up a short flake-crack and after a long reach follow the
right-hand edge of the buttress throughout. The occasional use
of the left arête of October Crack is difficult to avoid.

Kelly's Eliminate 10m HS 4a ★★   (1915-21)
A direct line up the centre of the face is very good and also
worth doing for historic interest. The start is steep and
strenuous, though on good holds, whereas the upper section is
much more delicate. The route was undergraded for years.

Kelly's Eye 10m HS 4a ★   (1993)
Climb the left-hand side of the face to enter a shallow groove
containing a flake. Finish directly.

Kelly's Crack 10m VD ★★   (1915-21)
Climb a prominent well-protected fissure just to the left. A
steeper section at half-height provides the crux and the loose
chockstone near the top has resisted generations of attempts
to release it from its socket.

Feathered Friends 10m VS 4b ★   (1979)
Start at a blunt rib to the left of Kelly's Crack and trend left
before climbing the steepening slab, and passing a perched flake
at half-height, to an awkward exit.

Perforation   9m   HVS 5b   ★   (1985)
Start from a flat block. Pull over the centre of an overlap and
make difficult moves to stand in a horizontal break. The slab
and wall above are easier.

Jim Crow   9m   HVS 5b   (1979)
Start in a small overhung niche four metres left of Kelly's Crack.
Climb a roof using a thin crack to continue up a short wall and
a shallow groove.

Rabbit's Crack   8m   HVS 5a   (1979)
Begin up a short rib four metres left of Jim Crow to a small
overhang and climb the thin, well-protected crack system to
finish up a groove.

So Many Classics, So Little Time   7m   E3 5c   (1984)
A short but serious (and misnamed) line up the wall to the left,
starting just to the left of a cruel-looking block and pulling
through a low roof. Finish up the centre of the wall above on
poor holds to a hideous finish; was HVS.

The edge deteriorates for approximately 110 metres before
reappearing at the south-facing wall known as the Seven Sisters.
In places the rock has a strange slippery texture, an example of
the geological phenomenon of 'slickenside'. This is polishing, caused
by the slow movement of the rock along a minor fault line. Between
Crow Chin and the Seven Sisters there are some low buttresses
which provide problems for those seeking solitude (if you must).

DESCENT ROUTE
The wide gully to the right of the face offers an easy way down.

SEVEN SISTERS

Sister Blister   8m   VS 4c   (1997)
The right-hand arête of the side-wall of the buttress is climbed
on its left-hand side past a bulge.

Not Richard's Sister Direct   8m   E1 6a   ★   (1989)
The first crack from the right leads up to a bulge and ends
there. Stepping left would be easy but, unfortunately, the true
way is straight on and is very tough. Strangely, and presumably
the reason for the name, the route is totally independent of the
true Richard's Sister.

7. Vena Cave-in	E3
8. Slap 'n Spittle	E4
9. Turtle Power	E6
10. Left-Hand Tower	VS

Richard's Sister 8m S (1961)
The second crack from the right (the first one to run to the top of the cliff).

Second Sister 10m VS 4c ★ (1961)
The next crack to the left (third from the right) is quite tricky.

Keep it in the Family 12m E1 5b (1997)
Between the two left-hand cracks is a shallow right-angled corner. Teeter up this (artificial but nice moves) to a bulge which is climbed directly, to finish on rounded holds.

1. Not Richard's Sister Direct — E1
2. Richard's Sister — S
3. Second Sister — VS
4. First Sister — VS
5. Tempskya — E3
6. Right-Hand Tower — HVS

First Sister 12m VS 4c ★★ (1957-60)
Start under the left-hand continuous crack. Make pleasing
moves up the thin lower section to reach and follow the more
continuous, and deeper, upper section of the crack.

Round to the left of the Seven Sisters is the west-facing :

CLEFT BUTTRESS

Tempskya 12m E3 5c ★ (1978)
Start from a collapsed wall and climb directly up a bulging face
to a finish up a short crack. The first of several routes which
feature steep climbing on spaced and rounded holds.

Wild and Woolly 16m E1 5b ★★ (1995)
Start carefully from the top of the collapsing wall and move out leftwards to good holds in a break. Climb straight up a bulging wall, initially on pockets and then on sloping breaks, keeping just to the right of the arête to reach the final ledge of Right-Hand Tower. Move left round the arête and finish with a long reach.

Right-Hand Tower 16m HVS 5b ★★★ (1957-60)
A spooky classic with a baffling collection of sloping ledges and flared breaks. If you have never climbed on grit before, don't start with this one. Begin at a thin crack just to the left of the arête and continue straight up on its left-hand side to the final break. Move right round the arete on to the south face and precarious moves to finish.

To the left is the deep, wide chimney (Easy Cleft) that gives Cleft Buttress its name. The left side of the chimney is actually a completely detached tower.

Vena Cave-in 16m E3 5c ★ (1981)
An entertaining trip up the right-hand wall of the cleft with good protection from large cams and, unfortunately, the possibility of cheating by bridging on to the opposite wall if things get too much. Start as for Right-Hand Tower and from the top of its initial crack trend gradually leftwards up well-spaced rounded breaks to stretchy final moves; 6a for the short.

Pacemaker 16m HVS 5b ★ (1983)
Bridge up the gradually widening chimney a couple of metres back from daylight until it gets a touch too 'squeaky' for comfort then hop on to the right-hand wall, just above the crux of Vena Cave-in, to finish.

The Jitters 14m VS 4b (pre-1964)
Bridge up the cleft and transfer to the left-hand wall early on to reach the arête and follow it on its right-hand side to the top.

Slap 'n Spittle 14m E4 6a ★ (1983)
The left-hand arête of the chimney is climbed on its left-hand side by faith and friction moves. Protection arrives after the crux but before the finish on the right-hand side of the arête.

Turtle Power 14m E6 6c ★★ † (1990)
The centre of a fine wall to the left of Slab 'n Spittle was a long-standing problem, now it is a challenging lead. Small RPs

offer limited protection for the crucial moves to reach the beckoning break where cams protect the crux section on the short steep wall above. The bottom wall keeps shedding pebbles but it doesn't appear to have affected the overall grade.

Left-Hand Tower   18m   VS 4c   (1923-51)
The steep crack left of the chimney leads to a ledge on top of a small subsidary tower. From the top of the tower step back right and finish up the arête.

To the left of Left-Hand Tower are a couple of fallen blocks, both of which have nasty, shelving tops, ideal venues for chin-grinding mantelshelves.

Hideous Hidari   8m   E3 6a   (1993)
Climb a broad rib to the left of the initial crack of Left-Hand Tower, then gain the slab above by a couple of baffling but well-protected moves. Walk off the back of the block.

Malc's Left-Hand Slab   18m   HVS 5b   ★   (1962-63)
A wandering trip with interesting moves. 'Boulder' on to the tip of the left-hand of the slabs and climb it to its top right-hand corner. Stride boldly on to the right-hand slab and pad up this to its crest. Move right and finish with a mantelshelf up the arête above the initial corner of Left-Hand Tower.

The next three routes are found by entering the cleft that splits **CLEFT BUTTRESS** and scrambling up into the darkness. They are only recommended in dry conditions as they rarely see the sun.

Easy Cleft   10m   M   (pre-1951)
The main right-angled corner in the back of the cleft is climbed up a series of blocks that make a pleasant but often green ladder. Not a great route but the easiest way to the cliff top.

DESCENT ROUTE
Competent climbers may use Easy Cleft as a way down. Care is needed as it is often damp.

Green Line   8m   E1 5b   (1984)
The thin, green seam in the slabby wall directly behind the tower is rarely in condition. When dry it provides thin and poorly protected climbing; at other times it is a luminous nightmare.

Back Door 10m VS 4c (1985)

Start at the 'back door' of the cleft and climb the chimney until an awkward and exposed exit is possible over the capping stone.

In a Big Way Yerself 9m E4 6b ★ (1990)

The north-eastern edge of the Left-Hand Tower block takes the form of an obvious curving arête, this being the right-hand edge (looking in) of Back Door. Climb the right-hand side of the arête past a hard but protectable semi-mantelshelf (crux).

To the left of the entrance of the Easy Cleft the path leads round past blocks into a bay containing the imposing blank corner of Nectar. This is the impressive Marble Wall Crag. 'The main face of Marble Wall stretches along for 100 feet and is of a steepness and smoothness unsurpassed by any other crag on Stanage'. 1951

The final chapters of Stanage Edge, from Marble Wall as far as Stanage End, represent a fitting finale to this fine crag. By now the bustle and scenes passed along the way will be long forgotten, and what is left are quiet, stately crags of the highest quality. Strolling along the mighty and well-named Marble Wall, along the little outcrops as far as the oft-deserted Stanage End, it is easy to forget other people. Easy to forget the thronging crowds of the Popular End, the busy classics and the desperate struggles. Easy to forget the massive cities that lie so close in every direction, the busy roads linking these cities less than half a mile away. In fact, it is virtually impossible to see any roads from this area, a fact that adds greatly to its sense of wilderness.

The two main areas, while similar in many ways, also have their own individual character. Marble Wall Area has been home to some of the fiercest technical challenges throughout the generations, its quarried smoothness and plumb verticality making for very powerful climbs. Indeed, it is home to the escarpment's hardest route, Marbellous, which had been Stanage's last great problem, and whose setting truly befitted such an accolade. In the area of rock around this wall lie a good number of fine powerful challenges; Goosey Goosey Gander, Harvest and Nectar are all desperate and rarely cruised testpieces, the latter being hailed as one of the most technical routes of its generation. Even the easier routes hereabouts are no giveaway and you had better have strong arms and good stamina.

A few hundred metres further on, Stanage End has a somewhat forgotten feel to it. This is no reflection on its quality; some of the best HVSs on the crag are there. Yet it is rare to see much chalk

Goosey Goosey Gander   E5 6a   (page 289)
Climber: Lucy Creamer   Photo: Ian Parnell

Orang-outang   E2 5c   (page 289)
Climber: Nigel Smart   Photo: Dave Wilkinson

on these holds. Yet for the mid-grade climber looking for well-protected challenges, or someone seeking out the solitude of an evening's soloing, then Stanage End is one of the finest places to sit, tired armed, watching the sun set.

MARBLE WALL CRAG

Don's Delight   8m   HVS 5b   ★   (1962)
An unusual route for this area, being delicate and by Whillans. Start up a short slab on the right-hand side of the bay and trend rightwards to where a precarious and unprotected layback leads into a shallow groove. Climb this to easy ground, or better, step left on to a ledge and follow a thin crack just left of the arête.

Goosey Goosey Gander   12m   E5 6a   ★★★   (1967/1976)
To the left an alluring, thin crack splits a series of bulges. This provides an arduous and action-packed route with good but hard-earned protection. Gain the crack by moving leftwards under the overlap. Follow this with a hard move over the bulge. The remainder is easier but still uphill. An exhausting pitch considering its diminutive length.

Marbellous   12m   E8 7a   ★★★   †   (1997)
The centre of the smooth wall to the left was possibly the true 'last great problem' of Stanage Edge. Climb a ramp three metres left of Goosey Goosey Gander, to the break and traverse left to place good cams in an obvious horizontal slot. Move back right and, using undercut flakes, scale the centre of the wall with the utmost difficulty to an easier finish. On attempts at the first ascent the bold start was soloed to the break, the gear was placed and the first ascensionist climbed down/jumped to the ground without weighting the rope. The gear was then left clipped for subsequent attempts. With a more direct start it would be awesome.

Orang-outang   12m   E2 5c   ★★★   (1962/1972-73)
Another brilliant route. Start round to the left of the arête. Climb up the cutaway and layback around the overhang to a poor rest. Follow a thin crack to ledges and a belay. Two direct starts have been reported; E3 5c on the left-hand side of the arête and E4 6a on the right. From just above the crux it is possible to follow the second pitch of The Lamia along its traverse and across the roof crack to reach the top. This is **Meisner's Link-up** 20m E3 5c ★★ (1990s), a sustained route on which good rope work proves essential.

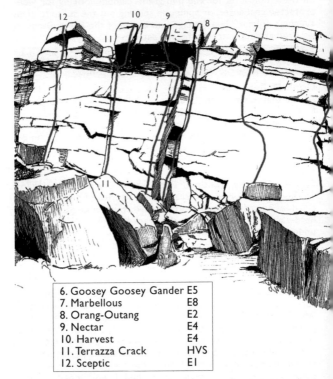

6. Goosey Goosey Gander	E5
7. Marbellous	E8
8. Orang-Outang	E2
9. Nectar	E4
10. Harvest	E4
11. Terrazza Crack	HVS
12. Sceptic	E1

Spinach Slab 12m E6 6c ★ †   (1990s)
The centre of the right wall of Nectar is climbed on well-spaced crimps and is protected by a runner close to Orang-outang. Despite the name it is not much of a slab.

Nectar 15m E4 6b, 6b ★★★   (1967/1976)
Technically sustained and with good protection the blank corner, that is the centrepiece of this area, provides a fine route. Omitting the second pitch (the norm) reduces the grade to E3.
1 11m. A delicate start and a demanding sequence of bridging moves lead up the corner past the deep horizontal break on the left to reach a welcome rest and belay under the roof.
2 4m. Leaning from the right, reach into the roof-crack above the corner. Shuffle towards the lip then follow the final section

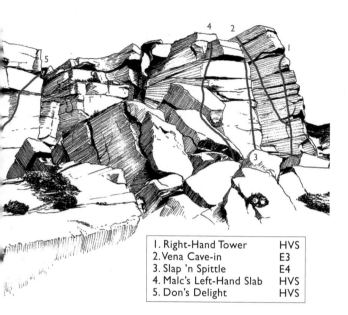

1. Right-Hand Tower	HVS
2. Vena Cave-in	E3
3. Slap 'n Spittle	E4
4. Malc's Left-Hand Slab	HVS
5. Don's Delight	HVS

of the crack with great difficulty. Purists and the short may have to climb all the way out from the back.

Terrazza Crack 11m HVS 5b ★★★ (1952)
The seductive crack in the steep face to the left gives a classic route. Superb jamming and laybacking lead strenuously to a 'lie-down ledge'. Escape left or try the following route.

Harvest 5m E4 6b ★★ (1975)
The short and savage roof crack above and right of Terrazza Crack yields to a classic struggle. Lean out and place good fist jams around the lip, cut loose and try to levitate that last metre to the top... so near and yet so far. A cruelly-placed pebble in the crack often leaves its mark.

Sceptic 11m E1 5b ★ (1970s)
Start from a convenient block two metres right of the arête of the wall. From the block move out right and then climb straight

up on flat holds to ledges. A spectacular finale leads over the capping roof on the some of the best holds around.

The Lamia   27m   E2 5b,5c   ★★★   (1975)
A superb girdle of the most continuous section of Marble Wall.
1 12m. Start as for Sceptic but move right to a developing horizontal break and follow it to Terrazza Crack. Hand-traverse to Nectar above all its difficulties and continue traversing to take a hanging belay, at the same level, on Orang-outang.
2 15m. Monkey along the obvious line until an awkward move by a diagonal overlap enables the wider break below the roof to be reached. Move right again and finish up the tough roof-crack to the left of Goosey's final crack.

Marble Tower Wall   14m   VS 4c   (pre-1951)
Start from blocks below the arête that bounds the left-hand edge of the main section of the face. Gain the first good ledge by a difficult move. Follow ledges that lead rightwards across the face to an exit below the overhangs. Variations described in the past include traversing back left to finish up the final moves of the arête (1951) or climbing over the roof as for Sceptic (1964).

Marble Arête   11m   VS 4c   ★★   (1960s)
Start as for the previous route and follow the arête throughout. Excellent climbing up exposed rock, which is not well-protected in its central section.

Marble Tower Flake   11m   S 4c   ★   (1950)
Gain the comfortable ledge on the arête with difficulty. Traverse left and leave the ledge via the huge flake above.

Green Crack   9m   VD   (1950)
To the left is a right-angled corner. Green by name, green by nature.

Spock Out   9m   VS 5a   (1978)
The thin cracks to the left of Green Crack, with a tricky start.

Bifurcated Headplate Max   9m   VS 4c   ★   (1978)
Taken direct from its base, the short arête to the left of Spock Out is surprisingly pleasant.

DESCENT ROUTE
Scramble down the left-hand side of the cliff then carefully cross the chaos of huge boulders that lie in front of the face.

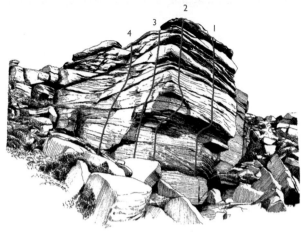

1. Clubbing	E3
2. Missing Link	E2
3. Brittle Bones	E1
4. Wetness Wall	VD

One hundred metres to the left of the northern extremity of the Marble Wall Crag is a solitary buttress with an undercut front face; this is the rarely visited and well-named:

LONELY CRAG

Flesh and Blood　6m　VS 5b　(1982)
A rippled wall to the right of the angular corner that bounds the right-hand side of the buttress has a tricky lower section.

Lonely Crag　9m　S　(1923-51)
The original route of the buttress follows a straightforward angular corner-crack on the right-hand side.

Mr Pemphigoid　7m　HVS 5c　(1982)
The right-hand arête of the buttress is started from the right and has tough moves to get established above the initial bulges.

Clubbing　8m　E3 6b　★　(1979-80)
Climb the centre of the roof on the front face with a very thin

293

pull on the lip which leads to easier, but still steep, rock and shelving holds.

Missing Link   9m   E2 5c   (1978)
Start on a block below the left-hand arête and from a good hold under a roof swing up and rightwards over it on to the front face to reach a delicate finish. The rock is a little loose in places. The left arête climbed direct is **Brittle Bones** E1 5c (1982).

Wetness Wall   7m   VD   (1961-63)
Paddle up the left-hand side of the north face of the buttress, a slimy expedition.

Two hundred metres farther north is a series of lower walls and blocky buttresses. In the past these have been dismissed, but explorations have unearthed a few worthwhile, if short, problems. These are clustered around the left-hand edge of the area where the rock is at its highest and a series of extended boulder problems is away to the right. Much of the rock is composed largely of rounded pebbles that have a habit of 'letting go' if you put too much pressure on them.

To the left of centre of the outcrop is a conspicuous bath-sized block resting on a double plinth on top of the cliff. About 100 metres right of this is a series of short buttresses and walls. The rightmost developed buttress has a tall flake standing against its left-hand (north-facing) wall and a metre-wide projecting rib in the centre of its front face. The first four routes are short and are: the pocketed centre of the wall to the right of the projecting rib is **Shining Jewel** VS 5a (1997) climbed trending rightwards to avoid a nightmare finish. The short shallow corner on the right-hand side of the rib is **Algol Corner** S (1997) while **Pillar Route** VS 5a (1997) ascends the front of the pillar and avoids the cracks on either side. The deeper corner to the left of the central rib gives **Greenman's Route** HVD (1997).

Drewitt, Drewitt   7m   VS 4c   (1997)
The arête that forms the left-hand edge of the wall is climbed mainly using holds on its right-hand side.

Flake Chimney   7m   D   (1997)
A pleasant chimney crack around the arête to the left.

Dennis's Harp   7m   HS 4b   (1997)
An arête to the left of the chimney is started from a convenient, pointed block.

The next three climbs are on the north-facing side-wall.

Medicus Curat 7m HVS 5b   (1997)
Start immediately to the left of the pointed block and climb
directly up the wall. Use of the block is to be avoided at this
grade.

Natura Sanat 7m HVS 5a   (1997)
Start just to the left at a pocket at waist level. Climb the wall
directly above this feature.

Two Pitch Climb 7m S   (1997)
Climb a short corner on the left to a ledge and finish up the
wall on the right.

To the left is a short, pebbly arête.

Ramps 8m HS 4c   (1997)
From the foot of the arête gain a ledge leading leftwards and
climb this to a move up on to a ramp; finish directly.

Ferret's Crack 6m S 4a   (1997)
The crack on the left-hand side of the face.

Eight metres to the left is an obvious square-cut chimney choked
by a huge, oblong block.

Scratch Wall 6m VS 5a   (1997)
Climb short cracks to the left of the chimney, awkward exit.

Scratch Arête 7m E1 5c   (1997)
The pebbly, left-hand arête of the wall on its right-hand side.

Thirty metres farther to the left is the bath-sized block, perched
on top of the cliff and mentioned in the introduction to this area.
Starting below and right of this is:

It's Scary Mary 8m S 4a   (1997)
Climb a short corner, go rightwards over blocks and climb the
south face of the capping block. The front face of the block can
be ascended at VS 4c.

Reptilian 15m VD   (1997)
Start at the lowest point of a rocky ridge to the left. Scramble
up the 'collapsed' ridge running towards the summit block Gain
its crest by an awkward move from the left. Descend from the
back with care.

1. Reptilian	VD
2. Flaked Out	HVS
3. Hard Nosed	HS
4. Hueco Heaven	HVS
5. Slab Happy	VS
6. Nosey Parkers	VS
7. Overhung	E1
8. Bamboozled	E1

To the left is a north-facing wall with a crack near its right-hand edge leading to a small, heathery ledge. The right-hand arête of the wall is capped by a square, projecting block.

Progressive Wall 8m E2 5c   (1997)
Climb the narrow, west-facing wall, starting from a couple of blocks and pass a jutting nose with difficulty. It is possible to traverse leftwards under the final nose and climb the short wall around the corner at HVS 5b.

The next two routes are located just to the left of the arête. The most logical way to climb them would be to swap their upper and lower sections, making a sustained HVS 5b and a sustained Severe.

Flaked Out 8m HVS 5b   (1997)
Climb the flake-crack just left of the arête passing a beak to reach a ledge. Continue up the wall just to the left of the upper arête to finish as for the left-hand variation to Progressive Wall.

Hard Nosed 8m HS 5b   (1997)
Climb the nose just to the left of the corner-crack with difficulty, to the ledge and finish up the easier flake behind.

Hueco Heaven 10m HVS 5a ★   (1997)
The best route hereabouts. Start one metre left of a blunt arête

and follow a steep wall trending leftwards to reach a block jammed in the final break. A long reach up and left should locate the heralded 'hueco'.

DESCENT ROUTE
To the left is an open gully that gives an easy way down.

Left of the descent route is a square, slabby block with two pleasant routes.

Slab Happy   8m   VS 5a   (1997)
Climb the centre of the slab with a couple of delicate moves and/or long reaches.

Nosey Parkers   8m   VS 4c   (1997)
The left-hand edge of the slab leads past an awkward bulge to easier ground.

Wedgewood   6m   S 4b   (1997)
The crack in the side-wall of the flake is tricky to start and a bit of a thrash to climb.

To the left is a wall with an overhang cutting across it just below half-height.

Overhung   8m   E1 5c   (1997)
Climb to the centre of the overhang and pass it using an undercut to reach sloping holds and a large, poor pocket. A quick pull leads to an easier finish.

Ram Jam Full   7m   HS 4c   (1997)
The short jamming crack to the left is pleasant while it lasts.

Bamboozled   7m   E1 5c   (1997)
The left-hand arête of the wall is climbed on its right-hand side and has a baffling starting sequence.

Brown Wall   6m   VS 4c   (1997)
The wall around to the left of the arête is started from a pointed block. Climb to a crack, move left along a horizontal break, and head for the highest point of the wall.

The rocks fade away again to reappear 400 metres or so farther north as a series of low, quarried walls. This is the start of Stanage End, often a great place to escape the crowds and particularly idyllic on a warm summer evening. Stanage End may be approached from either the A57 road or Dennis Knoll.

6. Arrow Crack	VS
7. Quiver	HVS
8. Twin Cracks	VD
9. Monad	E2
10. Valediction	HVS

STANAGE END

The first feature of any significance is the left-facing corner of Problem Corner. Across the quarried bay to the left (north) is the narrow buttress of Old Salt. One hundred and fifty metres right of Old Salt is a bulge on an obvious giant capstone, **I-Ro-Ha** E4 5c (1990s?) has desperate moves around the bulge leading to a break and a ball-bearing slap for the top.

Back in the quarried bay, the first short routes are: **Mr M'Quod and the Anti-rock Squad** HVS 5c (1983) is the right-hand arête of the aforementioned open corner of **Problem Corner** VS 5b (1961-63), while the centre of the wall right of the Corner is **Love Handles** HVS 5c (1983).

Crumbling Crack 6m HS 4b (1961-63)
This unpleasant route starts one metre left of Problem Corner and uses thin parallel cracks to gain a dirty cleft. Grovel up this to an easier exit.

298

I. Love Handles	HVS
2. Problem Corner	VS
3. Germ	E2
4. Microbe	E I
5. Thin Problem Crack	VS

Germ 6m E2 6a ★ (1980)
Climb straight up the wall midway between Crumbling Crack and the thin seam of Microbe. It features a technical lower wall and harrowing finishing moves.

Microbe 6m E I 5c ★ (1975)
Start in the centre of the wall at a small cutaway below a thin crack with an obvious pocket to its left. Climb directly, linking the previously mentioned features.

Thin Problem Crack 6m VS 5b (1983-89)
At the left-hand end of the wall is a thin crack which is started on finger jams and slippery foot holds. It eases immediately.

Vaccine Traverse 14m E2 5b (1988)
Start up Thin Problem Crack and follow a line of flat holds which lead across the wall at three-quarters height to an exit on the right-hand side of Problem Corner.

DESCENT ROUTE
To the left a series of large steps offers an easy descent, apart
from the two-metre drop at the bottom.

Balance 6m D   (traditional)
The shallow leftward-slanting ramp/groove around the arête to
the left has one awkward move.

Left again is a short, steep slab, split by a series of thin cracks.

Blinkers 6m VS 5b   (1983-89)
Climb the wall to the right of the right-hand crack to a
horizontal break and finish past a thinner break, with a long
reach for poor holds.

Arrow Crack 6m VS 5b   (1961-63)
The straight, right-hand, thin crack yields to good technique and
a layback move or two.

Quiver 6m HVS 5c   (1981)
Immediately to the left are two thin cracks. Climb the left-hand
one, which fades out at three metres, to reach a poor break.
The finish is hard and reachy.

Twin Cracks 6m VD   (1964-76)
Just to the right of a corner is a crack with jammed blocks.
Surmount the blocks and take either or both cracks to finish.

Boomerang Chimney 6m HS 4b   (1923-51)
The aptly-named cleft just to the left. Was undergraded at VD.

Monad 6m E2 6a   (1979)
An interesting problem up the wall immediately to the left of
the corner. Subtle hint — start by bridging the corner.

The Water Seller 8m E4 6a   (pre-1991)
Start as for Valediction but move out rightwards under its roof
to finish up a short steep wall.

Valediction 9m HVS 5a ★★   (1959)
Immediately before the arête is a steep smooth-sided crack,
which is climbed through overhangs to a rocky ledge. Contains
hidden delights.

Old Salt 10m HVS 5a ★★   (1963)
Climb the front of the buttress and make a long reach (or a
solid 5b move) to gain a small ledge. Move leftwards to follow

300

flakes out on to the steep face and finish airily with a final move left. **Rimmington Place** E2 5c ★ (1987) follows Old Salt to its small ledge, then moves upwards and rightwards with difficulty to pass the bulge. Finish up the exposed right-hand arête.

Exaltation   8m   E5 6c   ★★   (1989)
The blank wall around to the left is climbed by a desperate series of moves slightly rightwards and passing a slot (at this grade a hand-placed peg runner can be used but the route has been led without at E6) to finish direct on sloping holds. The original route **Saltation** E5 6c ★★ (1984) continued rightwards to join the final section of Old Salt.

To the left is the steep corner of February Crack.

February Crack   6m   HS 4b   ★   (1964-76)
Ascend the fine corner-crack in the main angle.

Acute Amnesia   6m   HVS 5b   (1981)
The thin crack in the wall just right can be climbed independently, though the start looks unlikely at the grade.

7% Soln   6m   HVS 5b   (1981)
Start from a block to climb the wall between Mars and February Crack, without touching either.

Mars   6m   VD   (1964-76)
A rightwards-slanting flake-crack to the left is awkward to start.

Tupperware   6m   E2 6a   (1997)
Climb the wall left of Mars to a good flake and slot, continue rightwards into the obvious scoop and a finish.

To the left is a short crack leading to a V-shaped groove then a taller tower of rock split by two cracks.

Mai   6m   VS 4b   (1992)
The thinner, right-hand cracks are followed throughout.

Avril   6m   S 4a   ★   (1964-76)
The wider crack which splits the left-hand side of the wall gives a short-lived but quality jamming pitch.

To the left is another V-shaped groove then a taller buttress split by a collection of thin cracks to the right of its centre.

5. Avril	S
6. Gameo	E2
7. Good Clean Fun	E4
8. Concept of Kinky	E6

Gameo 8m E2 5b (1986)
Climb the right-hand of the thin cracks, then move right to
finish up the arête.

Marathonette 7m HVS 5b (1997)
The arête right of Gameo is taken direct.

The Wobbler 9m HVS 5b ★★ (1962)
At the left-hand end of the wall, behind a large boulder is a
clump of shallow cracks which prove to be quite testing.

Good Clean Fun 9m E4 6b ★ (1984)
Start as for The Wobbler until a move leftwards allows a clean
face to be climbed, via a useful pocket. **'The Iain Farrar**

1. Old Salt	HVS
2. Saltation	E5
3. February Crack	HS
4. Mars	VD

Experience' E5 7a ★ † (2000) is the obvious direct start and without recourse to side-runners.

Concept of Kinky   9m   E6 6c   ★   (1989)
The hanging flake in the arête to the left of Good Clean Fun is climbed by a variety of techniques including a dynamic move. A nerve-testing tiny wire is supposed to offer protection.

Forty metres farther left is the tall tower split by the twin cracks of Surgeon's Saunter, to the right of which are some lower rocks. The most conspicuous feature of these is a square chimney capped by a tilted block. Six short routes climb this lower wall to the blocky floor of the amphitheatre above. From there it is possible to finish up Niche Climb, scramble out of the right-hand corner of the amphitheatre, or descend the easy crack right of Kelly's Corner.

The first climb is just right of a clean-cut, right-facing corner crack on the right-hand edge of these lower rocks.

Rib Tickler 7m VS 5a (1997)
Climb the short hanging crack and pull past a couple of blocks to finish up the arête above.

Manhattan Crack 6m VS 4b (1923-51)
Layback a steep crack in the corner to reach a rocky platform where there are a variety of ways off (see above).

New York, New York 6m E1 6a ★ (1986)
A technical laybacking exercise up the right-hand arête of the chimney to the left. Escape left at the break, or tackle the next route. Unfortunately the rumour that the route was so good that they climbed, and named, it twice is not true.

Sir Chilled 9m E4 6b ★ (1999)
The obvious arête above New York, New York gives a short exercise in safe, slappy fun.

Manhattan Chimney 6m HS 4b (1919)
The square, capstoned chimney is a back-and-footing cocktail of considerable vintage. Face whichever way you wish, passing the capping flake is the crux, though an escape can be made through a skylight.

Manhattan Arête 6m D (traditional)
Ascend the stepped left-hand arête of the buttress to the left of the square-cut chimney.

Kelly's Corner 5m VD (c.1915)
The left-hand side of the angle, immediately to the right of the soaring crack-line of Surgeon's Saunter, leads to the amphitheatre.

Niche Wall 9m VS 5a (1954)
The description, included in previous guidebooks, of this 'lost' route is recorded here for posterity in case there are any budding Doctor Livingstones out there. 'Step from a block and climb the face on very small holds, finishing to the left under the overhang'.

Niche Climb (The Niche) 9m S (1919)
At the back left-hand corner of the amphitheatre is a niche. 'A small fracture on the face and a finger-hold on the floor of the

1. Manhattan Crack	VS
2. New York, New York	E1
3. Manhattan Arête	D
4. Heath Robinson	E6
5. Surgeon's Saunter	HVS
6. Doctor's Chimney	S
7. Which Doctor	E5
8. Nursery Crack	VS

niche, enable the niche to be attained. Above is an overhanging crack. It is best to face right at first. Higher up a left arm wedge is used to overcome protruding rock. The position here is exposed and exhausting' 1951. Alternatively, climb the corner.

Heath Robinson 16m E6 6b ★★★ (1984)
The bulging arête right of Surgeon's Saunter is climbed directly to a harrowing exit where some inventiveness is needed. It is rounded in the extreme and a skin-shredding fall is highly possible.

Doctor of Physic 18m E5 6a ★ (1976)
Follow Heath Robinson to the last horizontal break on the arête, then traverse left to finish up the last couple of moves of Surgeon's Saunter. This variant avoids the crux.

Surgeon's Saunter 18m HVS 5b ★★★ (1953)
The twin cracks splitting the centre of the tower present a great route with a hard but protectable start and excellent jamming above. The original and easier start, **Doctor's Saunter** VS 4c ★★ (1923-51) is made by starting up Doctor's

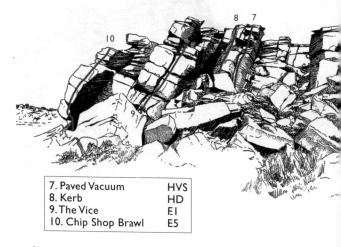

7. Paved Vacuum	HVS
8. Kerb	HD
9. The Vice	E1
10. Chip Shop Brawl	E5

Chimney for nine metres before traversing into the cracks just below the jammed block.

Doctor's Chimney 18m S 4a ★★ (1919)
To the left is a three-metre high pillar guarding access to a long chimney system. Climb either side of the pillar to reach the narrow soaring chimney. Tricky moves are needed to enter the main fissure which is followed without deviation to the top.

Which Doctor? 18m E5 6a ★ (1991)
Start around to the left of Doctor's Chimney at a shallow corner. Climb this and the wall above to gain the right-hand edge of the upper ledge on Physician's Wall. Make an intricate traverse out to the arête and slap wildly up this to reach safety.

Physician's Wall 12m E1 6a (1976)
The wall just to the right of Cripple's Crack provides one tough, but well-protected, move.

Cripple's Crack 12m HVD ★★ Nancy L 6.6.04 (1923-51)
Cloe S
The steep rightward-slanting crack that splits the centre of the north-facing wall.

306

1. Surgeon's Saunter	HVS
2. Which Doctor	E5
3. Cripple's Crack	HVD
4. Doctored	HVS
5. Nursery Crack	VS
6. Child's Play	HVS

Doctored 12m HVS 5c   (1983)
Climb the centre of the wall, to the left of the wide crack, with
one very long reach.

To the left of the tall tower of Surgeon's Saunter *et al* is a
broad, block-filled bay. Fifteen metres to the left of the previous
route is a narrow tower split by a 'wellington-width' crack.

Nursery Crack 8m VS 5a-ish   (1923-51)
The wide crack provides a good route for learning off-width
techniques. Using blocks on the right to get started is cheating,
but eminently sensible.

Child's Play 7m HVS 5a   (1984)
Climb the arête to the left of Nursery Crack on its left-hand
side, moving leftwards to finish.

Kindergarten 6m VS 4b   (1983-89)
Takes the centre of the north face of the tower and leads to a
finish close to Child's Play. The short north-facing wall five

metres to the left can be climbed up its centre, **Pie Face** VS 4b
(1960s).

Ten metres to the left and near the top of the cliff is a narrow
projecting buttress with a flake crack on its right side.

DESCENT ROUTE

The blocky gully to the right of the next small buttress gives an
easy way down.

Paved Vacuum 8m HVS 5a (1979)
Climb the flake-crack to a small ledge and tackle the stubborn
overhang above. The right arête of the block to the right of
Paved Vacuum is **And There's More** VS 5a (1992).

Kerb 8m HD (1992)
The slabby left-hand side of the arête is climbed to a finish up a
short corner to its the left.

Down and to the left is a taller buttress that has slumped to the
right. Its narrow front face is split by a slanting crack that smiles
in a strangely alluring kind of way.

The Vice 9m E1 5b ★★ (1962)
Starting from the ground (and not the boulder on the right)
attack the nasty overhanging crack by a variety of agonisingly
painful jams to a grotesque shelving exit that could leave you
shredded.

Around to the left is the first of a pair of attractive north-facing
slabs. The first one is bounded on its left-hand side by an inviting,
black, narrowing slit. This slab has some good lower grade routes.

Crab Crawl Arête 11m VS 4c ★ (traditional)
Start at the right-hand corner of the slab and follow the right-
hand arête as closely as possible.

The Crab Crawl 11m S ★★ (1919-23)
There is a small overlap at three metres. Start below the left-
hand edge of this and climb past it, then continue up the slab in
a direct line.

Prospero's Climb 12m VD ★★ (1921)
Start in the centre of the slab right of Caliban's Cave, at a crack.
Follow this to the first ledge and move left to gain the
prominent layback flake; finish up this.

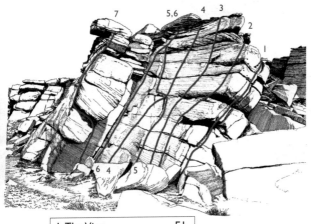

1. The Vice	E1
2. Crab Crawl Arête	VS
3. The Crab Crawl	S
4. The Tempest	VS
5. Prospero's Climb	VD
6. Caliban's Cave	HS
7. Chip Shop Brawl	E5

Miranda's Variation   12m   VD   ★   (1919-23)
Follow the previous route to the first ledge. Traverse right until
it is possible to move easily up to a higher ledge. This is
followed back left to the prominent flake, up which a finish is
made.

Green Ginger   11m   S   (1990s)
Start just to the left and climb directly to, and finish up, the
flake-crack on Prospero's Climb.

The Tempest   12m   VS 5a   (1996)
Begin just right of the black chimney and climb the slab to a
thin pocket. Make precarious moves up and right and continue
in the same line (above the lower crack of Prospero's Climb)
directly to the cliff top.

Caliban's Cave   11m   HS 4b   ★   (1921)
Awkward back-and-footing up the black, narrowing recess leads
to a rest on a ledge on the left before the difficult overhang.

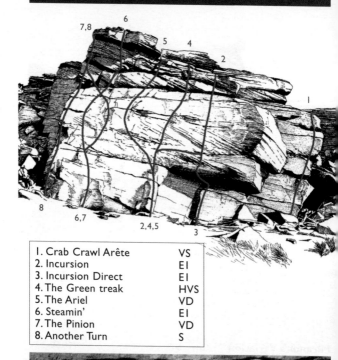

1. Crab Crawl Arête	VS
2. Incursion	E1
3. Incursion Direct	E1
4. The Green treak	HVS
5. The Ariel	VD
6. Steamin'	E1
7. The Pinion	VD
8. Another Turn	S

END SLAB

The final routes of substance in this area are on the sheet of rock which is End Slab. This leans back against the Crab Crawl Slab in a rather lazy manner. Unlike its neighbour the routes on End Slab are poorly protected and so a steady approach is required.

Chip Shop Brawl 11m E5 6c ★★   (1987)
From the tip of the block under the right edge of the overhang, leap on to, and slap desperately up, the brutish arête above.

High Flyer 11m E4 6a ★★   (1979)
Take off from the block under the overhanging right-hand arête and make a hard dynamic move (6b for the short) leftwards to gain the front face of the slab just left of Incursion. Follow the right-hand edge of this with an unforgettable move to gain the ledge; unprotected.

That Floating Fatman 11m E1 5c (1999)
Start between High Flyer and Incursion Direct below an
obvious pocket which is used to gain the slab; finish directly.
Unprotected and squeezed-in.

Incursion 13m E1 5b ★ (1962)
Go directly up the slab just left of the cutaway until a two-
metre traverse rightwards enables one to climb the centre of
the slab above the cutaway; unprotected. A direct start E1 6a
pulls directly out of the cutaway, using pockets, to the right-
hand end of the traverse of Incursion. A large puddle often
lurks below.

Slight Second 12m E1 5b (1979)
A blinkered approach enables one to squeeze between The
Green Streak and Incursion; unprotected.

1. Incursion	E1
2. The Green Streak	HVS
3. The Ariel	VD
4. Steamin'	E1
5. Another Turn	S
6. Bad Do	VS
7. Green Party	VS

The Green Streak 12m HVS 4c ★★ (1919-23)
A direct route up the slab just left of the cutaway with delicate
moves on pockets.

The Ariel 15m VD ★★ Clove L 6.6.04 (1919-23)
Nancy S
Start as for The Green Streak and trend diagonally leftwards to
gain a small projecting ledge, 'the Corbel'. From there climb to
the break and traverse to the left, around the corner and finish
close to the arête.

Steamin' E1 5b ★ (1983)
From one metre right of the edge of the slab climb directly up a
delicate slab, passing the right-hand edge of a thin overlap. From
the ledge, climb a short crack, a tricky wall and the final reachy
roof at its centre.

The Pinion 14m VD ★★ Nancy L 6.6.04 (1921)
Clove S
Start just to the right of the arête. Climb up for three metres,
make a long stride to an incut hole and move up to the small
ledge of 'the Corbel'. Go up to a break and rightwards for three
metres, and upwards again to finish on a large ledge.

1. Bathtime for Two	VS
2. You	VS
3. Splashing	HVS

Another Turn 11m S ★ (1976-83)
The left-hand arête of End Slab is climbed directly. The lower
section is delicate and poorly protected and the steeper, upper
part has good runners and large holds.

Bad Do 9m VS 4c (1987)
The narrow side wall of the slab is climbed starting from blocks.
The initial moves provide a delicate crux. From the ledge pull
over a juggy bulge and finish directly.

The Rack 11m D ~~Nancy~~ S *Clare L 6.6.06* (1951-64)
The wide crack in the left-bounding corner of the slab leads to
a finish up the short arête on the left.

Green Party 8m VS 5b (1989)
A mediocre route up the centre of a small, green slab to the
left of The Rack. The initial slab is puzzling but well-protected
and the remainder of the route is just plain green.

The Edge countinues northwards in the form of small unmarked
rocks, in a peaceful setting. The first block is 10 metres across the
open gully from End Slab.

START BUTTRESS

You 8m VS 4c (1992)
Climb a short crack in the recess on the right-hand side of the
wall, then swing leftwards along the break and make a powerful
pull into a short, finishing chimney.

Bathtime for Two 6m VS 5a (1989)
The steep wall just to the left of the start of You and crossing
its traverse has a tough initial move.

Splashing 6m HVS 5a (1989)
On the left-hand side of the buttress climb the blocky chimney
and swing rightwards below the first overhang on the right-
hand arête. Finish strenuously up this.

Goodtime 6m HS 4b (1989)
The flake-crack in the leaning wall to the left of the corner is a
mini-Rasp.

Seventy metres farther north is the final part of Stanage, a short
wall split by a central crack.

Slow Down 7m S (1992)

Start at a wide crack on the right-hand side of the face and follow it as it curves leftwards. Finish up the short wall above.

Faster 6m VS 5a (1992)

The face to the right of the central crack gives a pleasant pitch.

Move 6m HD (1992)

The short, central corner is followed without deviation.

Start 7m VS 5a (1992)

The face to the left of the central crack is climbed until it is necessary to use the left-hand arête.

1. Slow Down	S
2. Faster	VS
3. Move	HD
4. Start	VS

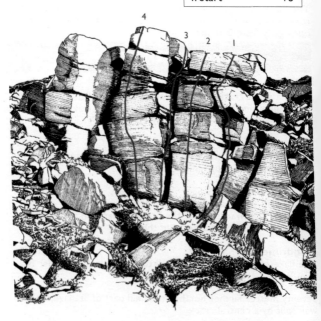

The Stanage Girdle Traverse
5000m (ish)   E5 6b (ish)   ★★★   †   (1992)
The crag has been girdled in its entirety by Ron Fawcett. The first ascent took Fawcett 6 hours 10 minutes to complete and is still unrepeated (2002). It is without doubt the longest route in the UK and the longest description ever featured in a UK guidebook.

Start easily by crossing breaks in green slab at left side of *End Slab*, foot-traverse a break and go up *Incursion* to a ledge. Cross right into *Caliban's Cave* on to a very sloping shelf near the top. Easy, mid-height traversing across the next slab to easy ground above the crux crack of *The Vice* and on to blocks. Cross the next two walls on very green breaks, awkward, and then low from *Child's Play* round into *Nursery Crack* and out on very dirty holds to blocks. Cross these to *Doctored*, traverse the obvious break to *Cripple's Crack* and head across and down to ledges. These lead on round into the chimney, then *Surgeon's Saunter* via the *Doctor's Start*.

Swing out on the big rounded pocket, very green, to easier ground and ledges leading to *The Wobbler* wall. Start high, cross some very impressive ground with hands just below the top leading to the final holds on *Good Clean Fun* — hard and green. From the top of *The Wobbler* continue on more dirty holds into *February Crack*. Swing out on to the very steep right wall on holds very near the top, which leads quickly across *Exaltation* into *Old Salt* and down this to a move across to *Valediction*. Finger-traverse the obvious break, hard, to *Monad* and on to the chimney.

Cross the next wall easily at half-height with the odd interesting move to ledges leading to *Microbe* wall. Swing on to the wall high on small finger-holds into *Microbe* and go down slightly to a finger ledge on *Germ*. Cross this to a crack and stretch into *Problem Corner*, from the bottom of this a very hard move gains a steep, green wall which leads to *Love Handles*, the arête and round this to the hillside.

Walk to *Wetness Wall*, cross delicately and carefully above the roof on rounded, dirty breaks to an easy corner. Finger-traverse the next short wall to the hillside. Walk to *Marble Wall*. Cross ledges on the aptly named *Green Wall* to the corner, then follow breaks to the arête and better rock to *Sceptic*. Follow *Lamia* to the final break below the roof, swing right on this to *Goosey Goosey Gander* and, at last, a rest on the top bit of *Don's Delight*. Cross blocks to *Cleft Buttress* and sneak around the back, bridging, until it is possible to swing on to *Vena Cave-in*, swing round the arête on the break and continue at the same level to the hillside.

Walk to *Crow Chin*. Easily cross the buttress at one third height to the hillside, walk to *Twin Buttress* and hand-traverse the break to below the hanging crack. Continue on ripples at the same level into the chimney, then on good holds to a horizontal crack leading to the arête, round this to the hillside. Walk to the next buttress, cross this on dirty ledges and breaks to another walk to *Deuteronomy Buttress*. From the first break of *Cheeky Little Number* swing across to *Exodus*, go down this a bit and stretch across to *Leviticus*. Go up to a high break and cross this to *Missing Numbers* and the arête. Cross the gully to *Treatment* and traverse the front face of the buttress on good holds to the hillside. Walk to *Pup*, go up this to cross via a finger-break, cross this to *Puss* and easier ground to the hillside.

Walk to the *Quantum Crack* area and easily cross this above the first roof to another walk to *Birthday Buttress*. Hand-traverse the obvious break to the arête, go up this to a ledge and along this to walk to *Heather Crack*, get into it at two thirds height and down it to delicate moves across *Flipside* into *Travesties*. Go up this to a swing out right on the top break, cross *Pig's Ear* at this level to a chimney. Go down this to very low moves out below *No More Excuses* to *The Knutter* and up this to a break above the crux and cross this to the hillside.

Walk to *The Blurter*. Easily cross ledges under *Overcoat's* crux roof to the gully, follow rounded breaks high out of this, very green, to *The Blurter* above its difficulties. Continue at the same level on ledges across the chimney to more ledges and round the corner to the hillside.

Walk to a small slab, go easily across this on horizontals to easier slabs and High Neb. Cross the bottom of the short wall to *Eric's Eliminate* at half-height, then into and down *Twisting Crack* to cross under the roof of *Kelly's Overhang* to *Inaccessible Crack*. Go across *Impossible Slab* under its hard stuff and continue on the same level under *Quietus* to *Norse Corner*. Cross to *King Kong* below its crux and down to breaks and awkward moves, low, into *Sogines* and *Neb Corner*. Move easily across to *High Neb Edge*, go up this to a green hand-traverse across *Old Friends*, just above the crux, to easier climbing leading to the end of the wall.

Walk to the next dirty buttress under *Mr Universe* and into the chimney. Go out on to the edge, up *Blockhead* and high across the next few short routes to a walk to some small walls. Cross these to low on *Anniversary Arête* then up to near the top of edge to a high traverse across *Grain of Truth* to gain the end of the wall.

Walk to *Broken Buttress*. Easily cross these to *Enclosure Buttress*. Traverse easily at mid-height to *Haze* then up, taking care with brittle holds, to a gully. Descend to a low level crossing of the remaining walls, very dirty. Continue along chossy walls and a very small buttress to *Count's Buttress*. From midway up the small buttress left of *Eden Arête*, cross it and into a chimney. Go up this to swing out on a horizontal break above *Nightmare Slab*. Follow the break across *Daydreamer* slab to the corner, go high out of this, very sloping and green, to the arête, and then at same level cross *Cool Curl* to the chimney. Descend to a horizontal crossing of *Count's Buttress* all the way to the arête, swing round this on jams to the crack and steeply climb into the corner. Easily cross breaks to a very difficult bit getting around the holly on *Prickly Crack*. Then on to *Shock Horror Slab* at two-thirds height on good horizontals into the grassy gully and down easily round the next buttresses, then walk on to the slab left of *D.I.Y.* wall. Cross the slab easily to ledges and swing round on to the sloping ledges of *Black and Decker*. Cross *D.I.Y.* on breaks and pockets to *Grime* crack, ascend to dirty holds on the right which lead into the top of *Sithee* and the gully.

Walk and scramble across the next wall and buttresses to *Wall End*. Cross very green breaks on *Outlook Buttress* into *Outlook Layback*, swing round high on to a hard, high traverse on awkward jams to the crack. Keeping high, cross the next few routes on green breaks to *Fern Crack*. Go down this to the traverse of *Fern Groove* and move easily into and across *Wall End Slab* to *Pure, White and Deadly*. Go up this to ledges and walk across to the next wall.

Cross low breaks on *Giro* to easy ground, up, down and then around into *Helfenstein's Struggle*. Hand-traverse out onto *Archangel* and into *Goliath's*, then out on *Doncaster's Route* onto ledges in the gully. Go through a slot round the back of *White Wand*, on to *Fairy Steps* and easily cross this and round the next wall. Walk down to *Spur Slab*, which is easy to *Living at the Speed*, cross this on the high break to a chimney and out on *Mark's Slab*. Continue on the same break to easy ground on *Pullover* and the hillside.

Walk to *Fina*, cross on high breaks then down to the first break to traverse low, dirty, into *Centaur*. Go up and move right into the chimney. Cross easily to *Cinturato*, gain it at half-height and ascend to a big horizontal, swing round into *Esso Extra* and from this reverse into the gully. Cross ledges above *Tower Crack* to move round corner above *Tower Face*.

Go down *Tower Face's* flake to a break, climb easily into the gully and out on to *Stretcher Case*. Continue traversing the top break on to *Nuke The Midges* and on to hillside. From *Strangler Buttress* cross *Swooper Slab* via a low traverse. Once in the gully traverse low, dirty break on to ledges, and round on to easy ground leading to *Small Dreams* buttress. Take a high green traverse out right to easy ground left of *Hathersage Trip*. From low on *Mercury Crack* swing round the first break above a nasty drop (feet scraping boulders but not the ground) to still hard moves but above a 'better' drop to *Overhanging Crack*. A strenuous hand-traverse across an obvious break leads to *Corner Crack* and up this before finger-traversing the high break across *National Breakdown* to the arête.

Finger-traverse the next walls on reasonable but very green breaks (good landing) to a high traverse into *Taurus Crack* and *Valhalla*. Go down this to foot-traverse with 'Thank God' finger pockets across into *Pegasus Wall*. Go up this to mid height, cross into *Pegasus Rib* and *Flake Gully*. A longish move on slopers leads to *Crossover*, then reverse this by a long stretch down for an undercut to good footholds. Climb *Overhanging Wall* to the arête, then steepish green moves cross *Flate* to short walls with green, slithery moves to the hillside.

From high on *Paradise Lost* go round the arête to easy high breaks leading into *Paradise Wall*. Go down this to ledges and a low traverse through a hollybush below *Comus* leads to *Sand Gully*. Go in and up *Sand Crack* and out on to *Billiard Buttress* taking a high break to *Millsom's Minion*. Very scary moves lead across the top break, green and hard, into *Cue*. Reverse this down into the top of the gully. Go over the back of the flake to a fingery traverse across *Between the Two* and on to *Tridymite Slab*, delicately cross this at half-height to easy ground. This leads to *Cannon* and *Slanting Crack*, from which go down this to a hardish low stretch into *Straight Ahead*. Even harder low moves on crumbly footholds and dirty undercuts lead to easier ground and on to ledges left of *Boys Will Be Boys*. Go low across this to a long, long lurch into *Capstone Chimney*.

Swing out low across *Moribund* to *Namenlos*, go up this to ledges on the right then easy ground to *August Arête*. Go up this to a break, cross *Telli* into a gully and out on a bendy flake to good holds leading into *Rib Chimney*. Hand-traverse out above *Nightsalt*, round the arête to *Calvary* and reverse the friable flake and hard mantel, very hard, to the first break, cross this under *Defying Destiny* into chimney. Go low and easily to ledges left of the *Unconquerable's* buttress. From below the crux pull of *Little Unconquerable*, hand-traverse (high up) into *Left Unconquerable* just under its crux. Reverse this to a low traverse into *Right Unconquerable*, continue at this level to the arête, go up this for a couple of moves and gain the chimney. Climb down and out on to *Curving Buttress*, go low across this and on to easy ground leading to a walk to *Twin Towers*. Very dirty and green climbing crosses here to another walk to a small wall with possibly the shortest routes on Stanage? Hand-traverse mid-level break on these walls to walk to a small wall. Easily cross this to *Dover's Wall* routes, where an easy traverse at half-height gains *Cleft Wing*. Go up and out on the wing to easy ground and *B.A.W.'s Crawl*.

From low out of the gully, no ground touching, reach the hand-traverse, go up the crux pull then continue traversing into the gully and out on good holds to *Pedlar's Rib*. Descend this to a low traverse leading to *Pedlar's Slab*. Go up this to an easy traverse into the crack/gully. Climb down this to a low swinging hand-traverse below *Plastic Dream* then on to and up *Old Dragon*. Easy hand-traversing from ledges cross *Greengrocer Wall* and *Verandah Wall* into a gully. Go out at half height to *Second Wind*. Swing round the arête on green breaks which lead into *Turf Crack*. Traverse easily across to *Martello Buttress* then take a low swing out right on to good hand-holds and breaks crossing *Saliva* into *Devil's Chimney*. Escape out of this and up *Step Ladder Crack* to a high traverse above the crux of *Dark Water* and into *Hell Crack*.

Continue at the same level into the gully. Go out on high and green holds to *Acheron* and into *Mississippi Chimney*. Descend this to swing round roofs heading down to a delicate shuffle across a foot ledge to below the crux of *Morrison's Redoubt*. Climb up this to a high traverse into the gully. Go high across a jumble of blocks, and *Balcony Buttress*, to caves. Virtually walking over ledges above *Wuthering* and continue at the same level, easily, to *Robin Hood Caves*.

From *Balcony Cave Direct*, traverse high on the break across *Pacific Ocean Wall* into *Desperation* at the big jugs and climb easily into *Staircase*. Green and sloping moves continue out around the next section to gain *Ellis's Eliminate*. Move out of this to the arête and into the top of *Inverted V*, from its right-hand variation and easy ground cross this to *Wright's Route*. Reverse this, very green, to a low traverse out on to *Whillans' Pendulum* and *Black Slab*. Cross the mid-level break to easy ground leading to *Topaz*. Take a very low, long stretch into *Green Crack* and easily cross *Rusty Wall* at half-height to easy ground with a pleasantly exposed bit around *Leaning Buttress Direct* at two thirds height.

Stroll across to *Flying Buttress*, go down this and across the slab under the roof to *Kirkus's Corner*. Climb this to a good hold then across the steep wall on green holds to a gully. Move out to the arête then delicately across the top of *Censor* to ledges. Walk across these to easy ground all the way to *Grotto Wall*. Go up this to good breaks and hand-traverse these to more strolling. Go high into *Rugosity Crack* then descend crossing *Plate Glass* and into *Mantelpiece Direct*. Perform its crux overhang to ledges and a well-deserved stroll to the hillside past *End Buttress*. Finish.

The Lamia E2 5c (page 292)
Climbers: Nigel & David Smart   Photo: Dave Wilkinson

Old Salt   **HVS 5a**   (page 300)
Climber: Seb Grieve   Photo: David Simmonite

Graded List

Just a few routes for discussion.

E8
Marbellous (7a)

E7
Careless Torque (7a)
Flight of Ideas (7a)
Black Car Burning (6c)
Groove is in the Heart (7a)
Little Women (7a)
Unfamiliar (6c)
Dreadnought (7a)
Cemetery Waits (6c)
Shine On (6c)

E6
Klingon (7a)
Sad Amongst Friends (6c)
Carpe Diem (6c)
Turtle Power (6c)
Boys will be Boys (6c)
Grace and Danger (6c)
My Herald
  of Free Enterprise (6c)
Skinless Wonder (6c)
Scapa Flow (6c)
Crypt Trip (6b)
Skidoo (6b)
9 o'clock Watershed (6c)
Master of Disguise (6c)
Ulysses (6b)
Wall of Sound (6b)
Back in the YMCA (6c)
Big Air (6b)
Defying Destiny (6b)
Weather Report (6b)
Star Trek (6b)
Paranoid (6b)
Heath Robinson (6b)
Indian Summer (6c)

E5
Shirley's Shining Temple (6c)
Chip Shop Brawl (6c)
Silk (6c)

Stanage without Oxygen (6c)
Headless Chicken (6b)
Pacific Ocean Wall (6b)
Trickledown Fairy (6b)
Saltation (6c)
White Wand (6a)
Punishment (6b)
Thunder Road (6a)
Goosey, Goosey Gander (6a)
Boc No Buttress (6a)

E4
Twin Cam (6c)
Nightsalt (6c)
Good Clean Fun (6b)
The Hathersage Trip (6a)
Snug as a Thug (6b)
Guillotine Direct (6b)
Nectar (6b)
In a Big Way Yerself (6b)
Quietus Right-hand (6a)
No More Excuses (6b)
Calvary (6a)
Grain of Truth (6b)
Old Friends (6a)
Chameleon (6a)
Direct Loss (6a)
Off With His Head (6a)
Harvest (6b)
High Flyer (6a)
Slap 'n Spittle (6a)
Comus (6a)
Stanleyville (5c)
Wolf Solent (5c)
Crime (5c)
The Strangler (5c)
Beautician (5c)

E3
Improbability Drive (6b)
Satin (6b)
Invisible Maniac (6b)
Crew Pegs Diffs (6a)
In-off (5c)

The Asp (6a)
Telli (6a)
Tippler Direct (6a)
D.I.Y. (6a)
Black Hawk Bastion (6a)
King Kong (6a)
The Logic Book (6a)
Archangel (5b)
Impossible Slab (5c)
Censor (5c)
Moribund (5c)
The Guillotine (5c)
Cave Eliminate (6a)
Vena Cave-in (5c)

E2

Daydreamer (6b)
Shock Horror Slab (6b)
Not to be Taken Away (6a)
Fading Star (6a)
Germ (6a)
Fern Groove (5c)
Quietus (5c)
Silica (5c)
Orang-outang (5c)
The Dangler (5c)
Count's Buttress (5c)
The Old Dragon (5b)
The Count (5c)
Yosemite Wall (5b)
The Lamia (5c)
Tower Face Direct (5b)
Wall End Slab Direct (5b)
Argus (5b)
Wuthering (5b)
Pot Black (5b)
Curving Buttress (5b)
Dry Rot (5b)

E1

Centaur (5c)
Nightmare Slab (5c)
The Mangler (5c)
The Unprintable (5b)
Incursion Direct (6a)
Desperation (5c)
Dark Continent (5c)
Punklet (6a)

Nuke The Midges (5c)
Pedlar's Rib (5c)
Anniversary Arête (5b)
Goodbye Toulouse (5b)
The Tippler (5b)
Greengrocer Wall (5c)
The Vice (5b)
Tower Chimney (5b)
Kirkus's Corner (5b)
The Left Unconquerable (5b)
Acheron (5b)
Tom-cat Slab (5b)
Morrison's Redoubt (5b)
Saliva (5b)
Easter Rib (5b)
Flying Buttress Direct (5b)
Millsom's Minion (5b)
Gullible's Travels (5b)
Incursion (5b)
Hearsay Crack (5a)
Crescent Arête (5b)
Namenlos (5a)

HVS

Suzanne (6a)
Rusty Wall (6a)
Kelly's Overhang (5b)
The Wobbler (5b)
Rugosity Crack (5b)
Pedlar's Slab (5c)
Paucity (5b)
Surgeon's Saunter (5b)
Black Magic (5b)
Travesties (5b)
Overhanging Wall (5b)
The Little Unconquerable (5a)
Deuteronomy (5b)
Leviticus (5b)
Terrazza Crack (5b)
The Link (5b)
Congo Corner (5b)
Black Magic (5b)
Eliminator (5b)
Fina (5b)
The Blurter (5b)
Apparent North (5b)
The Watch-tower (5b)
The Flange (5b)

Cave Arête (5a)
The Knutter (5b)
Billiard Buttress (5a)
Tower Crack (5a)
The Mississippi Variant (5a)
The Scoop/Ozymandis (5a)
BAW's Crawl (5a)
Goliath's Groove (5a)
Right-Hand Tower (5b)
Rusty Crack (5b)
Traversties (5b)
Cave Gully Wall (5a)
August Arête (5b)
Exodus (5a)
Pegasus Rib (5a)
Sudoxe (5b)
Cleft Wing (5b)
Queersville (5a)
The Right Unconquerable (5a)
Old Salt (5a)
Square Buttress Direct (5b)
Agony Crack (5a)
Harding's Super
   Direct Finish (5a)
Dover's Wall, Route 2 (5a)
Centre Stage (5a)
Tower Face Original (5a)
Fern Crack (5a)
Twin Chimneys Buttress (5a)
Retroversion (4c)
Grotto Wall (4c)
The Green Streak (4c)
Townsend's Variation (4c)

VS

The Groper (4c)
First Sister (4c)
Paradise Arête (4c)
High Neb Buttress (4c)
Count's Crack (4c)
The Little Flake Crack (5a)
Central Buttress (4c)
Cleft Wing Superdirect (4c)
Leaning Buttress Gully (4c)
Beggar's Crack (5a)
Inaccessible Crack (4c)
Ellis's Eliminate (4c)
Crab Crawl Arête (4c)

Cosmic Crack (4c)
Robin Hood's Cave
   Innominate (5a)
The Punk (4b)
Mississippi Buttress Direct (4c)
Tinker's Crack (4c)
Wall End Slab (5a)
Step-ladder Crack (5a)
Valhalla (5a)
Titanic (4c)
Wall Buttress (5a)
The Louisiana Rib (4c)
Norse Corner Climb (5a)
Hell Crack (4c)
Hargreaves' Original Route (4c)
Narrow Buttress (4c)
Heather Wall (4c)
Central Trinity (4c)
Milton's Meander (4c)
Marble Arête (4c)
Paradise Wall (4c)
Byne's Route (4c)
Gargoyle Buttress (4b)
Outlook Crack (4c)
Inverted V (4c)
Countess Buttress (4b)
Centrepiece (4c)
Gargoyle Buttress (4b)
Lucy's Delight (4b)
Zigzag Flake Crack (4a)
Rubber Band (4b)
Fairy Steps (4a)

HS

Manchester Buttress (4b)
Black Hawk (4c)
Castle Crack (4b)
April Crack (4b)
Martello Buttress (4b)
February Crack (4b)
Taurus Crack (4c)
Macleod's Variation (4b)
October Slab (4b)
Robin Hood's Right-Hand
   Buttress Direct (4a)
Christmas Crack (4b)
Holly Bush Gully Left (4b)
Kelly's Eliminate (4a)

Right-Hand Trinity (4a)

S
Avril (4a)
Jitter Face
Straight Crack (High Neb) (4b)
Marble Tower Flake (4c)
Broken Groove (4a)
Black Hawk Hell Crack (4a)
Balcony Buttress (4a) ✓
Robin Hood Zigzag (4a)
Twisting Crack
Amazon Crack (4a) ✓
Jitterbug Buttress (4a)
Crack and Corner (4b)
Aries
Bishop's Route (4a)
Outlook Layback (4b)
It's a Cracker (4b)
Dover's Wall, Route 1 (4a)
Doctor's Chimney (4a)
Kelly's Variation (4a)
Oblique Crack
The Crab Crawl
Flake Chimney
   (Robin Hood's Area)
Cave Buttress ✓
Lookout Flake

HVD
Verandah Buttress (5b)
Chockstone Chimney (4c)
✓Cripple's Crack
Slanting Chimney
Robin Hood's Crack ✓

VD
Hollybush Crack
Flying Buttress
Heaven Crack
Helfenstein's Struggle
Leaning Buttress Crack
Bent Crack ✓
Broken Buttress
Crack and Cave
Eckhard's Chimney
Robin Hood's Balcony Cave Direct
The Ariel ✓

Overhanging Chimney
Curving Chimney
Miranda's Variation
Hercules Crack
Meson
Black Hawk Traverse Left
Paradise Crack
Tango Crack
Broken Buttress
Mississippi Chimney
Prospero's Climb ✓
Hercules Crack
Rib Chimney
Leaning Buttress Indirect ✓
Kelly's Crack
The Pinion ✓
Intermediate Buttress
Crawly
Bow Crack
Right Twin Chimney ✓

HD
Boot Crack
Newhaven
Devil's Chimney
Duo Crack Climb

D
Black Hawk Traverse Right
Mantelshelf Climb ✓
Scraped Crack
Enclosure Crack
Holly Bush Gully Right
Dot's Slab
✓October Crack
Count's Chimney
Toxic
Boyd's Crack
Grotto Slab
Capstone Chimney
   (Grotto Slab Area)
Centurion's Slab
Spur Slab

M
Left Twin Chimney
Castle Chimney
Martello Cracks

First Ascents

1890-1903	**Count's Chimney, Hollybush Gully, Mississippi Chimney, Twin Chimneys** J W Puttrell
	Count's Chimney was named later by F C Aldous and Alf Schaanning after 'Count' Orloff, a friend of Schaanning whose first and last climb it was.
	High Neb Gully may have also been climbed around this time by Puttrell but no records exist.
1904	**Castle Chimney** (Black Hawk Chimney) J W Puttrell
1912-1914	**Eckhard's Chimney** Miss Eckhard
	'A redoubtable lead'.
1912-1914	**Boyd's Crack** W A Boyd
1912-1914	**Tango Crack** F C Aldous, Alf Schaanning
	'Aldous and Schaanning first gardened and then climbed Tango Crack one Saturday afternoon, but it did not get its name until the following morning when they were joined by Worthington. Aldous invited him to lead the route, and when he was about seven feet up he peeled off, landing safely but with a surprised expression on his face. Aldous smiled and said: "But this is an easy climb — that is, when you know the steps — just like the tango."'
1912-1914	**Black Hawk Traverse** (Bishop's Stride) Henry Bishop
1912-1914	**Inaccessible Slab, Wall End Crack, Castle Crack** (Black Hawk Slit), **Stomach-traverse, Neb Crack** (Corner?), **Hollybush Gully** (both branches), **Tower Chimney** (right of Tower Face, not described in the text), **Forked Chimney, Tunnel Crack, The Cave Chimney, Zigzag Climb, Boulder Chimney,** (last five routes not described in the text), **Blizzard Chimney, Cracks A, B** and **C** (possibly Nightride Corner, B Crack, and Scraped Crack), **The Ladder Cracks, Wall Crack** (between Count's Chimney and Wall End), **The Grotto** (Grotto Slab?), **The Grotto Chimney** (Capstone Chimney?), **The Christiania Swing** (known as Niche Wall prior to 1989 guidebook). Various climbers including Henry Bishop, Douglas Yeomans, F C Aldous, Claude Worthington, W F Boyd, W A Boyd (the bird-watcher), Bernard Garlick, Alf Schaanning, Miss Eckhard
	Above routes recorded in Rucksack Club Journal Volume 2 by F C Aldous.
1915	H M (Harry) Kelly appeared on the scene with his wife, Pat, who reluctantly accompanied him on several first ascents.
1915 Feb 21	**High Neb Girdle Traverse** (incomplete) Harry Kelly
	Climbed in two sections missing out the traverse across High Neb Buttress which was solved by Ivar Berg on 31 October 1915.
1915 March 14	**Inaccessible Crack** Harry Kelly
	Kelly started up Inaccessible Slab then traversed right.
1915 March 21	**Overhanging Chimney** Harry Kelly

1915 Oct 31	**High Neb Buttress** Ivar Berg (solo)
	Started on the left. Berg bivouacked at the crag and soloed the route before Kelly arrived.
1915 Oct 31	*Ivar Berg soloed the traverse across High Neb Buttress.*
1915	**Twisting Crack** Harry Kelly and party
1919-1923	**The Ariel, The Green Streak, Miranda's Variation, The Crab Crawl, Tango Buttress, Wall End Slab**
	These climbs, along with others above were recorded by R K Evans in the Rucksack Club Journal Volume 5 in 1923. Later on in that year published his Recent Developments on Gritstone which listed 48 climbs on Stanage. This contained, in addition to those already mentioned, the following routes; **Wall End Flake Crack, Robin Hood's Balcony Cave Direct, Robin Hood's Cave Gully, Robin Hood's Chockstone Chimney, Black Hawk Traverse Right, The Crack and Chimney** *(the last two are not in guidebook),* **Balcony Climb, Cave Buttress, Typical Grit, Mantelshelf Climb, Eckhard's Arête, High Neb Buttress** *(started direct and finished on right). Various climbers: including Fred Pigott, Morley Wood, Edgar Pryor, Lewis Coxon, George Bower, Cyril Ward, Frank Wallbank, Phil Barnes, Bernard Garlick, Rice Kemper Evans, Harry Kelly, Alf Schaanning and Fergus Graham.*
1919	**Doctor's Chimney, Manhattan Chimney, The Niche** A S (Fred) Pigott, Morley Wood, Rice Kemper Evans
	Rice Kemper Evans was the American Vice-Consul at Sheffield and was noted for his pleasantness, competence and strength rather than for exceptional skill. He is quoted as saying: "I guess I thought I'd write my name on Stanage, but it just didn't turn out that way." He is also credited with the invention of the word 'layback' with such a phrase as "You mean the pitch with the cute little layback." The routes were named in his honour.
1921	**Duo Crack, The Pinion, Caliban's Cave, Prospero's Climb** Harry Kelly, George Bower, Edgar Pryor, Rice Kemper Evans
1921 Aug 21	**High Neb Girdle Traverse** First complete ascent. Harry Kelly, Fred Pigott, Morley Wood, Bernard Garlick, Rice Kemper Evans
1921 Oct 21	*Kelly soloed High Neb Girdle Traverse in 15 minutes.*
1922	**Inverted V, Robin Hood Zigzag, Robin Hood's Right-Hand Buttress Direct, Garden Wall** Cyril Ward
	A superb collection of new routes. Robin Hood's Right-Hand Buttress Direct was also known as Buttonhook. Inverted V was probably the most difficult climb on the edge at that time and had been considered unjustifiable without a top-rope. Evans described it as "a whale of a climb, calculated to give some newspaper insurance scheme a nasty whack!"

1922	**Flying Buttress, Leaning Buttress Direct, Martello Buttress** Fergus Graham

1922 **Flying Buttress, Leaning Buttress Direct, Martello Buttress** Fergus Graham
Graham had a reputation for difficult solo climbing.

1922 **Robin Hood's Cave Traverse, Twin Chimneys Buttress** Lewis Coxon
Twin Chimneys Buttress still remains a committing lead.

1922 **Balcony Buttress** Lewis Coxon, Cyril Ward, Rice Kemper Evans

1923-1951 **Beech Tree Wall**
Inexplicably this has been called Birch Tree Wall *in recent editions of this guide. Perhaps even more odd is the fact that the birch on Birch Tree Wall at Black Rocks was identified as a beech in 1928.*

1926 **Hollybush Crack, Christmas Crack** George Bower
Bower's motto was, 'What man has done, other men can do'.

1926 **Kelly's Overhang** Morley Wood
An uncharacteristically bold and difficult climb for the time. Despite Phil Barnes's photographs the route was, unusually, not recorded and some sceptics have still to be convinced about its origins. Nevertheless it remains a fine struggle for many, who often doubt the grade.

1927 **The Mississippi Buttress Direct**
Top-roped by Albert Hargreaves and Roy Horsman
Rumoured to have been led eventually by Horsman although no actual record can be found of the first lead.

1928 **Black Slab** Albert Hargreaves
Hargreaves led the unprotected slab on sight at his first attempt; an impressive performance. A famous feature of the direct route, a rock button, was pulled off by Ken Davidson, making it much harder. Some time later in the Laddow cave two climbers were moaning that the vital rugosity had gone. "Some bastard has taken it away" said one of them. "Yes," said Davidson, producing it from his pocket, "here it is." 1966

1928 **Robin Hood Girdle Traverse** (not described in the guidebook) Roy Horsman, Albert Hargreaves
Considered to be one of the hardest routes on Stanage, the section across Black Slab being something of an epic; 'The crossing of Black Slab is very delicate and needs a steady leader...the traverse continues along to April Crack, the footholds gradually diminishing and the position being most exposed, until the last few feet become really tense'. 1951

1928 **Green Crack, Oblique Crack, April Crack, Rusty Wall** Herbert Hartley

1928 **Angle Crack** (not described in the guidebook) Maurice Linnell, Alf Bridge
Apparently 70 feet right of Manchester Buttress and 45 feet left of Crack and Corner.

1929 **Right-Hand Trinity, Central Trinity** Herbert Hartley
Two 'plums' which Hargreaves had also been after.

1929 **Robin Hood Flake Crack** Herbert Hartley?
This is almost certainly the route called Zigzag Flake Crack in the 1951 guidebook and The Great Flake in the 1964 guidebook.

1930s	**Curving Buttress** Possibly Eric Byne
	But as the route was originally graded Very Difficult and is now graded E2, there is some doubt.
1930s	**Mississippi Variant** Bernard Simmonds
	The route originally started up The Mississippi Buttress Direct route. The line described in the guide incorporates the original line of Stanleyville climbed in 1968. The current Stanleyville takes the wall to the right of this. Confused?
1930s	**Burgess's Variation** Frank Burgess
1930-1933	**Dover's Wall, Route 1** Harry Dover?
1930	**Wall End Slab Direct, Wall Buttress, Little Flake, Elliott's Variation** Frank Elliott, Harry Dover, Gilbert Ellis
	Their direct on Wall End Slab joined the original route at the break. Before the direct finish was added in 1983 it was graded E2 5b making it possibly the hardest route in the country at the time.
1932-1933	**Black Hawk, Black Hawk Hell Crack, Robin Hood's Crack, Byne's Route** (on Martello Buttress), **Count's Crack** Eric Byne, Clifford Moyer
	Black Hawk Hell Crack gained its name because 'all hell broke loose' when the resident hawk attacked the pioneers.
1932-1933	**Count's Buttress Direct?** Eric Byne, Clifford Moyer
	Until recently it was thought that Byne had climbed the 'traditional' Buttress route. However, Joe Brown was told by Byne that the climb went up the middle of the buttress. 'None of the Rock and Ice could do this, even on a top-rope. I eventually traversed right to the arete... I returned and led the arête a short time later'. Joe Brown, 1988. The route would have been Byne's finest lead being far above his usual standard. He reputedly found himself hopelessly committed and the route was 'unrepeated' until Al Parker's ascent in 1959 (which many people actually believe to be the first).
1932-1933	**Leaning Buttress Gully** Jim Lomas, ? Bannister
1932-1933	**Manchester Buttress, Black Hawk Girdle** (the latter not described in the guidebook) Maurice Linnell, Alf Bridge, Eric Byne, Clifford Moyer
1932	**Robin Hood's Cave Innominate, Cave Gully Wall** Alf Bridge
	The latter route was a remarkable lead on a snowy Sunday. Ascents of Cave Gully Wall saw probably the first use of double ropes in climbing. The same day, Eric Byne and Maurice Linnell discovered The Unconquerables.
1933	**Tower Chimney** Eric Byne?
	Given Exceptionally Severe in the 1951 guidebook.
1934	**Kirkus's Corner, The Kirkus Original** Colin Kirkus
	The Corner was a most outstanding display of climbing for the time. It was not repeated until September 2nd 1953 when it was top-roped by Peter Biven, T Turner, P Hassall and Joe Brown. That even Biven and Brown declined to lead it added considerably to its reputation. Kirkus also climbed a route on the Trinity Face but the line is unknown.

1930s-1940s	**Doncaster's Route** Michael and Tony Doncaster
	Although overshadowed by Goliath's Groove this route was
	a very difficult proposition, following the initial section of the
	groove.
1940	**Agony Crack** Len Chapman, Bernard Simonds
1946 May 12	**Harding's Super Direct Finish** Peter Harding,
	J Greaves, Ernest Phillips
	Originally called Cave Superdirect.
1947 Sept	**Goliath's Groove** Peter Harding, J N Millward,
	David Sampson, Ernest Phillips
	'It was suggested as a possibility by Alf Bridge during a
	walk along the edge with Harding and Moulam. The bottom
	half of the groove was already used by Doncaster's Route,
	but where this escapes out to the right Harding led directly on
	up. He and his two Stonnis companions used the jamming
	technique they had perfected on Black Rocks, but the fourth
	man, David Sampson, a powerfully built geologist from
	Sheffield University, laybacked the crack all the way and
	was pronounced a veritable Goliath by his friends. So the
	groove received its name'. 1966
1948	**Valhalla** Wilf White, Chuck Cook
	Cook and White were extremely powerful and talented
	climbers, whose abilities were largely overshadowed by the
	brilliance of Joe Brown.
1949	**The Left Unconquerable** Tom Probert, Albert Shutt
	Graded Exceptionally Severe in 1951. The climb was
	descended on a top-rope in 1932 by Maurice Linnell and Eric
	Byne and was soloed by Joe (Morty) Smith wearing plimsolls
	in the late '50s.
1949 Sept 4	**The Right Unconquerable** Joe Brown,
	Merrick (Slim) Sorrell, Wilf White
	The Unconquerables were discovered and named by Eric
	Byne and Maurice Linnell in 1932. They descended both of
	them on a top-rope but could not make an ascent. In the
	1930s Byron Connelly soloed down The Right Unconquer
	able but this apparently didn't count. Even Peter Harding
	failed on both the cracks in 1946 when he was climbing
	extremely well. Eric Byne wrote of the routes, 'Extreme
	severity on a rock climb usually implies technical severity
	coupled with exposure, sometimes strenuosity, and
	frequently an embarrassing lack of protection for the leader,
	all of which characteristics The Unconquerables certainly
	possessed, together with a reputation: and anyone who has
	made or repeated new climbs knows this can be the most
	formidable obstacle of all. Knowing nothing of Probert's earlier
	lead of the left-hand crack, Brown, seconded by Sorrell,
	proceeded to climb both of them with ease'. 1966.
	The Right Unconquerable was graded Exceptionally Severe
	in 1951 and Extreme in 1957.
1949	**Rugosity Wall** Chuck Cook (in nails)
1949	**Via Media, Townsend's Variation, Gargoyle Buttress,**
	Narrow Buttress Ron Townsend and members of the
	Peak Climbing Club

The Peak Climbing Club was formed in 1940, by Ron and Madge Townsend and was among the most outstanding contributors of new climbs in the Peak District'. 1966. Via Media was named after a route on the Teyrn Slab near Lliwedd.

1950	**Green Crack** Probably Eric Byne	
1950	**Marble Tower Flake, Marble Tower Wall** Eric Byne	

The latter route was superseded by Marble Arête in the 1960s.

1950 Nov	**Crack and Cave** Eric Byne, Charles Ashbury
1950 Nov	**Jitterbug Buttress** Eric Byne
1950 Late	**The Louisiana Rib** R A (Dick) Brown
1950	**Ellis's Eliminate** Top-roped by Gilbert Ellis, but who led it first remains a mystery.
1950-1951	**Tower Crack** Joe Brown, Slim Sorrell, Wilf White
1950-1951	**Overhanging Wall** Joe Brown, Slim Sorrell
1950-1951	**Namenlos** Joe Brown, Wilf White
1950-1951	**Step-ladder Crack** Ted Howard

Also climbed by Don Whillans and Joe Brown on April 27 1952 and named The Styx.

1951 Feb	**Via Dexter** AAJ (Tony) Moulam
1951 March	**Via Roof Route** Eric Byne, Charles Ashbury
1951 June 6	**Turf Crack, Little Tower** Dick Brown and party
1951	**Verandah Pillar** Dick Brown, Eric Byne
1951-1956	**Greengrocer Wall** Ray Burgess?
1952 April 27	**BAW's Crawl, The Z Crack** Joe Brown, JR (Nat) Allen, Don Whillans

If you were wondering as to the name: Brown, Allen and White's Crawl is obvious when you know the surnames.

1952 April 27	**The Unprintable** Don Whillans, Joe Brown, Nat Allen

Although overshadowed by The Dangler, many people find it as taxing a lead.

1952	**Terrazza Crack** Joe Brown, Don Whillans
1952	**Black Hawk Bastion** (1 peg for aid) Dick Brown, Donald Wooller, Frank Fitzgerald

'R A Brown, Donald Wooller and Frank Fitzgerald, fresh from pegging activities on Rivelin, assaulted the challenging Black Hawk Bastion with their ironmongery... Fortunately these three climbers then moved over to Matlock with eyes on the High Tor Bastion, Stanage took a deep breath of relief and the legitimate attacks began once more'. 1957.

The word Bastion is a corruption of the name given to the line before this trio proved that a peg in the right place could make even this ferocious buttress yield. Many people still think the route is a bit of a 'bastion' today.

Climbed free in 1975.

1952	**M Route** Reg Pillinger

Originally credited to Don Morrison et al in the early 1960s.

1953 Oct 6	**Quietus** Pete Biven

Biven top-roped the route and reputedly led it with one point of aid. It was free-climbed the following year.

1953 Oct 7	**Surgeon's Saunter** Peter Biven
	The upper section was already followed by Doctor's
	Saunter. (This route of ascent was graded VD in 1951.)
1953	**Indignity Wall** (not described in the guidebook)
	Slim Sorrell, Don Chapman
	This route, which appeared only in the 1957 Further
	Developments guidebook, appears to have been on the wall
	now climbed by Boys Will Be Boys, E6 6b.
1953	**The Little Unconquerable** Joe Brown, Wilf White
1953	**Cleft Wing** Joe Brown, Slim Sorrell
1954 April 21	**Niche Wall** Peter Biven, HTH (Trevor) Peck
	An enigmatic route.
1954 Oct 3	**Congo Corner** Pete Biven, Trevor Peck
1954	**Quietus** Joe Brown, Don Whillans
	Believing that Biven had led the route free, Whillans set
	about making a 'repeat' ascent only to fly off leaving Brown
	to take the prize. 'I can remember fixing a runner near the lip
	on two opposing stones in a horizontal crack'.
	Joe Brown 1988.
1954	**Butcher Crack** Peter Biven
1954	**The Nose** Joe Brown, Don Whillans
1954	**The Dangler** Joe Brown, Ron Mosely
	Their ascent 'astonished the Stanage clientele'. 1957. The
	route's and Brown's reputations were further enhanced by
	pictures of him casually hanging from one hand whilst
	smoking a cigarette. A pre-placed sling was used for
	protection. The first lead without pre-placed protection was
	made by Ted Howard shortly after the first ascent.
1955 Sept 3	**Saliva** Peter Biven
1955	**Count's Buttress** Joe Brown, Slim Sorrell
	Mistakenly thought to have been climbed by Eric Byne, whose
	line actually followed that taken by The Direct.
1956 April 8	**The Flange, Easter Rib** Peter Biven, Trevor Peck
1956 April	**B P Super, Tower Face Direct, The Roundabout,**
	Ferryboat Highway Pete Biven, Trevor Peck
	Undoubtedly one of the hardest routes on grit at the time,
	B P Super was given the grade 'Excessively Severe'. As a
	result of losing holds, the 1964 guidebook stated that 'The
	route of B P Super is now considered impossible, and so is
	not listed'. It was reclimbed in 1965 and incorporated into
	Indian Summer in 1986.
1956 Sept 17	**Flying Buttress Direct** (4 pegs for aid) D A Lomas
	Led free in 1966.
1957 May	**Esso Extra** Joe Brown, Wilf White
1957 Sept 20	**Hangover** Bob Brayshaw, N K T Froggatt, G S Kitt
1957 Nov	**Aries** Al Parker, Richard McHardy, Peter Bamfield
	The first new route by Al Parker, who along with his friends in
	the Alpha Club, has made a major contribution to the
	climbing on Stanage.
1957 Nov	**Mother's Day** Al Parker, Peter Bamfield
1957-1960	**Titbit** Don Morrison and others
1957-1960	**Right Twin Crack** Rodney Wilson
1958 Jan	**Pullover** Allan Austin, Brian Evans

1958 April	**Jeepers Creepers** Joe Brown
1958 Nov 11	**Lusitania** Al Parker, Peter Bamfield, B Platt
1958 Nov	**Fina** Al Parker, Peter Bamfield
1958 Dec	**Heather Crack, Green Wall** B Platt, Al Parker
1958	**Seranata** Al Parker, Peter Bamfield
1958	**Titanic** Al Parker, Hugh Banner, Lew Brown
1958	**The Coign** Geoffrey Sutton
1958	**Centaur** Don Whillans, Joe (Morty) Smith
1958	**Slab and Crack** Nat Allen, Joe Brown
	Climbed, claimed and named by Bob Brayshaw, Al Parker in 1960 as Sickle, under which name it appeared in the 1976 guidebook.
1958	**N Route** Nat Allen, Nip Underwood
	Also claimed by Bob Brayshaw and N K T Froggatt in August 1958.
1958	**Whillan's Pendulum** Don Whillans
1959 Feb 22	**Enclosure Crack, Slanting Chimney** Al Parker, Peter Bamfield
1959 Feb 28	**Angus** Al Parker, Paul Nunn (both solo)
1959 Feb 28	**Blockhead** Richard McHardy, Al Parker
	Very quickly superseded by The Direct six days later.
1959 Feb 28	**The Wedge** Bob Brayshaw, Al Parker
1959 March 1	**Parallel Cracks, Central Chimney, Central Buttress** Al Parker, Peter Bamfield
1959 March 1	**Keith's Crack** Keith Taylor, Al Parker, Andy Garvey
1959 March 1	**Letter-box, Turnover** Al Parker, Peter Bamfield, B Platt
1959 March 1	**The Confectioner** Bob Brayshaw, Al Parker
1959 March 2	**Lino, Setsquare** Al Parker, Peter Bamfield
1959 March 6	**Blockhead Direct** Bob Brayshaw, Al Parker
1959 March 15	**Cosmic Crack** Al Parker, Bob Brayshaw
1959 March 22	**Beanpod** Al Parker, Bob Brayshaw, Peter Bamfield
1959 April 4	**Exodus** Richard McHardy, Al Parker, Paul Nunn, Bob Brayshaw
1959 April 4	**Genesis** Paul Nunn, Al Parker
1959 April 5	**Kitten** Al Parker, Peter Bamfield
1959 April 18	**Anniversary Arête** Al Parker, Hugh Banner, Paul Nunn
1959 May 6	**Valediction** Geoffrey Sutton, G F Mansell
	One month earlier, Sutton had reached the upper part of the route by soloing what is now the start to Old Salt, grading it Severe!
1959 May 16	**Surprise** Al Parker, Bob Brayshaw
1959 May 16	**Desperation** Bob Brayshaw, Al Parker
	Desperation was well ahead of its time in terms of steepness and technical difficulty. Originally given a 'solid VS' some people consider it to be E2.
1959 June 20	**Gnat's Slab, Dot's Slab** Al Parker, Peter Bamfield
1959 Aug 2	**August Arête, Traversity** Al Parker, Peter Bamfield
1959 Aug 22	**Billiard Buttress** Al Parker, Paul Nunn, Bob Brayshaw
1959 Aug 22	**Cue** Bob Brayshaw, Al Parker
	Possibly climbed earlier by Les Gillott.
1959 Oct 3	**The Blurter** Al Parker, B Platt
1959 Oct 17	**Birthday Buttress, Typhoon** Al Parker (on his birthday), B Platt

1959 Oct 17	**Count's Wall** (1 nut for aid) Al Parker, B Platt	

Free-climbed in 1976.

1959 Oct 17 **Count's Buttress Direct** Al Parker, B Platt
Possibly led by Eric Byne in the early 1930s.

1959 Nov 18 **Nightmare Slab** Al Parker, Peter Bamfield,
Bob Brayshaw, Paul Nunn, Richard McHardy
The route originally traversed right at the bulge; the direct finish was added in the 1970s.

1959 **The Mangler, Crescent** Don Whillans,
Audrey Whillans, Nat Allen

1959 **The Scoop** Rodney Wilson, Al Parker
Lost for many years, the route was later claimed as Ozymandias.

1959 **Tea-leaf Crack** Members of the Alpha Club
The name comes from the old-time bivouackers' dirty habit of tipping the 'mashings' from their brew can down the line of the route.

1960s **Marble Arête** Paul Nunn, Al Parker
Strangely the route was never described until it was reclaimed and named by Chris Craggs for the 1983 guide.

1960s **Countdown,** Al Parker
Again unclaimed and unnamed until the 1990s when Chris Craggs described it for the current guide.

1960 Jan 1 **Meson** Peter Bamfield

1960 Jan 1 **Scorpion Slab** Bob Brayshaw, Al Parker, Paul
Nunn, Peter Bamfield

1960 March 6 **Daydreamer** Bob Brayshaw, Al Parker
"There was a pebble... and Brayshaw could stand on that pebble and reach the ledge halfway up. So it wasn't all that hard. I remember Gray West doing it in a pair of Klets. He stood on the pebble and the pebble fell off and he did." Richard McHardy. *The route was originally given VS!*

1960 March 20 **Obstinance, Gardener's Groove, Gardener's
Crack, Corner Crack** Al Parker, Peter Bamfield

1960 Aug 2 **Countess Buttress** Al Parker, Peter Bamfield, B Platt

1961 Dec 24 **Milton's Meander** Alan Clarke, Les Gillott

1961-1963 **Fern Groove** (2 slings for aid) Pat Fearneough
Two slings were almost certainly used to enter the groove, but were not considered aid at the time by certain people.

1961-1963 **Scraped Crack, Prickly Crack, Flaked Crack,
Flaked Traverse, Canton, Grime, Toxic, Short
Crack, Dry Crack, Flute Chimney, Outlook Crack,
Lookout Flake, Ladder Corner, Jammed Stone
Chimney, P. O. Crack, Slanting Chimney, Terrace
Gully, The Chute, Grooved Arête, Pizza Slab,
Paradise Lost, Pool Cracks, Pool Wall, Tridymite
Slab, Cannon, Slanting Crack, Straight Ahead,
Holly Crack, Straw Crack, Curving Buttress
Corner, Chockstone Crack, Pillar Arête, Scoop
and Corner, Pal, Pal Joey, Dover's Wall, Route 3**
Les Gillott, Alan Clarke (varied leads and solos)

1961-1963 **Tom-cat Slab** Alan Clarke (solo)

1961-1963	**Fairy Steps, Unpredictable** Alan Clarke, Les Gillott
1961-1963	**The Groper** Les Gillott, Alan Clarke
1961-1963	**Pedlar's Slab** Barry Pedlar (solo)
1961-1963	**Pedlar's Arête, Hidden Crack, Verandah Cracks, Verandah Wall, Bauble, Beads, Narrowing Chimney, Fallen Pillar Chimney, Fairycastle Crack, Fairy Chimney, The Flue, Scoop Crack, Balcony Corner, Upanover, Upanover Crack, Paucity, Cave Arête, Hybrid, Wright's Route, Oblique Buttress, Albert's Pillar, Wedge Gully, Wedge Rib, Tinker's Crack, Tier Climb, Two Tier Climb, Cakestand, Cool Groove, Chimps Corner, Little Ernie, Hoaxer's Crack, Mantelpiece Buttress Direct, Zip Crack, Square Buttress Routes, Gashed Crack, Ding Dong, Finale** Various combinations of Don Morrison, John Loy, Albert Hattersley and H Woods
1961-1963	**Gullible's Travels** (1 point of aid) Brian Pallet
	The line was spotted and named by Pat Fearneough who pointed the gullible Pallet at it. The indiscretion was removed in 1963.
1961-1963	**Rugosity Crack** Pat Fearneough
1961-1963	**Apparent North, True North** Len Millsom
1961	**Second Sister, Richard's Sister** Richard McHardy, Al Parker
1961	**X-ray** Al Parker, Bob Brayshaw, Peter Bamfield
1961	**Rinty** Clive Rowland, Al Parker
1961	**Afterthought** Clive Rowland, Al Parker
1962-1963	**Morrison's Redoubt, Retroversion** Don Morrison
	Retroversion was one of Ron Townsend's 'secret lines', that was until he let Don in on the secret.
1962-1963	**Thrombosis, Rigor Mortis, Paralysis** Don Morrison
1962-1963	**Zagrete** John Loy
	Possibly climbed before by Alan Clarke.
1962-1963	**Malc's Left-hand Slabs**
	Soloed regularly but not recorded until 1998.
1962 April	**Creepy** Peter Bamfield, F Johnson
1962 May	**Incursion** Paul Nunn, Oliver Woolcock, Dave Roberts
1962	**The Vice** Clive Rowland
1962	**The Wobbler, Orang-Outang** (2 points of aid) Pete Crew
	The latter route used two slings for aid and was free-climbed in the either 1972 or 1973.
1962	**Don's Delight, The Knutter** Don Whillans (solo)
1962	**Millsom's Minion** Len Millsom
	Climbed, as usual for Len, in bendy boots.
1963 March	**Old Salt** Paul Nunn, Al Parker
	The start had already been climbed as an alternative start to Valediction in 1959.
1963	**Gullible's Travels**
	Climbed free and solo by Alan Clarke; An outstanding climber, on one occasion he led The Tippler while it snowed.
1964 Aug 9	**Electron, Quantum Crack** Alan Clarke, Mike Parkin

1964	**The Tippler** Barry Webb
1965 May 29	**B P Super** Reclimbed after loss of holds by G Dimmick (unseconded)
1965 June 17	**Saul's Arête Indirect** G Dimmick, H Richardson

Starting in Helfenstein's Struggle Dimmick traversed the break rightwards to climb the upper part of Archangel.

1965 June 17	**Tower Face Direct**

Reclimbed by G Dimmick after loss of holds.

1965 June 28	**The Actress, Eliminator** Alan Clarke, Mike Parkin
1965 July 4	**Queersville** Alan Clarke, Mike Parkin
1965 Aug 17	**Yosemite Wall** Alan Clarke, A Watson

Was graded HVS in 1976 guidebook.

1965 Sept 5	**Suzanne** Reg Addey (solo)
1966 April 30	**Flying Buttress Direct** Paul Gray, David Johnson

Climbed free, Gray utilised a peg runner but nevertheless it was a superb effort. Sadly, he died in 1969 on the Isle of Harris and as a tribute his ashes were scattered over Flying Buttress.

1966 Oct	**Gunter** T Norcliffe, C Smith
1967 Jan	**Cinturato, Dracula** John Gosling, Mike Simpkins, Eddie Thurrell
1967 March 5	**Titanic Direct** (finish only) Al Parker, Jud Jordan, Eddie Thurrell

A direct start Dive, Dive, Dive was added in 1979 by Gary Gibson.

1967 April	**Gibbon** (Nectar) (1 sling for aid) John Gosling, Mike Simpkins, Eddie Thurrell

Free-climbed in 1976.

1967 April	**Buffoon** (Goosey Goosey Gander) (3 slings for aid) John Gosling, Mike Simpkins, Eddie Thurrell, Oliver Woolcock, Al Parker

It received its renaissance in 1976.

1967 May	**Acheron** Jim Perrin, R Bowker
1967 June	**Phlegethoa, Lethe** Jim Perrin
1967 July	**Pedlar's Rib** Jim Perrin
1967 Aug	**Censor** Jim Perrin

An extremely serious climb which saw few ascents until the 1980s and the development of RPs. Reputedly top-roped 23 times before the first ascent.

1968 June 15	**The Old Dragon** (1 sling for aid) Bill Birch, T Norcliffe

Ron Mosely is rumoured to have climbed a similar line in the 1950s. Climbed free in 1973 by John Allen or possibly earlier by Mike Hammill.

1968	**'Stanleyville'** Bill Birch, T Norcliffe

Effectively a direct start to Mississippi Variant and now incorporated into that route. It was originally thought to take the wall further right and consequently acquired an awesome reputation. To add to the confusion this line has been called Stanleyville and was probably first led (by accident) in 1973.

1969 Aug 11	**Right Wall** Geoff Milburn, Dave Gregory
1970 June	**Calvary** (1 peg for aid) Mike Simpkins, John Gosling

A nut for protection was pre-placed in the flake. The aid-peg was in the top break. Climbed free in 1976.

1970 Nov 15	**Anji** D Constable, Angela Illingworth, Terry Bolger	
1971 Sept	**The Guillotine** (1 point of aid) Ed Drummond, Hamish Green Armitage	

1971 Sept   **The Guillotine** (1 point of aid) Ed Drummond, Hamish Green Armitage
On the first ascent the leader rather lost his head and placed a peg for aid. Free-climbed in 1973 by John Allen.

1971 Oct   **Premier** John Allen, Neil Stokes
John's first new route. He was only 12 at the time.

1972 April 13   **The Archangel** Ed Drummond, Hamish Green Armitage
Originally named Saul's Arête it was top-roped by Don Whillans in 1954 with a 'little support from the rope' and, reputedly, a rubber inner tube between his knees for grip. The arête was later soloed on its right-hand side in 1985.

1972 Aug 3   **Rubber Band** John Allen, Neil Stokes
Only the last section of the route is included the guide.

1972 Aug   **Tower Traverse** John Allen, Neil Stokes

1972-1973   **Orang-outang** Terry King may have made the first free ascent in 1972, but it was certainly led clean the following year by John Allen and Steve Bancroft.

1972-1973   **Margery Daw** Neil Stokes, John Allen

1972-1973   **Pegasus Rib** John Allen, Neil Stokes

1972   **Undercut Crack, 49th Parallel, QE2, Mantelpiece** Bill Birch, Al Parker

1972   **Bottomless Crack** Al Parker (solo)

1972   **Persuader** Al Parker, B Jones

1972   **Ritornel** Al Parker, R Stevens

1973 April 29   **Wuthering** Ed Drummond, Hamish Green Armitage

1973 July 31   **Stanleyville** John Allen, Neil Stokes, Steve Bancroft
The day that the Allen/Bancroft partnership began. A side-runner was employed in Mississippi Variant.

1973 Aug 5   **The Punk** Steve Bancroft, John Allen, Neil Stokes

1973 Aug 26   **Mouthpiece** Steve Bancroft, Neil Stokes, John Allen

1973 Sept 2   **Old Friends** John Allen, Neil Stokes, Steve Bancroft
A superb plum picked by a 14-year-old who was to revolutionise gritstone climbing.

1973 Oct 27   **The Stretcher** R Franklin, G Young.
The Direct Start was added in 1996 by Chris Craggs and Jim Rubery.

1973 Dec 25   **Cold Turkey** John Allen, Steve Bancroft
Climbed what is now the upper section of Thunder Road. "I had persuaded my father to run us out to Stanage and hold my rope on Christmas Day. We were due back for Christmas dinner and things were taking longer than expected and dad began ranting about how the turkey would be cold by the time we got home." It was claimed again in 1993 as Lightening Lane by Jim Rubery after it had been 'lost' for twenty years.

1973   **The Guillotine, The Old Dragon** First free ascents by John Allen and Neil Stokes.

1973   **Cave Eliminate, Constipation** John Allen, Neil Stokes

1974 June 16   **Symbiosis** Mark Scott, John Woodhouse, Graham Hoey

1974   **Deuteronomy, Puss** John Allen, Steve Bancroft

1974	**The Link** Chris Craggs
1975 May 28	**Microbe** Steve Bancroft (solo)
1975 May 28	**The Lamia** Steve Bancroft, John Allen (alternate leads)
1975 July 18	**White Wand** John Allen, Steve Bancroft

Ed Drummond top-roped the route in the morning then returned in the evening to solo it then naming it Wind. Unbeknown to Drummond, Allen had top-roped and soloed it in the afternoon. The hardest route in the 1976 guidebook; which stopped dead, virtually all tickers! Gabe Regan reputedly used to down-climb from above the crux.

1975 July 18	**Not Much Weak Stack Battered or What** John Allen, Nick Stokes

A friend's description of what would happen to John if he fell off.

1975 Aug 27	**Black Hawk Bastion** Climbed free by John Allen and Steve Bancroft
1975	**Harvest** John Allen, Tom Proctor
1975	**The Asp, Chameleon** Ed Drummond, John Young

A few days prior to Drummond's ascent of The Asp, John Allen took a nasty fall after pumping out whilst trying to place a runner on an on sight foray. From the road below, Drummond watched the episode through binoculars and returned to snatch a fine route.

1976-1981	**Kenneth** Ken Bridges
1976-1982	**Stage Fright** Martin Veale (solo)
1976 April 16	**Punklet** Steve Bancroft, John Allen (both solo)
1976 May 8	**Nectar** John Allen, Steve Bancroft (alternate leads)

A free ascent of the aided route Gibbon and a new second pitch. For a while it was heralded as one of the hardest routes in Britain. 'Stickies' have now rendered it 'mild'.

1976 June 23	**Pot Black, Black Magic** Giles Barker, John Oldroyd
1976 July	**Travesties** Robin Miller, Pete Steward, Steve Cannon

Named after the play by Tom Stoppard.

1976 Aug	**Doctor of Physic** Andy Parkin

Parkin traversed left below the horrendous bulging finish: later climbed, when the route was renamed Heath Robinson, in 1984.

1976 Aug 10	**Calvary** Climbed free by Gabe Regan.
1976 Aug 19	**Incursion Direct** Andy Parkin, Giles Barker (both solo)
1976 Aug 19	**Physician's Wall** Andy Parkin, Giles Barker, Ruth Norton
1976 Aug 24	**Crab Crawl Arête** Andy Parkin, Giles Barker, Bill Briggs (all solo)
1976 Sept	**Ono** Brian Cropper, Paul Cropper
1976 Oct	**Protractor** Al Parker (solo)
1976 Oct 11	**Meddle** Paul Millward, Jon de Montjoye
1976 Nov 19	**Goosey Goosey Gander** (Buffoon free) Gabe Regan, Al Evans

An outstanding effort by this talented climber. On his first attempt Gabe used a nut to rest, then led the route clean. Buffoon was first climbed with three points of aid in 1976.

1976	**Count's Wall** Climbed free by Dave Mithen and Dave Morgan

1976	**Abacus** Dave Mithen, Dave Morgan, Jim Worthington
1976	**The Count** Dave Morgan, Dave Mithen, Jim Worthington
1976	**Warlock** Dennis Carr, Al Parker, Lew Brown, Tony Cowcill
1976	**Crescent Arête** Gabe Regan (solo)
1976	**Not To Be Taken Away** John Allen (solo)

Named after an inscription scraped on the large block behind, (climbed by The Photograph); which is no longer visible.

1976	**Right Spur** John Allen (solo)
1976	**Miserable Miracle** John Allen, Neil Stokes
1976	**Tippler Direct** Jim Reading, Clive Jones

This may have been done in the 60s by Martin Boysen.

1977 April 8	**Good Friday** P Green, Mike Nugent

Incorrectly credited to Phil Burke as Ginny Come Lately in the 1983 guidebook.

1977 April 9	**Silica** John Fleming, John Street
1977 May	**Sleepwalker** Chris Calow (solo)
1977 May	**Out for the Count** Chris Calow, Tim Carruthers
1977 May 28	**Sithee** Jim Lawrenson, Giles Barker (both solo)

Started on the right.

1977 June 18	**The Graduate** Chris Lawson, Mike Nugent
1977 June 19	**Jean's Line** Ron Kenyon
1977 June 26	**5.9 Finish** Clive Jones, Ray Jardine
1977 Summer	**The Strangler** Gabe Regan, Allan Manson, Steve Webster
1977 Summer	**Nuke the Midges** Allan Manson

Named by Paul Mitchell on a subsequent 'first' ascent.

1977 Aug 10	**Crew Pegs Diffs** Steve Bancroft, Nick Stokes, 'Cool' Pete Lowe

Named after a scurrilous inscription that was once scratched on one of the boulders below Goliath's Groove.

1977 Aug 31	**Plastic Dream** Ed Wood, Colin Banton, Nigel Riddington
1977 Sept	**Scavenger** S Thorpe
1977	**Ma's Retreat** Al Parker

Named, after Ma Thomas retired and closed her cafe in Hathersage: a sad loss.

1977	**Argus** Tim Carruthers (roped-solo)
1977	**Little Blondie** John Stevenson, Howard Johnston

The route traversed out of Paradise Wall to climb what is now the upper section of Comus but not described in the route text.

1978 May 7	**Wolf Solent** Martin Berzins, Nic Hallam
1978 May 28	**Outlook Slab** Martin Veale, 'Wild' Bill Lucas
1978 June 2	**Lancashire Wall** Dave Kenyon, Paul Cropper
1978 June 14	**Missing Link** Al Parker, Graham Fyffe
1978 June 14	**Death and Night and Blood, Nephron** Gary Gibson
1978 June 17	**Side Effect, Icy Crack** Bill McKee, Rob Jarret
1978 Summer	**Pig's Ear** Jonny Woodward (solo)
1978 July 9	**Telli** Steve Bancroft, Robert Carey, Dave Humphries

On the first ascent Steve Bancroft had somebody (tied on)

dangle their legs down the final moves.

1978 July 16	**Fate**, **Cent** Gary Gibson, Ralph Hewitt, Derek Beetlestone	
1978 July	**Europa**, **Small Dreams** Chris Calow, Tim Carruthers	
1978 Aug 20	**Cornflakes** A Mallinson	
1978 Aug	**Dark Continent** Phil Burke	
1978 Aug	**Tip Off** Phil Burke, John Yates	
1978 Oct	**King Kong** Al Parker, Graham Fyffe	

A good find that still sees many (tall) notables grovelling.

1978 Oct 4	**Squiggle** Gary Gibson (solo)

Now forms the bottom section of Don't Bark, Bite, *climbed in 1980.*

1978 Oct 8	**Meiosis** Gary Gibson
1978 Oct 8	**Goodbye Toulouse**, **Providence** Gary Gibson, Ralph Hewitt, Derek Beetlestone
1978 Dec 5	**Spock Out**, **Bifurcated Headplate Max** Colin Banton (solo)
1978 Dec	**Lucy's Delight** Lucien Taylor (solo)
1978	**Tempskya** Clive Jones

Originally graded HVS by the first ascensionist!

1978	**Limbo** Chris Craggs (solo)
1978	**Sinew Stretch** Bill Sutton, Steve Bancroft
1978	**Stairway Crack**, **Lucy's Slab** Al Parker, Graham Fyffe
1978	**Jean's Route** Graham Fyffe, Al Parker
1978	**Mark's Slab** Mark Whitfield (solo)
1978	**Improbability Drive** John Hart, Andy Freem
1978	**Nothing to do with Dover** Clive Jones (solo)
1978	**Withered Thing** Chris Hamper, Mike Sayer, Jim Reading
1978	**South Sea Charmer** Paul Williams
1979 April 1	**Direct start to Robin Hood's Crack**, **Space Junk** Gary Gibson (solo)
1979 April 4	**Living at the Speed** Gary Gibson

Direct start added in 1984.

1979 April 18	**Flate**, **Zero Point** Gary Gibson (solo)
1979 April 20	**Paved Vacuum**, **Treatment**, **Pure Gossip** Gary Gibson
1979 April 22	**E.M.F.**, **Mr Universe**, **Magazine**, **Cringe**, **Titanic Direct** (start) Gary Gibson (solo)

The latter was named Dive, Dive, Dive.

1979 April	**Slight Second** Bill McKee (solo)
1979 April	**Monad** Steve Bancroft (solo)
1979 June 30	**Comus** Martin Berzins (solo)
1979 July 13	**The 3-D Wall** Gary Gibson
1979 July 15	**The Aeneid** Gary Gibson
1979 July 15	**Fading Star** Gary Gibson, Ian 'Hotshot' Johnson

The line was climbed two months later by Gabe Regan, John Regan and Steve Webster who named it After the Fire *believing it to be new.*

1979 July 17	**Zel** Gary Gibson(solo)
1979 July 22	**Topaz** Gary Gibson (solo)
1979 Sept 9	**Bloodshot** Gabe Regan, John Regan, Steve Webster
1979 Sept 16	**Thunder Road** Gabe Regan

	Soloed by Mark Stokes in 1980, a rarely repeated effort. Superseded by the arguably better route of Cold Turkey, climbed in 1973.
1979 Sept 24	**Silence** Ed Wood, Chris Craggs
1979	**High Flyer** Lee Bower (solo)
	Also climbed in April by Steve Bancroft.
1979	**Feathered Friends** Terry Bolger, Dave Dunn
1979	**Jim Crow** Terry Bolger, Steve Punshon, Chris Astill
	Optimistically graded 4c in the 1989 guide.
1979	**Rabbit's Crack** Chris Astill (solo)
1979	**Editor's Vaseline** Paul Mitchell (solo)
1979	**Fear and Loathing** Mark Stokes (solo)
1979	**Boc No Buttress** Steve Bancroft, Nick Stokes, Pete Lowe
	Boc No is back-slang for what Steve had that day.
1979	**Last Bolt** Martin Boysen, Phil Burke
1979-1980	**Clubbing** Paul Mitchell (solo)
1970s	**Sceptic** Al Parker?
	Also claimed by Dave Gregory, Clive Jones. Claimed again and named by C Craggs in the late '70s.
1970s	**Little Things** Martin Boysen
	Claimed again and named by C Craggs in the late '70s.
1980 July	**The Mersey Variant** Trevor Pilling, Ian Carr
1980 Sept 14	**Don't Bark, Bite** Gary Gibson
	This appears to have been recorded as Mortuary Steps VS in the 'olden days.'
1980	**Germ** Chris Sowden (solo)
1980	**Nightrider** Chris Hamper (solo)
	Superseded Little Blondie climbed in 1977.
1980	**Shock Horror Slab** Steve Bancroft (solo)
1980	**Moribund** Steve Bancroft, Nick Stokes, Pete Lowe
1981 Jan 31	**Missing Numbers** Graham Hoey (solo)
1981 Jan 31	**Anxiety Attack** Gary Gibson, Derek Beetlestone
1981 Feb 11	**Coconut Ice, Ice Boat** Gary Gibson, Hazel Gibson
1981 March 23	**Dry Rot** Gary Gibson, Derek Beetlestone, Dave Light
1981 March 28	**Puzzlelock, Melancholy Witness** Gary Gibson, Derek Beetlestone, Dave Light, Duncan Munroe
1981 April 3	**Quietus Right-Hand** Ian Maisey, Jonny Woodward
1981 April 10	**The Watch-tower** Gary Gibson
1981 April 11	**7% Soln., Acute Amnesia** Gary Gibson (solo)
1981 April 11	**Vena Cave-in** Gary Gibson, Derek Beetlestone
1981 May 1	**Paranoid** Jonny Woodward
	Desperate: waited nearly two decades for it's first known repeat.
1981 May 23	**D.I.Y., Sithee Direct Start** Graham Hoey (solo)
	Sithee previously traversed in from the right.
1981 May 25	**Spartaciad** Gary Gibson
	Superseded by Smash Your Glasses in 1988
1981 May 30	**Counterblast** Gary Gibson
1981 June 15	**Haze** Gary Gibson, Hazel Gibson
1981 June 18	**Quiver** Graham Hoey (solo)
1981 July 4	**Grain of Truth** Chris Calow, John Jefferies
1981 July	**Vanishing Point** Chris Craggs, Ed Wood

1981 Aug 5	**Stretcher Case** Chris Jackson, Roy Small, Andy Kassyk
1981 Aug 10	**Neutrons For Old** Chris Jackson, Roy Small
1981 Summer	**Centrepiece, Bon Ami** Chris Calow (solo)
1981 Summer	**Ashes** John Fleming, John Street
1981 Summer	**Right Wall** John Fleming (solo)
1981 Nov 15	**Meninblack II, Waiting for M.I.B.** Gary Gibson (solo)
1981 Nov 22	**Overcoat** Chris Calow
1981 Nov 22	**Enigma (Youth Meat)** Bob Berzins, Chris Calow
1981 Nov 30	**Arsenic Poisoning, Duchess, Trench Deadlock, Motor Mile** Gary Gibson (solo)
1981 Nov 30	**Touched** Gary Gibson, Phil Gibson
1981 Nov 31	**Central Buttress Direct Start** Gary Gibson (solo)
1981 Sept 23	**The Logic Book, Four Winds; Eight Directions** Gary Gibson

Hazel (Gibson) wouldn't have been tall enough to reach the break over the roof on Four Winds; Eight Directions *and she was fed up with 'the winch'.*

1981 Sept 23	**Teenage Lobotomy** Gary Gibson, Hazel Gibson, Elaine Wroe
1981	**Marmite, Prowler** Chris Calow (solo)
1981	**Parasite** Chris Craggs, Colin Binks
1981	**Monday Blue** Ernie Marshall, Nick Longland
1982 Feb 23	**Skin Grafter** Gary Gibson (solo)
1982 Feb 23	**A Problem of Coagulation** Gary Gibson
1982 March 27	**Certainly Parakeratosis, Hardly Hyperkeratosis, Cheeky Little Number** Gary Gibson, Neil Harvey

The former two routes were named after a week of intense study of Dermatology.

1982 March 30	**Brittle Bones, Mr Pemphigoid, Flesh and Blood** Gary Gibson (solo)
1982 March 31	**American Gritfeati** Todd Swaid, Giles Barker
1982 April 23	**No More Excuses** Graham Hoey, Giles Barker
1982 April 23	**Leaps and Bounds** Simon Yearsley, Lee Clarke
1982 April 24	**Spasticus Artisticus** Paul Cropper, Nadim Siddiqui
1982 Spring	**Four Star** Simon Horrox (solo)

Simon was a very popular local climber who died in The Alps later that year. The 1983 Stanage Millstone guidebook is dedicated to him.

1982 May	**The Hathersage Trip** Bob Berzins (solo)

So named because his foot slipped off as he was just reaching the top whilst soloing the first ascent. If he had fallen off he would have ended up in Hathersage.

1982 July 9	**Off With His Head** Andy Barker

The original line followed what is now taken by Tarzan Boy to the loose flake, then traversed right and was led with a pre-placed nut. Climbed more directly and led without the nut by Andy Barker on 11 September 1982.

1982 July 22	**Mating Toads, Massacre, Petty Larceny, Grand Theft** Andy Barker (solo)
1982 July 25	**The Photograph** Paul Mitchell

Led with a pre-placed wire.

1982 Aug 28	**Pure, White and Deadly** Tony Credland (solo)
1982 Sept 11	**Last Ice Cream** Paul Mitchell

341

1982 Oct	**Defying Destiny** Bill Turner, Iain Edwardes
1982	**Direct Start to Typhoon** Paul Clark
	Done on sight in error, thinking it to be Wolf Solent.
1982	**Giro** Martin Veale, Chris Craggs
1982	**Magnetic North** Simon Horrox
	The line many thought was True North.
1983 Feb 19	**Frigid Witch** Paul Mitchell (solo)
1983 April 14	**Ulysses** Jerry Moffatt (solo)

This last great problem fell not just to a pair of 'stickies' but also to a good deal of technique, cool and top-rope practice. Soloed on-sight by Johnny Dawes in April 1984. The second on-sight attempt ended in a shattered ankle for Neil Foster one day after climbing (the subsequently named) Ulysses or Bust on Curbar Edge.

1983 April 15	**Snug as a Thug on a Jug** Paul Mitchell

The route was described by Paul as 'An excellent route, a must for masochistic thugs'.

1983 May	**Bandits in the Woods, Autumn Gold, Ventured Point** D Leversidge, M Ellis (both solo)
1983 May	**Mary Whitehouse** Paul Mitchell (solo)
1983 May 6	**The Modest Carpenter** Paul Mitchell

A wire was pre-placed in the flake of Old Friends. Led without by Roger Greatrick on 18 June 1983.

1983 June 9	**Eminence Grise** Paul Mitchell
1983 June 15	**Tram Eaters** Paul Mitchell, John Allen, Andy Barker
1983 June 15	**Boobagram** John Allen, Paul Mitchell, Andy Barker
1983 June 18	**The Dalesman** Roger Greatrick, Keith Ainsworth
1983 June 22	**Spearing the Bearded Clam** Paul Mitchell (solo)
1983 June	**Blow Out** Chris Craggs (solo)
1983 Summer	**Doctored, Pacemaker** Colin Binks, Chris Craggs.
1983 Summer	**21 Today** Martin Veale, Chris Craggs
1983 Summer	**Time and Tide** Martin Veale (solo)
1983 Summer	**Look Before You Leap** Chris Craggs, Graham Parkes
1983 Summer	**Pacific Ocean Wall, Wall of Sound, Stanage Without Oxygen** John Allen, Mark Stokes

John returns to his native grit with vision.

1983 Summer	**Swings** Named by Paul Mitchell but climbed before by Tony Walker (solo).
1983 Summer	**Little Sarah** Chris Horsfall (solo)
1983 July 2	**Thalidomide** Paul Mitchell, Andy Barker
1983 Aug 14	**Slap 'n Spittle** Andy Lewandowski, Colin Brooks
1983 Oct	**Overflow** Chris Calow
1983 Dec 4	**Dark Water** Al Rouse & 'others'
1983 Dec 7	**The Crypt Trip** Ron Fawcett

In typical style Fawcett scoops another plum line.

1983	**Steamin'** Chris Craggs, Nigel Baker
1983	**Love Handles, Mr M'Quod and the Anti-rock Squad** Mark Stokes, John Allen (both solo)

Also claimed around this time by Stuart MacKay

1983	**Wall End Slab Direct Finish** Chris Craggs, Martin Veale
1983	**Bumblies in Red Socks, Rabies** Paul Mitchell (solo)
1983	**Wax Museum** John Allen (solo)

1983	**Bobsnob** Chris Craggs (solo)
1983	**Bob's Jolly Jape** John Allen

Named after Bob Berzins decided not to 'prat about' putting runners in and fell off attempting to on sight solo the first ascent. After coming round Bob staggered around in a daze but John refused to take him to hospital until the route was in the bag.

1983	**The Thin End** Nic Hallam (solo)
1983	**Randolf Cheerleader** Mark Stokes
1983	**Whatever Happened to Bob?** Bob Berzins (solo)

He got married and took up running.

1984 Feb 15	**Reagent** Al Rouse (solo)
1984 March 2	**Timothy Twinkletoes** Chris Hardy (solo)

"The worst name I could think of."

1984 March 5	**Good Clean Fun** John Allen, Mark Stokes
1984 March 9	**Shirley's Shining Temple** John Allen (solo)

A much desired line. Allen originally started on the right returning later to straighten out the route via some thoroughly desperate climbing.

1984 March 2	**The Cool Curl** Johnny Dawes, Nigel Slater

Originally graded E4 6b until the loss of pebbles. Re-led in 1987 by Mike Lea.

1984 April 7	**Nihilistic Narl** John Allen (solo)
1984 April 10	**Vision Set** Johnny Dawes, Nigel Slater
1984 April 29	**So Many Classics, So Little Time** John Allen (solo)

Originally graded HVS by an on-form John Allen.

1984 May 17	**Breadline** John Allen (solo), Mark Miller (spotting)
1984 May 24	**Basil Brush** Nigel Slater, Alistair Ferguson
1984 May 31	**Mitch Pitch** John Allen (solo)

Named after Paul Mitchell's eye for a line.

1984 May	**Green Line** Al Rouse (solo)
1984 May	**A Thousand Natural Shocks** Crispin Guest (solo)
1984 May	**Weather Report, I Didn't Get Where I am Today** Johnny Dawes (solo)

The latter was originally graded E2 5b by a very on-form Dawes and described as climbing the still unclimbed wall to the left of Outlook Chimney.

1984 June 15	**Flipside** Gabe Regan, John Regan
1984 June 18	**Marie Celeste** Gabe Regan, John Regan
1984 June	**Badly Bitten** Paul Pepperday, Chris Hale
1984 July 16	**Scrole Not Dole** John Allen, Nick Stokes
1984 August 1	**Zero Zero Sputnik, Waffti** Keith Ashton (solo)
1984 Sept	**Regret** Al Rouse, Neil Foster
1984 Oct 14	**Walking the Whippet** John Allen
1984 Nov 13	**Creepy Crawly** Keith Ashton (solo)
1984 Nov 17	**Non-toxic** Keith Ashton (solo)
1984 Nov	**The Beautician** Steve Bancroft, John Allen
1984 Nov	**The Unthinkable** Paul Williams, Mark Stokes, John Allen
1984	**Heath Robinson** Johnny Dawes

A typically bold solution.

1984	**Saltation** Johnny Dawes
1984	**Satin** Johnny Dawes (solo)

1984	**The Introvert** Johnny Dawes, Crispin Guest
1984	**Youth Meat** Johnny Dawes (solo)

A direct start to the route Enigma climbed in 1981.

1984	**Anxiety Attack 2** Mark Stokes, John Allen, Paul Williams
1984	**Amoeba on the Edge of Time** Paul Williams (solo)
1984	**Narlavision** John Allen (solo)
1984	**Silk** Johnny Dawes (solo)

A remarkable on-sight solo of some of the thinnest moves on Stanage.

1984	**Gnome Man's Land** John Arran, Dave Turner
1984	**Swooper** Johnny Dawes (solo)

He climbed the route on-sight, wire-brushing as he went.

1984	**Michelle My Belle** Paul Pepperday, Chris Hale
1984	**Old Pals, Child's Play, For Ever and Ever** Paul Harrison (solo)

Child's Play was incorrectly credited in the 1989 guidebook to Harry Venables and Jon Heydon

1984	**Nightsalt** John Allen (solo)
1984	**Twin Cam** Johnny Dawes
1984	**Sad Amongst Friends** Johnny Dawes (solo)

An outstanding feat, especially since good runners exist.

1984	**Led A Dance** Chris Plant, Brian Davidson, Alan Dance

Note the name of the third man.

1985 April 12	**Black and Decker** Greg Griffith (solo)
1985 April 15	**Torture Garden, Splinter** Greg Griffith (solo)
1985 April 16	**Headbanger, Sneaking Sally Through the Alley** Keith Ashton, Dave Allsopp
1985 April 18	**Skidoo** John Allen

So-named after his feet slipped on the unprotected 6c crux, facing a horrible fall. Johnny Dawes had previously attempted an on-sight first ascent in 1984.

1985 April 24	**Miss World, Left, Right** Doug Kerr (solo)
1985 April 24	**Head Over Heels** Doug Kerr (self-protected solo)
1985 April	**Non-stop Pedalling** Steve Bell
1985 May 12	**African Herbs** Al Rouse, Richard Hazsko
1985 May 17	**Boris the Bold** Chris Gilbert, Dave Woolgar
1985 May	**Perforation, May Crack** Chris Craggs, Colin Binks

The first route follows an incorrectly positioned dotted line in the 1983 guide, hence the name.

1985 Spring	**Back Door, Bright Eyed** Chris Craggs (solo)
1985 Spring	**Our Version** Chris Craggs, Graham Parkes
1985 June 2	**Count Me Out** John Allen
1985 June	**Tower Block** Al Rouse
1985 Sept	**High and Wild** Chris Craggs, Colin Binks, Nigel Baker
1985 Sept	**Don** Ed Drummond (solo)

Named in memory of Don Whillans.

1985 Dec 7	**Feminist's Breakfast** John Allen, Paul Williams

A lemon if you're wondering.

1985	**Scraps** Chris Craggs (solo)
1985	**Help the Aged** Johnny Dawes (solo)
1985	**Comet** Jonathan Wyatt (solo)

1985	**Tribute to Kitty** Mike Lea
	Following the loss of crucial pebbles and without the use of side runners it was reclimbed by Dan Honneyman on January 21, 1999 and offered a new name, not a practise to be encouraged.
1985	**Al** Al Rouse, Steve Bancroft
1985	**Breakdance** Johnny Dawes
1985	**Pudding** Mark Clark, Steve Bancroft
1985	**Chips, Peas** Steve Bancroft, Mark Clark
1986 April 27	**Second Wind** Tony Ryan (solo)
1986 April	**Clegg** John Judson, Tony Williams, N Croston
1986 May 5	**Way Fruitsome Experience** John Allen (solo)
1986 May 8	**Insomniac** Graham Hoey (solo)
1986 May 8	**Leroy Slips a Disc** John Allen (solo)
1986 May 8	**Head Spin** Mark Stokes, John Allen, Johnny Dawes
1986 May 8	**Traverse of the Gritstone Gods** Johnny Dawes, John Allen, Mark Stokes
	With this first ascent team it should be called Traverse of the Gritstone Gobs.
1986 May 13	**Mini Micro** Tony Ryan (solo)
1986 June 11	**Left Spur** John Allen (solo)
1986 June 19	**Crime** Martin Veale
1986 June 19	**Punishment** John Allen (solo)
1986 June 19	**Passover** Steve Bancroft, John Allen, Pete Lowe
1986 July 8	**Plugging the Gaps** Ian Riddington, Keith Sharples, Ian Smith
1986 July 16	**Boys Will Be Boys** John Allen (solo)
	John had previously soloed the route in winter above a huge snowdrift only to fail at the cornice. A rarely repeated outing for which a grade of E7 has been mooted.
1986 July 16	**Direct Loss** John Allen, Martin Veale, Steve Bancroft
1986 July 20	**Video Nasty, Grace and Danger** John Allen (solo)
	The latter route was a surprising find, opening the mind to new possibilities.
1986 July	**Preston's Wall** John Regan, Keith Ashton, Harry Venables, John Sonczak
1986 July	**The Amazing Harry Greystoke II** Keith Ashton, John Regan, Harry Venables, John Sonczak
1986 August 1	**Marmalade's Lost Start** Tony Walker, Noel Croach
1986 August 2	**Dark Angel** John Allen
1986 Summer	**Black Adder's Fortress** Alec Burns, Paul Evans, Nick James
1986 Sept 9	**Indian Summer** John Allen, Dave Gillott
	A good route which used the lower section of B P Super. It had been inspected by many climbers, but nobody was prepared to pull on the wafer-thin friable flakes. John solved the problem by knocking the tops off them!
1986 Sept 20	**Walrus Butter** Paul Mitchell
	"A hard dyno off pebbles. If pebbles go, tough titty!"
1986 Sept 28	**New York, New York, Gameo** John Allen (solo)
1986	**Dream Boat** Alan Doig (solo)
1986	**Lucky Strike** Andy Cave, Chris Hale
1987 Feb	**Life Begins at 40** John Allen

1987 April 14	**Hairless Art** Graham Hoey, John Allen, Mark Stokes (all solo)

1987 April 14   **Big Air** Martin Veale (solo)
Even the jump was practised on a top-rope.

1987 April 22   **Chip Shop Brawl** John Allen (solo)

1987 April   **Bad Do** John Allen, Mark Stokes

1987 Spring   **Rimmington Place** Shaun Ainley, H Bradley

1987 Spring   **Careless Torque** Ron Fawcett (solo)
Definitely one of the last great problems on Stanage. Ron practised for the ascent by jumping off Not To Be Taken Away from increasing heights!

1987 Sept 9   **The Cool Curl** Re-led by Mike Lea after the loss of some 'crucial' crystals and upgraded to it's present E6 from E4.

1987 Sept 13   **Mounting Frustration, Pretty Petty?** John Allen (solo)

1987 Sept 19   **Too Cold to be Bold** Keith Sharples, Graham Hoey, Bill Gregory
A side-runner provided the safety, the cold the excuse.

1987 Sept 21   **Guillotine Direct, Tarzan Boy** John Allen, Mark Stokes
Only the finishing traverse of Tarzan Boy was new, the lower section had been climbed in 1982 as part of an indirect version of Off With His Head.

1987 Oct 17   **Straightsville** Bill Birch, Rick Gibbon

1987 Oct   **The Deliverance** Quentin Fisher (solo)
One giant leap for Quentin, a ladder for mankind.

1987   **Suitored** Steve Bancroft, Sue Bird

1987   **Nairobi** Paul Mitchell (solo)

1987   **National Breakdown** Greg Griffith (solo)

1988 April 24   **Have a Break, Basil Half-tail** John Allen (solo)
The latter route was named after Graham Hoey's rat? (cat?) as John couldn't think of a name.

1988 April   **In-off** Steve Bancroft, Sue Bird, Adrian Hughes

1988 May 17   **Zit** Graham Parkes, Chris Craggs, Dave Vincent

1988 June 22   **The Trickledown Fairy, Smash Your Glasses** John Allen, Paul Mitchell

1988 June 22   **Toothcomb** John Allen (solo)

1988 June   **Manchester United** Chris Craggs (solo)

1988 July 3   **Vanquished** Tony Ryan, Gary Ryan

1988 Aug 22   **Scuppered** John Allen (solo)

1988 Sept 5   **Foetus on The Eiger** Paul Mitchell, John Allen
The media reported that Alison Hargreaves, whilst six months pregnant, had just climbed The Eiger.

1988 Sept 19   **Early Starter** Chris Craggs, Dave Spencer

1989 Jan 20   **Public Image** Keith Ashton, Mike Berresford

1989 Jan   **Calvary Direct** Matt Carr, Hedda Graham

1989 March 8   **My Herald of Free Enterprise** Dave Thomas
Named in honour of a newly purchased Triumph Herald which allowed a new freedom to climb.

1989 March 1   **A Day Without Pay** Mike Lea (solo)
Possibly the shortest E6 in the world?

1989 Spring   **Not Richard's Sister Direct** John Allen

1989 May 22	**Greg's Retreat** Mike Snell (solo)	
1989 May	**I Never Said It Was Any Good** Chris Craggs, Dave Spencer, Martin Veale, Ros Cullen	
1989 May	**Where did my Tan Go** Chris Craggs (solo)	
1989 June 29	**Gnat's Slab Direct** Mike Snell (solo)	
1989 July 3	**Hot and Bothered, Body Roll Finish** John Allen, Martin Veale	
1989 July 5	**Corner Crack** Martin Whittaker (solo)	
1989 July 17	**Cosmos, Lapton** Mike Snell (solo)	
	Named at a later date.	
1989 July 20	**The Concept of Kinky** John Allen	
1989 July	**Jersey Boys** Chris Craggs, Kevin Eloury, Phil Brown	
	Visitors from the island picked the wettest weekend of the year. The Monday morning before they flew back was better, something was salvaged.	
1989 Aug 22	**Trimming the Beard** Chris Horsfall (solo)	
1989 Aug	**Turnbull's Trajectory** Mark Turnbull, Jan Turnbull	
1989 Sept 2	**Exaltation** Paul Smith	
1989 Sept 4	**Back to School** Chris Craggs, Graham Parkes, Jim Rubery, Rab Carrington	
1989 Sept 4	**Star Trek** Graham Parkes, Chris Craggs	
	Other notables 'played' on the route but lost interest before the deed was done. Originally climbed with a low side runner, Andy Popp did 'the right thing' a couple of years later.	
1989 Sept 29	**Little Weed** John Barr, Andy Wallam	
1989 Nov 3	**Paping about Like a Man with No Arms** Nigel Prestige (solo)	
1989 Nov 15	**Point Five Crack** James Thomas, Justin Ansell	
1989 Dec 29	**Bathtime for Two, Goodtime, Splashing** David Simmonite, Roy Bennett (both solo)	
1989 Dec 29	**Green Party** David Simmonite (solo)	
1989 Dec 29	**Dijon Dip** Mike Lea, Chris Wright, Rob Harwood, Bill Hein	
1989 Dec 31	**New Years Eve** Lee Bower (solo)	
	Possibly done before.	
1989	**The Go Player** Paul Mitchell, Tim Freeman	
1989	**Moriarty** Robin Barker (solo)	
1989	**Nordes with Attitude** John Allen, Paul Mitchell	
1980s	**Quietus Middle Leg** Mark Stokes	
1980s	**Via Trivia** Mike Snell (solo)	
1980s	**Rose and the Self-employed Business Man** Jason Myers	
1990 April 1	**Malarête** Falko Rech, Peter Brayshaw, Richard Boryshevich	
1990 April 6	**Wearing Thin** Mike Lea, Chris Wright	
1990 May 1	**Boc No Buttress Direct** John Allen	
1990 May 6	**In a Big Way Yerself** Neil Travers, Dave Barrel	
1990 May 7	**Lysteria Hysteria** Mike Lea, Rob Harwood	
1990 May 13	**Tying the Knot** Mike Lea, Caroline Killick	
	Climbed a week before the wedding.	
1990 May 20	**Black Attack** John Allen (solo)	
1990 June 10	**Blue Fluff** John Allen	
1990 June 26	**Lamia Antics** Mike Snell (solo)	

1990 July 1   **That Sad Man**   Clive Rockcliff, David Simmonite
1990 July 22   **Turtle Power**   Neal Travers, Mike Lea
1990 Aug 9   **Elephant in the Doghouse**   David Simmonite, Roy Bennett
1990 Aug 9   **Billy B**   Roy Bennett, David Simmonite
1990 Aug 14   **Louis the Loon**   Rob Harwood, Pete Pounds
1990 Aug 27   **Tears and Guts**   Stuart Lancashire, Stephen Whiteman
1990 Sept 12   **Dope Test**   Martin Veale, Tez, Gegs
1990 Oct 14   **Savage Amusement**   Paul Fearn, Stephen Fearn
Pre 1991   **The Water Seller**   Paul Mitchell
        Named after privatisation of the water industry.
1991 Feb 25   **Rib and Face**   Mike Snell (solo)
1991 March 27   **Lucky**   David Simmonite (solo)
1991 April 10   **Back in the Y.M.C.A**   Neil Travers
1991 April 14   **Lamb's Tail**   David Simmonite (solo after top rope)
1991 April 14   **Shout it out**   David Simmonite, Roy Bennett
1991 May 12   **The Old Bag's Head**   Steve Bancroft, Sue Bird
1991 May 14   **Keep Pedalling**   Chris Craggs, Jim Rubery, Dave Spencer
1991 May 14   **Divine Providence**   David Simmonite, Dave Hauton
        Probably done before, the top half in particular as a cop out to Providence
1991 June 22   **Memory Loss**   Chris Craggs, Jim Rubery, Colin Binks (all led), Dave Gregory
1991 June 22   **The Edale Trip** (Beyond Hope)   Colin Binks, Jim Rubery, Dave Gregory, Chris Craggs
1991 June 22   **Squally Showers**   Chris Craggs, Colin Binks, Jim Rubery (all led)
1991 June 22   **Big Screams, Shelf Life**   Chris Craggs, Colin Binks, Jim Rubery (all led), Dave Gregory
1991 June 22   **Gripe Fruit Juice**   Jim Rubery, Chris Craggs
        The spotting of a 'blank on the map' led to a busy and productive day.
1991 July 1   **Which Doctor?**   Martin Veale, Chris Craggs
1991 July 13   **Double Act, Ride Him Cowboy, Wall End Slab Super Duper Direct**   Chris Craggs, Jim Rubery (both led)
        The latter was initially led with a side runner. Chris returned two days later, when the wind had dropped and led the route 'clean'.
1991 Sept 1   **Have a Nice Day**   Chris Craggs (solo)
1991 Sept 22   **Ain't Nobody Here but us Chickens**   Paul Harrison, Shane Lucas
1991   **Woolly Pully**   Chris Craggs (solo)
        This may well have been done before in mistake for Pullover but had never been recorded.
1992 April 1   **Mini Motor Mile**   Dave Gregory, John Street
        Work on the new 'topo' guide began. Many new and previously unrecorded routes came to light. Some will have been climbed before and their first recorded ascentionists are listed from here.
1992 April 5   **You**   B Middleton, G Mason
1992 April 5   **Slow Down**   C Drinkwater, Bruce Goodwin

1992 April 5	**Faster** G Mason, B Middleton
1992 April 5	**Move** Bruce Goodwin and party
1992 April 5	**Start** Bruce Goodwin, C. Drinkwater
1992 April 15	**Gathering Gloom** Chris Craggs, Dave Spencer
1992 May 5	**Top Block Rock, Pisa Pillar** Bill (The Sausage) Tayor, Dave Gregory
1992 May 5	**Recess Rib** Dave Gregory, Bill Tayor
1992 May 15	**Bill & Ted's Lobotomy** Adrian Jones, Paul Scorer
1992 June 18	**Ice Cream Flakes** Dave Gregory (solo)
1992 June 18	**Side Plate, Warm Afternoon, Pulse, Staircase Rib, Solo Slab, Erica Micra** Dave Gregory, John Street
1992 July 7	**Stirrup, Hot Spur** Dave Gregory, John Street
1992 July 22	**Little Slab, Spectacle** John Street, Dave Gregory
1992 July 22	**Lost Soul, Radox, Jam Good** Dave Gregory, John Street
1992 July 22	**Pixie, Bean, Four, Stringer, Muesli, Soft Shoe** Bruce Goodwin, John Street
1992 July 29	**Awl, Dun, Be** John Street, Bruce Goodwin
1992 July 30	**Don't Tell Maurice** D.M.Whittaker, P.Buckle
1992 Aug 11	**Triplet, Albert's Amble** Bruce Goodwin, John Street
1992 Aug 16	**Jude** Chris King (solo)
1992 Aug 16	**Unfamiliar** Robin Barker
	One of the last great 'last great' problems, top roped and then led the same day. The first of a series of significant new routes by an accomplished sport climber, turning limestone-induced power to some of the gritstone challenges which the previous generation had failed on, including Johnny Dawes for whom it was a 'ground up' project for a long time.
1992 Aug19	**Mai, Sinister, Nice One, Dissuader, Broken In, Kerb, Balance** Dave Gregory, John Street
1992 Aug 28	**Scrag End, Spare Rib, Miny, Meeny, Eeny** Dave Gregory, John Street
1992 Sept 5	**Another Game of Bowls Sir Walter?** Chris Craggs, Brian Rossiter
1992 Sept 5	**Choux, Choux Fleur** Brian Rossiter, Chris Craggs
1992 Sept 5	**Scapa Flow** Andy Barker
	One of the fingerholds had been 'scraped' before Barker came along to clean the line.
1992 Sept 8	**Bolt Buttress, Warm September, No Man, Sharpener** Dave Gregory, John Street
1992 Sept 11	**Cheapest Topping, Stacked Blocks** Dave Gregory, John Street
1992 Sept 11	**Nasty Green Dwarf** John Street, Dave Gregory
1992 Sept 15	**Shaky Gully, Cheque, Corduroy, The Mark Devalued, Roll Neck, Unleaded, Stealth, Whimper** Dave Gregory, John Street
1992 Sept 18	**Horn, Quartz** Dave Gregory, John Street
1992 Sept 20	**Beaky** Jim Rubery (solo)
1992 Sept 20	**Naughtical Slab, High Tide, The Big C, Bastille, Mate** Jim Rubery, Dave Gregory
1992 Sept 20	**Prairie Dog** Jim Rubery
1992 Sept 20	**Balcony Bulge** Chris Young, Steve Wright, Tanya Aloneida, Steve Sergeant, Rob Gormley

1992 Sept 24	**Short Straw** Dave Gregory, John Street
1992 Oct 1	**Modesty, Pinch, Jammy, Delovely, Delightful, Tumble Down, Dieppe, Eyes** Dave Gregory, John Street
1992 Oct 1	**Delirious, Delicious, Jon's Route** John Street, Dave Gregory
1992 Oct 15	**Shine On** Robin Barker
	Eventually climbed solo after several days of top roping.
1992 Oct 19	**The Traverse** Ron Fawcett (solo)
	The ultimate girdle by the ultimate climber. The traverse of the full length of the crag was done at the third attempt.
1992 Oct 23	**Snap Shot** Andy Crome (on-sight solo)
1993 March 11	**Kangaroo, Beady Eyed, Cocktails, Original Scoop** Dave Gregory, John Street
1993 March 11	**Twinkle Toes** John Street, Dave Gregory
1993 March 18	**Salt and Vinegar** Dave Gregory, John Street
1993 March 25	**Shuffle, Big Al, Spring Sunshine, Kelly's Eye** John Street, Alan Lawson
1993 March 28	**Trinket, Velcro Arête, Toggle, Button Wall** Dave Gregory, John Street
1993 April 10	**49 Bikinis, The Levee** Bill Briggs, Dave Gregory, Dave Farrant
1993 April 15	**Hideous Hidari** Paul Mitchell, Martin Boysen
1993 Spring	**Curving Buttress Direct Finish** Pete O'Donovan, Chris Craggs
	According to 'sources' this had been done for years, but was never claimed. The production on the 1993 Stanage Topo Guide showed the gaps for all to see.
1993 May 5	**In Earnest, Big Chris, The El Cap Finish, Still in Limbo** Chris Craggs, Dave Gregory
1993 June	**Big Yin** Chris Craggs (solo)
1993 June 10	**Happy Hips** Andy Chrome
1993 July	**Grovel, you don't know the meaning of the word** Chris Craggs, Colin Binks (both solo)
1993 July 28	**Standing Around Trying, Sittin' here Drinkin'** David Simmonite (solo)
1993 Aug 10	**Mental Peace** David Simmonite, Alex Thackway
1993 Aug 15	**Straight Variations, Pull and Step** Bruce Goodwin (solo)
1993 Aug 16	**Dave's Little Route** David Simmonite (solo)
	May have been climbed before.
1993 Aug 19	**My Crazy Head, Scary Canary** David Simmonite (solo)
1993 Sept 4	**Gashed Knee, Fragile Mantel, Carborundum** Chris Craggs (solo)
1993 Sept 4	**Centre Stage, Exit Stage Left** Chris Craggs, Dave Spencer
1993 Sept 6	**Just One Cornetto** Chris Craggs
1993 Sept 15	**Black Car Burning** Robin Barker
1993 Oct 1	**Skinless Wonder** Richie Patterson
	The name gives a clue to what would happen in the event of a fall!
1993 Oct 15	**Following On** Tony Nicholls (solo)

1993 Oct 16	**Hands** Bruce Goodwin (solo)
	Probably done before.
1993 Oct 16	**Feet** Bruce Goodwin, N Bishop, Tony Nicholls
1993 Oct 17	**What I've Done** Simon Royston, John Whistow,
	Malc Baxter, Flossy Glossop
1993	**Pleasant Slab** Bruce Goodwin
1994 April 11	**Flight of Ideas** Simon Jones

A superb effort up the oft-eyed and stunning arête but not without first trying the swooping 30-foot fall. It has seen repeated attempts by many talented climbers and still awaits a repeat.

1994 May 1	**Brittle Star** Mike Przygrodzki, Ian Hirst,
	Frances Przygrodzki
1994 May 15	**Friction** Adrian Berry
	A 'lost' route above Tower Face.
1994 May 18	**Carpe Diem** Neil Foster, Howard Lancashire,
	Huw Perkins

The first of four tough but fine offerings as Neil eyes up some of the cliffs more obvious gaps.

| 1994 June 14 | **Master of Disguise** Neil Foster |
| 1994 June 30 | **The 9 o'clock Watershed** Neil Foster |

A very early start before work for Neil and his belayer David Simmonite to take advantage of the cool conditions.

1994 July 3	**Self Propelled, Petazautte** Bruce Goodwin (solo)
1994 July 5	**Headless Chicken** Neil Foster, Steve Hartley
1994 July 15	**Limitsville** Paul Mitchell (solo)
1994 Aug 7	**Armchair Buccaneer** David Simmonite,
	Roy Bennett, Ian Carey
1994 Aug 8	**Hard Head, Stumpy, Old Slob**
	David Simmonite (solo)
1994 Aug 9	**Little Pete, Jaygo's Pipe** Bruce Goodwin, John Street
1994 Aug 15	**Mop Up** Tony Nicholls (solo)
1994 Aug 30	**Feeding the Pony** David Simmonite (solo)
1994 Sept	**Three Lanky Sassenachs and One Wee Jock**
	Oliver Addey, John Addey, Chris Craggs, Willie Jeffrey.
1994 Oct 9	**Seduced by the Dark Side of Climbing** Bill Birch,
	Rick Gibbons
1994 Nov 6	**Moss Side** Bill Birch, Richard Hyde
1994	**Madhouse** Paul Tattersall
1994	**Brad Pitt** Jason Myers

At the time it was one of the hardest boulder problems in the world. Jason spent 25 days trying it with his dynamic jump method. He was hitting the top hold within a few days and eventually managed to hold it. It has since been climbed via a new static sequence that was found to be easier. The jump method was eventually repeated in 2000 by visiting German, Thomas Ballinger, who added a desperate sit-down start.

1995 April	**Wild and Woolly** Chris Craggs, Dave Spencer,
	Angela Soper
1995 April 10	**Side Wall** Bruce Goodwin (solo)
1995 April 29	**Sands of Time** Bill Birch, Rick Gibbon,
	David Simmonite

Two starts were climbed, both are described in the text.

1995 May 10	**Introversion** Bill Birch, David Simmonite (both led), Rick Gibbons	

Birch and Simmonite turned up at the same time to make the first ascent. A toss of a coin decided who went first.

1995 May 14	**Echoes** Bill Birch, Rick Gibbon
1995 June 6	**Lucy's Joy** Brue Godwin, Guy Fox-Kelly, Alan Cowburn
1995 June 22	**Warm Love** Johnny Dawes
1995 July 20	**Full Blown Finish** Warren Trippet, Malc Baxter
1995 July 23	**Cemetery Waits** Joe Brown, Tim Hulley

Not to be confused with the older Brown!

1995 Aug 15	**Flatlander** T O'Rourke, Stu Sagal
1995 Sept 14	**Dithering Frights** Chris Craggs, Graham Parkes, Dave Vincent
1995 Oct 15	**Andrea** Mike Stacey
1996 Feb	**Mr Twitch** Paul Mitchell
1996 March 10	**Balcony Balustrade** Chris Craggs, Graham Parkes
1996 March 10	**Spring into Action** Graham Parkes, Chris Craggs
1996 March 10	**Orinoco Flow** Graham Parkes, Chris Craggs, John Godding
1996 March	**Sneezy** Chris Craggs, Jim Rubery
1996 April 10	**Invisible Maniac** Richie Patterson (solo)
1996 April 27	**Tributary** Bruce Goodwin, Brian Middleton, Guy Fox-Kelly
1996 April	**The Tempest** Chris Craggs, Dave Spencer
1996 May	**Barmy Brian's Flake Crack** Brian Rossiter, Chris Craggs (both solo)
1996 June 2	**Three Steps to Heaven** Chris Craggs (solo)
1996 June 2	**Sustenance** Chris Craggs, Martin Veale, 'Ant', 'Walt'
1996 June 24	**Before Dunne** T O'Rouke (solo)
1996 June 30	**Worth Travelling Four Hundred Miles For?** Chris Craggs, Graham Parkes, Dave (Smiler) Cuthbertson

Smiler arrived at the crag hot from Inverness.

1996 June	**Marked Up** Chris Craggs, Dave Gregory
1996 June	**Central Reservation** Chris Craggs (solo)
1996 June	**Caved In** Chris Craggs, Graham Parkes
1996 July 7	**Hebden's Heights** Wil Jones, R.Cawthray
1996 July 28	**Kinell** Stuart Ryder, Peter Simpson
1996 Aug 15	**Going Grey** Paul Harrison (solo)
1996 Sept 1	**Long Reaches** Chris Craggs, Martin Veale (both solo)

Their differing heights led to discordant opinions of the route's grade.

1996 Sept 1	**Falaise de Douvre** Chris Craggs, Graham Parkes, Dave Spencer
1996 Sept 1	**Ramsgate, Older Still** Chris Craggs (solo)
1996 Sept 1	**Taking a Winger, On a Wing and a Prayer** Graham Parkes, Chris Craggs
1996 Sept 7	**Skippy** Chris Craggs, Martin Veale (both solo)
1996 Sept 14	**Pollyfilla** Chris Craggs, Graham Parkes, Dave Vincent
1996 Sept	**Left Twin Crack** Chris Craggs (solo)
1996 Oct	**The Long and the Short** Chris Craggs, Martin Veale (both solo)
1996 Oct 26	**Big Dave's Wall** Percy Bishton, David Simmonite

Cripple's Crack **HVD** (page 306)
Climber: Graham Sutton Photo: David Simmonite

The Green Streak HVS 4c (page 312)
Climber: Ian Hey Photo: Niall Grimes

1996	**Happy Amongst Friends** Johnny Dawes
	(on-sight solo)
1996	**Little Side Line** Dave Gregory
1996	**Help the Young** Paul Mitchell (solo)
1997 Jan 25	**One Stop Shopping, Fit as a Butcher's Dog**
	Graham Parkes, Chris Craggs
1997 Feb 9	**Small Reward, Small Change** Joe Rhodes
1997 Feb 9	**Imposter** Malc Baxter, Dave Whiteley
1997 March 7	**Sister Blister** Chris Craggs, Graham Parkes
1997 March 7	**Keep it in the Family** Graham Parkes, Chris Craggs
1997 March 8	**The End of All Things, The Be All and End All**
	Chris Craggs, Dave Gregory (both solo)
1997 March 8	**Three Calm Men** Malc Baxter, Jim Campbell,
	Dave Whiteley
1997 March 8	**Blown Away** Malc Baxter, Simon Royston
1997 March 8	**Gypsy Moth** Malc Baxter, Simon Royston, Joe Rhodes
1997 March 8	**Clegg Direct, Flecky Wall, Flecky Wall Arête,**
	Serapis, Osiris, Apis, White Hare Malc Baxter
	(all solo)
1997 March 9	**Little Women** John Welford
	Powerful climbing plugs the penultimate gap on True North
	Buttress.
1997 March 13	**The Big C Left-Hand, Whacky Attack** Malc Baxter,
	Joe Rhodes
1997 March 13	**Interlude** Joe Rhodes (solo)
1997 March 15	**Skidoo II** Niall Grimes
	Climbed in mistake for the original Skidoo.
1997 March 18	**Th'ickle Buttress** Malc Baxter, Al Parker, Rick Hibbert
1997 March 18	**Undercoat** Al Parker
1997 March 18	**Hale Bopp** Malc Baxter, Al Parker
	Named after the 1997 'Comet of the Century'.
1997 March 22	**Cixtot, Shard, Bell Heather** Chris Craggs (solo)
1997 March 29	**Spring Plum** Malc Baxter, Paul Durkin, Simon Royston
1997 March 29	**Blown Drie** Paul Durkin, Simon Royston, Malc Baxter
1997 March 29	**Darthuader** Simon Royston, Malc Baxter, Paul Durkin
1997 March 29	**Broken Arête** Paul Durkin
1997 March 30	**Tomcat, The Other Effect** Simon Royston,
	Malc Baxter
1997 April 5	**Square Chimney Arête** Chris Craggs (solo)
1997 April 16	**Holiday Quartet** Bruce Goodwin, Dave Gregory,
	Alan Cowburn, Graham Fletcher
1997 April 27	**Bodypopping** Nick Taylor (solo)
1997 June	**It's a Cracker** Chris Craggs, Jim Rubery
1997 June 1	**Reptilian, Wedgewood, Ram Jam Full** Chris Craggs
	(solo)
1997 June 1	**Hard Nosed** Graham Parkes, Chris Craggs
	(both solo)
1997 June 1	**Hueco Heaven, Bamboozled, Overhung**
	Graham Parkes, Chris Craggs
1997 June 1	**Slab Happy** Chris Craggs, Graham Parkes
1997 June 1	**Nosey Parkers** Chris Craggs, Graham Parkes
	(both solo)
	Some of these routes had certainly been climbed before.

1997 June 6	**Fruitcake** Phil Meats
1997 June 6	**Squat, Teeter, Grunt, Fun in the Sun, Short and Sweet, Shuffle, Reach for the Sky, Drewitt Drewitt, Heather Heaven, Flaked Out, Hold Your Breath** Chris Craggs, Dave Gregory in a variety of combinations. *The day did not start well when the team was locked out of their car in Sheffield, eventual arrival at the crag was 'better (five hours) late than never'.*
1997 July	**Wild West Wind** Chris Craggs (solo)
1997 July	**Angel in the Stars** David Simmonite
1997 July	**Newborn** David Simmonite, Ann Stuart-Gibson, John Daley
1997 July 4	**Shining Jewel, Algol Corner, Pillar Route, Dennis's Harp, Ferret's Crack, Brown Wall** Bruce Goodwin (solo)
1997 July 4	**Greenman's Route, Flake Chimney, Two Pitch Climb** Dave Gregory (solo)
1997 July 4	**Medicus Curat, Natura Sanat, Scratch Wall, Scratch Arête, Progressive Wall, Flaked Out** Bruce Goodwin, Dave Gregory
1997 July 4	**Ramps, It's Scary Mary** Dave Gregory, Bruce Goodwin *Acting on a tip, the two 'old timers' had a busy day, with 18 new routes.*
1997 July 5	**Ugly Mugs** Chris Craggs, Dave Gregory
1997 July 5	**Right On** Dave Gregory, Chris Craggs
1997 July 6	**Meaty Bugs** David Simmonite, Ian Smith
1997 July 6	**Jenny Wren** Ian Smith, David Simmonite
1997 July 13	**Marathonette** Mathew 'Joe' Rhodes, Simon Royston and others
1997 July 27	**Tupperware** Miles Gibson (on-sight solo)
1997 Aug 19	**Rib Tickler** Malc Baxter, Malcolm Seal
1997 Aug 25	**Mythology** Tony Edwards
1997 Sept 1	**A Paucity of Independent Climbing** Pete Robins, Graham Parkes, Chris Craggs
1997 Sept 15	**Marbellous** Robin Barker *The biggest gap on the edge falls to extreme technical ability and considerable boldness. On the first attempted lead, the scary start was soloed to the break, the gear was placed and then Barker down climbed and jumped off to the ground. The gear was then left clipped for subsequent attempts. The belaying team for attempts spread over several days included Rachel Nicholson, Jon Barton, Neil Bentley, John Welford, Nic Kidd, Piff Oates, Richard Heap, Mark Turnbull, Paul Twomey and Jean Minh Trien Thieu. Despite the size of the team a human pyramid was not employed.*
1997 Sept 16	**The Beast of Endcliffe** Percy Bishton, Lucy Atkinson, David Simmonite
1997 Sept 19	**Hard Men in Lycra** Pete Robins, Graham Parkes, Chris Craggs
1997 Sept 28	**Counterfeit, Conundrum,** Graham Parkes, Chris Craggs
1997 Oct 5	**Block Buster** Chris Craggs, Graham Parkes

354

1998 March 15	**Regret Direct Start** Graham Parkes, Chris Craggs	
1998 March 15	**Finger Licking Good** Graham Parkes, Chris Craggs	
1998 April 29	**Spring Wall** Bruce Goodwin, Alan Cowburn, Dave Gregory, Les Gorham, Brian Davies	
1998 June 28	**O D G's Chimney** Dave Gregory (solo) *Named after the man, not the pub.*	
1998 June 28	**Men Only** Brian Rossiter, Nigel Baker, Chris Craggs, Dave Gregory	
1998 June 28	**Don't Fluff It** Brian Rossiter, Nigel Baker, Chris Craggs, Dave Gregory	
1998 Aug 7	**5 See Plus** Bruce Goodwin, Dave Gregory, Tina Priestly, Brian Davies	
1998 Aug 8	**Gothic Armpit** Dave Thomas, Richard Heap	
1998 Aug	**The Cutting Room Floor** John Arran, David Ashe	
1998 Sept 2	**Right Side, Pedlar's Wall**, **Topo Mania** Brian Middleton, Bruce Goodwin, Alan Cowburn, John Street	
1998 Sept 2	**Elastic** Bruce Goodwin, John Street, Alan Cowburn, Brian Davies, John Warburton, Les Gorham	
1998 Sept 19	**Billiard Buttress Direct** Martin Veale, Chris Craggs, Dave Gregory	
1998 Sept 25	**Old Smoothie** Bruce Goodwin, Dave Gregory, Brian Davies, Tina Priestly, Glynn (A. N. Other)	
1998 Sept 25	**Probably Done Before, Paste** Bruce Goodwin, Dave Gregory	
1998 Sept 25	**Obviously Done Before** Dave Gregory, Bruce Goodwin	
1998 Oct 10	**Outside Exit** Dave Gregory, Chris Craggs *Scant reward for a tough day checking the chimneys of Stanage.*	
1998 Dec 15	**Groove is in the Heart** Neil Bentley *The last gap on True North Buttress utilised a pre-placed wire.*	
1999 Feb 1	**Beneath the Breadline** Pat King (solo)	
1999 March 1	**Four Star, E10, 7b** Don Honneyman, Nick Jennings	
1999 March 1	**Scrittalacious** Nick Jennings, Don Honneyman	
1999 March 6	**Broken Arrow** Graham Parkes, Chris Craggs	
1999 March 10	**The Descrittalizer** Don Honneyman, Nick Jennings	
1999 March 19	**Groovy** Andy Healy, 'Albert Spansworthy' *Could Albert be Mark Turnbull?*	
1999 March 20	**Dark Reign** Mark Turnbull, Andy Healey	
1999 April 1	**Sky Bouldering** Dan Honneyman	
1999 May 2	**Frankie Ferocious** James Boosey, David Simmonite, Steve Bell, Tony Penning, Dave Viggers *Led on sight and James's first day on grit.*	
1999 May 15	**Twin Set** Dave Gregory, Chris Craggs (both solo)	
1999 May 15	**Frank Sinatra** Chris Craggs, Dave Gregory	
1999 June 12	**The Muted Trumper** Richard Heap, Catherine Schirmacher (The Muted), Nic Sellars (The Trumper)	
1999 June 16	**Sir Chilled** Richard Heap, Patty Desroy, Dawi Lee	
1999 June 26	**Olly Wall** Chris Craggs, Dave Gregory (both solo)	
1999 June 26	**Forethought** Dave Gregory, Chris Craggs, Graham Parkes, Phil Robins	

1999 June 26	**Moments of Inertia**	Graham Parkes, Phil Robins, Chris Craggs, Dave Gregory
1999 July 3	**New Balls Please**	Graham Parkes, Chris Craggs
	The name was connected to the Wimbledon semi-finals and in no way related to the leader's bottle or lack of.	
1999 Aug	**Flying Butt**	John Arran (on-sight solo)
1999 Sept 1	**Darkness Falling**	Thomas de Gay
1999 Sept 3	**That Floating Fatman**	Darren Stevenson
1999 Oct 15	**The Nays**	Bruce Goodwin, Dave Gregory (both solo)
1999 Oct 15	**The Grey Cliffs of ..., Dover's Wall Route 1.5**	Bruce Goodwin, Dave Gregory
1999 Oct 20	**Deadline**	Richie Patterson (solo)
1999	**Dreadnought**	Mike Lea
1999	**Savage**	Chris Savage (on-sight solo)
1990s	**Spinach Slab**	Andy Popp
1990s	**Meisner's Link Up**	Mike Meisner
1990s	**Green Ginger**	Lee Bower (solo)
1990s	**Wakamono**	Paul Mitchell
1990s	**I-Ro-Ha**	Andy Barker, Paul Mitchell
2000 March	**Small Time Crook**	John Boyle, Steve Adams
2000 April	**Klingon**	Mike Lea
2000 May	**An Other Ology**	Dave Gregory, John Street
2000 July 26	**One Two Eight**	Bruce Goodwin, John Street
2000 October	**Overexposed**	Don Honeyman, Nick Jenning
2000	**The Ace**	Jerry Moffatt
	Superceeded The Joker, an earlier problem by Moffatt	
2000	**Pressure Drop**	Adam Long (solo)
2000	**'The Iain Farrar Experience'**	Dan Honneyman
2001 Jan 28	**Lichen Alive**	Dan Honneyman
2001 May 28	**Flake Gully Slab, Flake Gully Crack**	Steve Clark, Lynn Robinson
2001 May 29	**Impure, Grey and Mildly Threatening**	Steve Clark, Lynn Robinson
2001 May 29	**Spur Slab Left-Hand**	Steve Clark (roped solo)
2001 June 5	**Edgar Rice Burroughs**	Steve Clark, Iain Mount Brian Reynolds

In an attempt to record a more comprehensive history and first ascent's list of Stanage Edge in the future all of the routes named in the main route text but which no details are forthcoming are listed below in chronological order. If you know of any details or corrections to any first ascent details please drop a line (contact details at the front of the guide).

1910s	Capstone Chimney
1912-14	Norse Corner Climb
1914-21	Kelly's Variation
1914-23	Cave Buttress, Cave Buttress Right-Hand, Typical Grit
c.1915	Kelly's Corner
1915-21	The Marmoset, Bent Crack, Kelly's Eliminate, Kelly's Crack
1919-23	Wall End Crack, The Y Crack
1920s	Bishop's Route (Zigzag Variations), Fergus Graham's Direct Route, Leaning Buttress Crack
1922	Leaning Buttress Indirect, Balcony Climb Direct

1923-51	Monkey Crack, Square Chimney, Mantlepiece Buttress, Plate Glass Slab, Ground Glass, Small Crack , Black Chimney, Right Wall Route, Recess Wall, Grotto Wall, Heather Wall, Crack and Corner, Beggar's Crack, Anatomy, Sociology, Physiology, Flying Buttress Gully, Straight Crack, Twin Cracks, Robin Hood's Staircase, Little John's Step, Amazon Crack, Heaven Crack, Devil's Chimney, Mistella, Martello Cracks, Intermediate Butress, Verandah Buttress, Wing Wall, Wing Buttress, Wing Buttress Gully, Curving Chimney, Cleft Wall Route 2, Cleft Wall Route 1, Chockstone Chimney, Curved Crack, Flake Gully, Pegasus Wall, Taurus Crack, Overhanging Crack, Mercury Crack, Hercules Crack, Tower Gully, Waterloo Branch, Spur Slab, Fern Crack, Ampitheatre Face, Outlook Layback, Heather Slab, Broken Buttress, Burgess Crack, Eric's Eliminate, Straight Crack, October Slab, Left-Hand Tower, Lonely Crag, Manhattan Crack, Doctor's Saunter, Cripple's Crack, Nursery Crack, Boomerang Chimney
1923-57	Wall End Holly Tree Crack
1930s	Bridge's Variation, Helfenstein's Struggle, Tower Face Indirect, Chockstone Direct
1930-51	Dover's Wall, Route 2
1932-33	Black Hawk Tower
1933	Tower Face Original
1946-51	Wall End Traverse
Pre-1951	Conolly's Variation, Macleod's Variation, Easy Cleft, Marble Tower Wall
1951-56	Crossover, Sand Crack, Pisa Crack, Mantlepiece Lower Hand-Traverse, Nicheless Climb, Niche Wall Direct
1951-64	Tower Chimney and Face, The Rack
1955-56	Gargoyle Variant
1957-60	Hearsay Crack, First Sister, Right-Hand Tower
1958	Cleft Wing Superdirect
1960s	Pie Face
1960	Seesaw
1961-63	Additive Chimney, Outlook Chimney, Eden Arete, Broken Groove, Crawly, Cracked Wall, Sogines, Impossible Slab, Youth, Sudoxe, Leviticus, Wetness Wall, Crumbling Crack, Arrow Crack, Straight Chimney, Flake Chimney
Pre-1964	The Jitters, Right Edge
1964-76	Dover's Wall, Route 4, Palermo, Paradise Arete, Flaky Wall, Outlook Buttress, Count's Buttress Right-Hand Finish, Pertinacious, Wall and Slab, Pup, Quadrille, Bow Crack, Twin Cracks, February Crack, Mars, Avril
1970s	Surprise Direct Start, Public Face, High Neb Edge
1976-77	Twintrin
1976-79	War Zone
1976-80	Leave Heather Alone
1976-81	The Cracks Between
1976-82	Stage Fright, Between the Two, Fulcrum, Percy's Prow, Compost Corner, Kitcat, Heather Wall Variation, The Famous Ed Wood
1976-83	Count's Crack Left-Hand Finish, Cracked Wall Direct Start, Another Turn
1979-89	Fading Star Direct
1980s	Historical Arete, Historical Crack, Wokamono, Topaz Copout, The Green Traverse, Rotor
1981	Straight and Narrow
1982	Big Bob's Bazaar
1983	Quark
1983-89	Gnat's Slab Arete, Twisting Crack Variation, Thin Problem

	Crack, Blinkers, Kindergarten, Finale Direct, Tip Off Right
1984	Millsom's Minion Direct, Tales of Yankee Power, The Anamolous Snail
1986	Midge
1988	Vaccine Traverse
1990s	Cock o' the Rock, Mantlepiece Upper Left Hand, Adults Only
1992	Poor Pizza
1999	Stay in the Light
Traditional	Square Buttress Corner, Easy Jamming, Trainer Failure, The Real 20 foot Crack, Mantlepiece Crack, Scrappy Corner, The Bishop's Move, Pedestal Chimney, Robin Hood's Staircase Direct, The Scoop, Left Flank, Viridescent Corner, Corner Crack, Green Chimney, Newhaven, A Black Ying, Capstone Chimney, Sand Gully, Flake Chimney, Pebble Arete, Centurion's Dexter, Centurion's Slab, The Wide Crack, It's a Cracker, Ami, High Neb Buttress Variation, Frosty, Uno Crack, Stairway Crack, Deep Chimney, Manhattan Arete, Curving Chimney Left Arete, Right Unconquerable Direct Start, Telli Right-Hand

Index